2196835   34.00 ᘓ
           68c

D1552923

HEATING, VENTILATING, AND AIR CONDITIONING:

Design for Building Construction

John E. Traister

PRENTICE-HALL, INC., Englewood Cliffs, New Jersey 07632

Library of Congress Cataloging-in-Publication Data

Traister, John E.
  Heating, ventilating, and air conditioning.

  Includes index.
  1. Heating. 2. Ventilation. 3. Air
conditioning. I. Title.
TH7222.T72 1987   697   86-30415
ISBN 0-13-385196-6

Editorial/production supervision: *Raeia Maes*
Cover design: *Photo Plus Art*
Manufacturing buyer: *Rhett Conklin*

Figures 7-1, 7-3, and 7-4 are from John E. Traister,
Residential Heating Operations and Troubleshooting,
© 1985 by Prentice-Hall, Inc.

Figures 11-1 through 11-54 and 12-14 are from John E. Traister,
Practical Drafting for the HVAC Trades, 2nd ed.,
© 1984, 1975 by Prentice-Hall, Inc., pp. 50, 52,
53–78, and 229.

Printed in the United States of America

10 9 8 7 6 5 4 3 2 1

ISBN 0-13-385196-6   025

Prentice-Hall International (UK) Limited, *London*
Prentice-Hall of Australia Pty. Limited, *Sydney*
Prentice-Hall Canada, Inc., *Toronto*
Prentice-Hall Hispanoamericana, S.A., *Mexico*
Prentice-Hall of India Private Limited, *New Delhi*
Prentice-Hall of Japan, Inc., *Tokyo*
Prentice-Hall of Southeast Asia Pte. Ltd., *Singapore*
Editora Prentice-Hall do Brasil, Ltda., *Rio de Janeiro*

CONTENTS

PREFACE

The analysis of working drawings and specifications prepared by professional engineers has long been a major part of the serious engineering student's method of study. Unfortunately, most mechanical engineering students preparing for a position in a consulting engineering firm lack the wealth of material needed to aid him or her. Prints or construction documents for mechanical systems are relatively plentiful, but few—if any—explain why and how a certain design is performed. Necessary calculations leading up to the final design are also omitted, usually leaving the student completely confused. The basic purpose of this book is to remedy this situation by giving the budding professional a means of seeing and analyzing actual working drawings that were prepared by consulting engineers and used by contractors and their personnel to install HVAC systems in buildings of all types. Furthermore, since the personal computer is being used more and more in engineering firms and contractor's offices, practical computer programs are also included in this book to demonstrate their use in actual HVAC applications.

But the student is not alone. Practicing professional mechanical designers must constantly keep abreast of all the latest products and techniques available to the HVAC industry. Architects and their clients trust professionals to design the best mechanical system within a predetermined budget, and it is the responsibility of the professional engineer to do so. This book is also designed to show the professional some of the latest developments in HVAC systems and how they should be indicated on working drawings and described in written specifications.

The reader will note that this book deals only briefly with theories, since hundreds of previous books have taken ample care of this. This book attempts to get right to the "meat" of the matter by dealing mainly in the application of practical mechanical designs that must be dealt with by professional engineers and designers in consulting firms. Because of this practical approach, HVAC construction supervisors and technicians, as well as sales representatives for HVAC material suppliers, should also find this book invaluable in their daily work.

Practically all the examples given are in working-drawing format, with written explanations to clearly illustrate at a glance exactly what is taking place and for what purpose. No further data are necessary to understand the examples except for the material found in the appendixes.

A deep and grateful bow must be made in the direction of the architects, drafters, designers, and engineers who furnished most of the drawings that appear in this book. Their names are listed elsewhere in this book under the appropriate illustrations.

Suggestions for improvement of this book from readers will be most welcome to both the publisher and the author.

John E. Traister

1

THE ESSENTIALS

The fundamental objective of this chapter is to give the reader an overall picture of the building construction industry and the mechanical designer's relationship to it. Familiarity with these relationships is considered necessary to give designers a proper background for approaching their work more intelligently.

This chapter also introduces fundamental design procedure, mechanical drawings and symbols, and other basic essentials necessary to the mechanical design profession.

CONSTRUCTION OF A BUILDING

In almost all instances, when an owner decides to have a building constructed, an architect is hired to prepare the complete working drawings and specifications for the building. The drawings usually include the following:

1. A plot plan indicating the location of the building on the property.
2. Elevations of all exterior faces of the building.
3. Floor plans showing the walls and partitions for each floor or level.
4. Sufficient vertical cross sections to indicate clearly the various floor levels and details of the foundation, walls, floors, ceilings, and roof construction.
5. Large-scale renderings showing such details of construction as may be required.

The architect often represents the owner in soliciting quotations from general contractors and advises the owner as to the proper award to make. The architect also usually represents the owner during construction of the building and inspects the work to ascertain that it is being performed in accordance with the requirements of the construction documents (drawings and specifications).

On very small projects, the architect may merely show a one-line diagram of the ductwork on the architectural floor plans with the volume of air and British thermal units of heat required for each area. The ductwork is often sized, in cases like this, by the mechanical contractor installing the job. For jobs of any consequence, the architect usually includes drawings and specifications covering the design of plumbing, heating, ventilating, air conditioning, and electrical work.

In larger buildings, where the mechanical systems are more extensive and complex, architects normally hire consulting engineers to handle the details of the mechanical (HVAC) construction from the time the design and layout of the work are started, through the bidding and construction sequences, to the final approval and acceptance of the finished job.

The relations of the consulting engineer parallel those of the architect, inasmuch as the consulting engineer often represents the architect and owner in soliciting from the contractor's quotations that pertain to the engineer's responsibility. The engineer also inspects his or her portion of the work to assure the architect that this portion is carried out according to the working drawings and specifications. The engineer also approves shop drawings (material submittals), checks and approves progress payments, and performs similar duties—all pertaining only to the engineer's phase of the construction.

Architects sometimes require the engineer to prepare an approximate cost estimate of the mechanical work to aid them in determining the probable cost of the building prior to the actual request for formal quotations. This is especially true when government projects are being developed.

The mechanical engineer or designer uses the architect's drawings as a reference when designing a suitable HVAC system for the building in question. This design usually involves calculating the heat gain for air conditioning, the heat loss for heating, the required air changes per hour for ventilation, the size and shape of duct to deliver the required volume of air to the various areas within the building, control wiring, and similar details.

Draftsmen, in turn, are responsible for translating the engineer's design into neat, detailed, and accurate working drawings that indicate, beyond any question of a doubt, exactly what is required to install a correct HVAC system in a building. In doing so, the draftsman uses lines, symbols, dimensions, and notations to convey the engineer's design to the workers on the job. Usually, a set of written specifications describing in detail the requirements of the design accompanies these drawings. Together with the working drawings, it forms the basis of the contract requirements for the construction of the project.

HVAC DRAWINGS

Mechanical drawings, as applied to the HVAC trades, are basically accurate, neat, clear line representations of the entire mechanical system, including all related controls. Most of these drawings are highly diagrammatical and are used to locate ductwork, equipment, and other necessary details of the system.

The exact method of showing mechanical layouts varies with the engineering or consulting firm commissioned to design the system. However, the following description is typical.

In general, HVAC drawings indicate the location of all equipment; the supply, makeup, and return air ducts, the fans for ventilation; the size and location of grilles, registers, and diffusers; and any other items falling under the HVAC specifications. The drawings also include equipment schedules and large-scale construction details when they are required.

QUALITY OF DESIGN

Consulting engineering firms should strive to produce designs and working drawings that are no less than excellent in quality. They should not only be correct as far as heating and cooling methods, duct sizes, pipe sizes, and the like are concerned, but they should also be presented in a way that is easily interpreted by the mechanical contractor, estimators, inspectors, and workers on the job. The mechanical drawings combined with the written specifications should leave no doubt as to exactly what is required of the mechanical contractor for the proper installation of the mechanical system for the project.

2

TAKING ACCURATE MEASUREMENTS

The most common measurements are those of length, area, and volume. In HVAC practice, all three of these measurements are frequently used in calculating the size of a room or area to be heated or cooled. The volume of air ducts must be determined to maintain the proper amount and speed of conditioned air, the physical dimensions of ductwork must be measured and sized to fit in a given area, and so on. The cases are endless in the HVAC trade.

Two common measuring systems are in use today, the English inch system, which is most commonly used in the United States at the present time, and the meter system, which is a European standard of length in general use in a number of countries. The two systems are interchangeable, in that the meter equals 39.37 inches (in.) and the inch equals 25.4 millimeters (mm).

The use of measuring tools in the sheet-metal shop or on the job is principally concerned with the thirty-sixth subdivision of the yard, or the inch. The inch is subdivided into various lengths down to as short as one ten-thousandth part or less; but for all practical use in the HVAC trades, $\frac{1}{16}$ is considered adequate for the great majority of all measurements required.

For laying out work on sheets of sheet metal, the most common tools used are steel rules, dividers, protractors, straight edges, and steel squares. Workers are also required to use the architect's scale, which is described in Chapter 3.

The discussion to follow deals with conversions from English to the metric system of measurement since many drawings and diagrams utilize both to relay the dimensions to the worker or engineer. Two BASIC computer programs are also included at the end of this chapter to make the conversion much simpler. An engineer or contractor, for example, may need to convert English measurement to metric for use on a project, say, in Canada, or vice versa, when drawings from other countries are used in the United States. The two BASIC programs have been tested and proved accurate enough for all HVAC calculations. To use, merely type in the program once the computer has been placed in the BASIC mode. Run the program to check for typing errors and then save the program for later use, giving it an easy to remember name such as "Metric." The temperature-conversion program could be called "Temp" to facilitate remembering it's program name when it has to be used. Both should find constant use in HVAC shops around the world.

It is recommended that the temperature-conversion program be studied, entered into the computer's memory, and tried with several examples before typing in the longer metric conversion program, since typos and other errors will be spotted more easily on the shorter program.

THE METRIC SYSTEM

The metric system is an international language of measurement. Its symbols are identical in all languages. There are some basic rules to the metric system, which is called the International System of Units (SI). A few units outside SI that are acceptable for use with SI are also described in the following.

RULES FOR WRITING METRIC QUANTITIES

Capitals

Unit names, including prefixes, are not capitalized except at the beginning of a sentence or in titles. Note that in degree Celsius the unit "degree" is lowercase. (In the term "degree Celsius," "degree" is considered to be the unit name, modified by the adjective "Celsius," which is always capitalized. The "degree centigrade" is obsolete.)

Symbols: The short forms for metric units are called symbols. They are lowercase except that the first letter is uppercase when the name of the unit is derived from the name of a person. See Table 2-1.

EXAMPLES:	Unit Name	Unit Symbol
	meter	m
	liter	l
	gram	g
	newton	N
	pascal	Pa

Printed unit symbols should have upright (Roman) letters, because sloping letters (italic) are reserved for quantity symbols, such as for mass and length.

TABLE 2-1

Quantity (1)	Common Units	Symbol	Acceptable Equivalent	Symbol
plane angle	degree (2)	°		
length	kilometer	km		
	meter (3)	m		
	centimeter	cm		
	millimeter	mm		
	micrometer	µm		
area	square kilometer	km²		
	square hectometer	hm²	hectare	ha
	square meter	m²		
	square centimeter	cm²		
	square millimeter	mm²		
volume	cubic meter	m³		
	cubic decimeter	dm³	liter (3,4,5)	l
	cubic centimeter	cm³	milliliter (4)	ml
velocity	meter per second	m/s		
	kilometer per hour	km/h		
acceleration	meter per second squared	m/s²		
frequency	megahertz	MHz		
	kilohertz	kHz		
	hertz	Hz		
rotational frequency	revolution per second	r/s		
	revolution per minute	r/min		
mass	megagram	Mg	metric ton	t
	kilogram	kg		
	gram	g		
	milligram	mg		
density	kilogram per cubic meter	kg/m³	gram per liter	g/l
force	kilonewton	kN		
	newton	N		
moment of force (6)	newton-meter	N·m		
pressure	kilopascal (7)	kPa		
stress	megapascal (8)	MPa		
energy, work, or quantity of heat	megajoule	MJ		
	kilojoule	kJ		
	joule	J		
	kilowatt-hour (9)	kW·h	kilowatthour	kWh
power or heat flow rate	kilowatt	kW		
	watt	W		
temperature	kelvin	K		
	degree Celsius	°C		
electric current	ampere	A		
quantity of electricity	coulomb	C		
	ampere-hour (10)	A·h		Ah
electromotive force	volt	V		
electric resistance	ohm	Ω		
luminous intensity	candela	cd		
luminous flux	lumen	lm		
illuminance	lux	lx		
sound level	decibel	dB		

NOTES

(1) Listed in same sequence as ISO 1000.

(2) For efficiency in calculations, plane angles should be expressed with decimal subdivisions rather than minutes (') and seconds (").

The SI unit for plane angle is radian (symbol rad), defined as "the plane angle between two radii of a circle which cut off on the circumference an arc equal in length to the radius".

(3) For information regarding spelling, see Preface. The spellings "meter" and "liter" are preferred by ANMC but "metre" and "litre" are recognized to be in widespread use.

(4) To be used only for fluids (both gases and liquids) and for dry ingredients in recipes.

(5) Do not use any prefix with "liter" except "milli".

(6) Torque or bending moment.

(7) See Rule 10.

(8) Except for very weak materials.

(9) To be abandoned eventually. 1 kW·h = 3.6 MJ

(10) 1 A·h = 3600 C

Prefix Symbols: All prefix names, their symbols, and pronunciation are listed in Table 2-2. Notice that the top five are uppercase and all the rest are lowercase. The importance of following the precise use of uppercase and lowercase letters is shown by the following examples:

    G for giga; g for gram

    K for kelvin; k for kilo

    M for mega; m for milli

    N for newton; n for nano

    T for tera; t for metric ton

TABLE 2-2 SI Unit Prefixes

Multiplication Factor	Prefix	Symbol	Pronunciation (USA) (1)	Meaning (in USA)	In Other Countries
1 000 000 000 000 000 000 = 10^{18}	exa(2)	E	ex´ a (a as in about)	One quintillion times (3)	trillion
1 000 000 000 000 000 = 10^{15}	peta(2)	P	as in petal	One quadrillion times (3)	thousand billion
1 000 000 000 000 = 10^{12}	tera	T	as in terrace	One trillion times (3)	billion
1 000 000 000 = 10^{9}	giga	G	jig´ a (a as in about)	One billion times (3)	milliard
1 000 000 = 10^{6}	mega	M	as in megaphone	One million times	
1 000 = 10^{3}	kilo	k	as in kilowatt	One thousand times	
100 = 10^{2}	hecto	h (4)	heck´ toe	One hundred times	
10 = 10	deka	da (4)	deck´ a (a as in about)	Ten times	
0.1 = 10^{-1}	deci	d (4)	as in decimal	One tenth of	
0.01 = 10^{-2}	centi	c (4)	as in sentiment	One hundredth of	
0.001 = 10^{-3}	milli	m	as in military	One thousandth of	
0.000 001 = 10^{-6}	micro	μ (5)	as in microphone	One millionth of	
0.000 000 001 = 10^{-9}	nano	n	nan´ oh (an as in ant)	One billionth of (3)	milliardth
0.000 000 000 001 = 10^{-12}	pico	p	peek´ oh	One trillionth of (3)	billionth
0.000 000 000 000 001 = 10^{-15}	femto	f	fem´ toe (fem as in feminine)	One quadrillionth of (3)	thousand billionth
0.000 000 000 000 000 001 = 10^{-18}	atto	a	as in anatomy	One quintillionth of (3)	trillionth

(1) The first syllable of every prefix is accented to assure that the prefix will retain its identity. Therefore, the preferred pronunciation of kilometer places the accent on the first syllable, not the second.

(2) Approved by the 15th General Conference of Weights and Measures (CGPM), May–June 1975.

(3) These terms should be avoided in technical writing because the denominations above one million are different in most other countries, as indicated in the last column.

(4) While hecto, deka, deci, and centi are SI prefixes, their use should generally be avoided except for the SI unit-multiples for area and volume and nontechnical use of centimeter, as for body and clothing measurement. The prefix hecto should be avoided also because the longhand symbol h may be confused with k.

(5) Although Rule 1 prescribes upright type, the sloping form is sometimes tolerated in the USA for the Greek letter μ because of the scarcity of the upright style.

Plurals and Fractions

1. Names of units are plural when appropriate.

> *Examples:* 1 meter, 100 meters, 0 degrees Celsius

Values less than 1 take the singular form of the unit name.

> *Examples:* 0.5 kilogram or $\frac{1}{2}$ kilogram

Although decimal notation (0.5, 0.35, 6.87) is generally preferred, the most simple fractions are acceptable, such as those in which the denominator is 2, 3, 4, or 5.

2. Symbols of units are the same in singular and plural.

> *Examples:* 1 m, 100 m

Periods

A period is *not* used after a symbol, except at the end of a sentence.

> *Examples:* A current of 15 mA is found . . . The field measured 350 × 125 m.

The Decimal Marker

A dot on the line is used as the decimal marker. In numbers less than one, a zero should be written before the decimal point. This prevents the possibility that a faint decimal point will be overlooked.

> *Example:* The oral expression "point seven five" is written 0.75.

Grouping of Numbers

1. Separate digits into groups of three, counting from the decimal marker. A comma should not be used. Instead, a space is left to avoid confusion because many countries use a comma for the decimal marker.

2. In a four-digit number, the space is not required unless the four-digit number is in a column with numbers of five digits or more.

> *Examples:* For 4,720,525   write 4 720 525
> For 0.52875   write 0.528 75
> For 6,875   write 6875 or 6 875
> For 0.6875   write 0.6875 or 0.687 5

Spacing

1. In symbols or names for units having prefixes, no space is left between letters making up the symbol or the name.

   Examples: kA, kiloampere; mg, milligram

2. When a symbol follows a number to which it refers, a space must be left between the number and the symbol, except when the symbol (such as °) appears in the superscript position. The symbol for degree Celsius may be written either with or without a space before the degree symbol.

   Examples: 455 kHz, 22 mg, 20 mm, 10^6 N, 30°, 20°C, or 20 °C

3. When a quantity is used in an adjectival sense, a hyphen should be used between the number and the symbol (except ° and °C).

   Examples: It is a 35-mm film; but, the film width is 35 mm.
   I bought a 6-kg turkey, but the turkey weighs 6 kg.

4. Leave a space on each side of signs for multiplication, division, addition, and subtraction, except within a compound symbol.

   Examples: 4 m $\times$ 3 m (not 4 m$\times$3 m); kg/m^3; N·m

Squares and Cubes

When writing symbols for units such as square meter or cubic centimeter, write the symbol for the unit, followed by the superscript ^{2} or ^{3}, respectively.

   Examples: For 14 square meters, write 14 m^2.
   For 26 cubic centimeters, write 26 cm^3.

Compound Units

1. For a unit *name* (not a *symbol*) derived as a quotient, for example, kilometers per hour, it is preferable not to use a slash (/) as a substitute for "per" except where space is limited and a symbol might not be understood. Avoid other mixtures of words and symbols.

   Examples: Use meter per second, not meter/second, meter/s, or m/second.

   Use only one "per" in any combination of units.

   Example: meter per second squared, not meter per second per second

2. For a unit *symbol* derived as a quotient, for example, km/h, do not write k.p.h. or kph because these are understood only in the English language, whereas km/h is understood in all languages. The symbol km/h can also be

written by means of a negative exponent, for example, km · h⁻¹. Do not use more than one slash (/) in any combination of symbols unless parentheses are used to avoid ambiguity.

Examples: m/s², not m/s/s; W/(m · K), not W/m/K

3. For a unit *name* derived as a product, a hyphen is recommended (or a space is permissible) but never a "product dot" (a period raised to a centered position). For example, write newton-meter or newton meter, not newton · meter.

4. For a unit *symbol* derived as a product, use a product dot, for example, N · m. Do not use the product dot as a multiplier symbol for calculations.

Example: Use 6.2 × 5, not 6 · 2 · 5.

5. Do not mix nonmetric units with metric units, except units for time, plane angle, or rotation.

Example: Use kg/m³, not kg/ft³.

6. Eliminate the problem of what units and multiples to use. A quantity that constitutes a ratio of two like quantities should be expressed as a fraction (either common or decimal) or as a percentage.

Examples: The slope is 1/100 or 0.01 or 1%, not 10 mm/m or 10 m/km.

Prefix Usage

1. Although hecto, deka, deci, and centi are SI prefixes, their use should generally be avoided except for the SI unit multiples for area and volume and nontechnical use of the centimeter, as for body and clothing measurements.

2. In broad fields of use, or in a table of values for the same quantity, or in a discussion of such values within a given context, a common unit multiple should be used even when some of the numerical values may require up to five or six digits before the decimal point.

Examples: mm	for mechanical engineering drawings
kPa	for fluid pressure
MPa	for stress
kg/m³	for density

3. When convenient, choose prefixes resulting in numerical values between 0.1 and 1000, but only if this can be done without violating the preceding rules 1 and 2.

4. To avoid errors in calculations, prefixes may be replaced with powers of 10, for example, 1 MJ = 10⁶ J.

5. Generally avoid the use of prefixes in a denominator, except for kilogr: for example, kJ/m^3, not J/dm^3, and kJ/kg, not J/g.

6. Do not use a mixture of prefixes unless the difference in size is extreme.

   Examples: Use 40 mm wide and 1500 mm long, not 40 mm wide and 1.5 m long; but 1500 meters of 2-mm-diameter wire.

7. Do not use multiple prefixes.

   Examples: Use 13.58 m, not 13 m 580 mm.

   Use nm, not m m.

   Use milligram, not microkilogram.

8. Do not use a prefix without a unit; for example, use kilogram, not kilo.

Units for Pressure

Kilopascal (kPa) is the only unit recommended for fluid pressure for all fields of use except high-vacuum measurements of absolute pressure, for which Pa, mPa, and so on, may be more convenient.

Do not use bar (10^5 Pa) or millibar (10^2 Pa) because they are not SI units and are accepted internationally only for a limited time in special fields because of existing usage. They are also objectionable because they introduce too many different units. This requires frequent conversions to the preferred SI unit kPa (10^3 Pa), with the consequent chance for decimal point errors (1 bar = 100 kPa).

Gage pressure is absolute pressure minus ambient pressure (usually atmospheric pressure). It is positive or negative (called vacuum) according to whether the pressure is higher or lower, respectively, than the ambient pressure. Absolute pressure is specified either by (1) using the identifying phrase "absolute pressure," or (2) adding the word "absolute" after the unit symbol and separating the two by a comma or a space. Do not add (to the unit symbol) either "g" for gage or "a" for absolute.

Spelling of Vowel Pairs

In three cases the final vowel in a prefix is omitted; megohm, kilohm, and hectare. In all other cases, both vowels are retained and both are pronounced. No space or hyphen should be used.

PRONUNCIATION OF METRIC TERMS

The pronunciation of most of the unit names is well known and uniformly described in American dictionaries, but four have been pronounced in various ways. The following pronunciations are recommended.

candela: Put the accent on the second syllable and pronounce it like dell.

joule: Pronounce it to rhyme with pool.

pascal: The preferred pronunciation rhymes with rascal. An acceptable second choice puts the accent on the second syllable.

siemens: Pronounce it like seamen's.

For the pronunciation of unit prefixes, see the SI Unit Prefixes (Table 2–2 and footnote 1).

WEIGHT, MASS, AND FORCE

Considerable confusion exists in the use of the term weight as a quantity to mean either force or mass. In commercial and everyday use, the term weight nearly always means mass. Therefore, when one speaks of a person's weight, the quantity referred to is mass. This nontechnical use of the term weight in everyday life will probably persist. However, in physics, weight has usually meant the force of gravity. American dictionaries define weight as either the heaviness or the mass of an object.

To avoid the ambiguity of this dual use of the term weight, avoid its use in technical practice except under circumstances in which its meaning is completely clear. Instead, the terms mass and force of gravity (or gravity force) should be used, together with the appropriate units of kilogram (kg) and newton (N), respectively.

A floor-load rating or a capacity rating of a vehicle (or other load-supporting machine) is intended to define the mass that can be supported safely. The rating should be expressed in kilograms rather than newtons. Similarly, the area density of floor loading should be expressed in kilograms per square meter rather than pascals (newtons per square meter). In engineering calculations involving structures, vehicles, or machines on the surface of the earth, the mass in kilograms is multiplied by 9.8 to obtain the approximate force of gravity in newtons. (The force of gravity acting on a mass of 1 kg varies from about 9.77 to 9.83 N in various parts of the world.)

TYPEWRITING RECOMMENDATIONS

Superscripts

With an ordinary typewriter keyboard, figures and the minus sign can be raised to the superscript position by rolling the platen half a space before typing the figure. When this is done, the figure may tend to run into the text in the line above. This interference can be avoided by using care and double-spacing. In printing, interference is avoided by making superscripts of smaller type than the body of the text; however, this procedure would be available with a typewriter only by modifying the keyboard.

Special Characters

For technical work, it is useful to have a number of Greek letters available on the typewriter. If all metric symbols for units are to be properly typed, a key with the Greek lowercase μ (pronounced "mew" like a cat, not "moo" like a cow) is necessary. This is the symbol for micro, meaning one millionth. It can be approximated on a conventional machine by using a lowercase u, and adding the tail by hand (u). Those planning typed work can choose whether to use this procedure, use the transfer characters known as press-ons, or spell the unit name out in full.

For units of electricity, the Greek uppercase omega (Ω) for ohm will also be useful. But when it is not available, the word "ohm" can be spelled out.

The Letter "El" for Liter

On most typewriters there is no difference at all between the lowercase el (the recognized symbol for liter) and the numeral one. Accordingly, it is preferable to spell the word in full, for example, 24 liters/100 km (fuel consumption). However, there is no problem with ml (milliliter).

If the space for the full word liter is not available, and you do not want to use a lowercase symbol "l" because it looks like a numeral "1", a capital "L" is preferable to a script ℓ. However, the L is not yet recognized in any American National Standard or International Standard.

Typewriter Modification

When frequently used, the following symbols should be included on typewriters: superscripts ^{2} and ^{3} for squared and cubed, Greek μ for micro, ° for degree, for a product dot for symbols derived as a product, and Greek Ω for ohm. The positions in which these are placed on the keyboard will depend partly on the design of the keyboard and partly on the frequency with which the new characters are needed. A special type-ball is available for some typewriters that contains all the superscripts, μ, Ω, and many other characters used in technical reports. Some typewriters have replaceable character keys.

Longhand

To assure legibility of the symbols m, n, and μ, it is recommended that these three symbols be written to resemble printing. For example, written ᶯᶆ not ᵚᵚ. The symbol μ should have a long distinct tail, μ.

Shorthand

Stenographers find that the SI symbols are generally quicker to write than the shorthand forms for the unit names.

PRACTICAL BASIC PROGRAMS

The program in Fig. 2–1 provides a fast method of converting between Celsius and Fahrenheit temperatures. This is an extremely short program and one that can be typed and proofed in 10 minutes or so; it is a good one to start with. Once the program has been entered into the computer, run the program and answer the

```
Ok
LIST
10 REM **TEMPERATURE CONVERSION PROGRAM**
40 INPUT "DO YOU WANT TO CONVERT CELSIUS TO FAHRENHEIT? (Y OR N)";T$
41 PRINT
50 IF T$="N" THEN 70
60 IF T$="Y" THEN 100
70 PRINT "SINCE YOU THEN WANT TO CONVERT FAHRENHEIT TO CELSIUS, ENTER"
80 INPUT "THE FAHRENHEIT TEMPERATURE IN DEGREES";F
90 C=(F-32)*5/9
91 PRINT "THE CELSIUS TEMPERATURE IS:   ";C;" DEGREES"
92 GOTO 220
100 INPUT "ENTER THE CELSIUS TEMPERATURE IN DEGREES";C
110 F=(C*9/5)+32
120 PRINT "THE FAHRENHEIT TEMPERATURE IS:   ";F; "DEGREES"
130 GOTO 220
220 PRINT
230 PRINT
240 STOP
Ok
RUN "PRNSCRN



Ok
RUN
DO YOU WANT TO CONVERT CELSIUS TO FAHRENHEIT? (Y OR N)? N

SINCE YOU THEN WANT TO CONVERT FAHRENHEIT TO CELSIUS, ENTER
THE FAHRENHEIT TEMPERATURE IN DEGREES? 72
THE CELSIUS TEMPERATURE IS:   22.22222  DEGREES


Ok
RUN
DO YOU WANT TO CONVERT CELSIUS TO FAHRENHEIT? (Y OR N)? Y

ENTER THE CELSIUS TEMPERATURE IN DEGREES? 25
THE FAHRENHEIT TEMPERATURE IS:   77 DEGREES


Ok
RUN "PRNSCRN
```

Figure 2-1

```
80 M=8
90 M1=9
100 M2=6
110 M3=8
120 DIM L1$(8)
130 DIM L2$(8)
140 DIM L3(8)
150 DIM A1$(9)
160 DIM A2$(9)
170 DIM A3(9)
180 DIM W1$(6)
190 DIM W2$(6)
200 DIM W3(6)
210 DIM V1$(8)
220 DIM V2$(8)
230 DIM V3(8)
240 FOR I = 1 TO M
250 READ L1$(I),L2$(I),L3(I)
260 NEXT I
270 FOR I = 1 TO M1
280 READ A1$(I),A2$(I),A3(I)
290 NEXT I
300 FOR I = 1 TO M2
310 READ W1$(I),W2$(I),W3(I)
320 NEXT I
330 FOR I = 1 TO M3
340 READ V1$(I),V2$(I),V3(I)
350 NEXT I
360 REM **********
370 REM **** PROCESSING AREA *****
380 PRINT "DO YOU WISH TO CONVERT LENGTH (L), AREA (A),"
390 PRINT"                        MASS (M), OR LIQUID VOLUME (V)?"
400 INPUT A1$
410 PRINT
420 PRINT"                        CONVERSIONS AVAILABLE"
430 PRINT
440 PRINT TAB(9);"NBR";TAB(14);" FROM";TAB(39);" TO"
450 PRINT TAB(9);"---";TAB(14);"----------";TAB(39);"-------------"
460 IF A1$="L" THEN 520
470 IF A1$="A" THEN 650
480 IF A1$="M" THEN 780
490 IF A1$="V" THEN 910
500 PRINT"ENTRY MUST BE L, A, M, OR V"
510 GOTO 380
520 PRINT
530 FOR I = 1 TO M
540 PRINT TAB(10);I;TAB(15);L1$(I);TAB(40);L2$(I)
550 NEXT I
560 PRINT
570 PRINT"ENTER THE NUMBER OF THE CONVERSION TO BE USED (0 WHEN DONE)";
580 INPUT N
590 IF N=0 THEN 1040
600 PRINT"ENTER THE NUMBER OF ";L1$(N)
610 INPUT L0
620 L=L0*L3(N)
630 PRINT L0;L1$(N);"=";L;L2$(N)
640 GOTO 560
650 REM **** PRINT OF AREA ****
660 FOR I = 1 TO M1
670 PRINT TAB(9);I;TAB(14);A1$(I);TAB(39);A2$(I)
680 NEXT I
```

Figure 2-2

15

```
690 PRINT
700 PRINT"ENTER THE NUMBER OF THE CONVERSION TO BE USED (0 WHEN DONE)"
710 INPUT N
720 IF N=0 THEN 1050
730 PRINT"ENTER THE NUMBER OF ";A1$(N);
740 INPUT A0
750 A=A0*A3(N)
760 PRINT A0;A1$(N);"=";A;A2$(N)
770 GOTO 690
780 REM ******** PRINT OF MASS ********
790 FOR I = 1 TO M2
800 PRINT TAB (10);I;TAB(15);W1$(I);TAB(40);W2$(I)
810 NEXT I
820 PRINT
830 PRINT"ENTER THE NUMBER OF THE CONVERSION TO BE USED (0 WHEN DONE)";
840 INPUT N
850 IF N=0 THEN 1050
860 PRINT"ENTER THE NUMBER OF ";W1$(N);
870 INPUT W0
880 W=W0*W3(N)
890 PRINT W0;W1$(N);"=";W;W2$(N)
900 GOTO 820
910 PRINT
920 FOR I = 1 TO M3
930 PRINT TAB(10);I;TAB(15);V1$(I);TAB(40);V2$(I)
940 NEXT I
950 PRINT
960 PRINT"ENTER THE NUMBER OF THE CONVERSION TO BE USED (0 WHEN DONE)";
970 INPUT N
980 IF N=0 THEN 1050
990 PRINT"ENTER THE NUMBER OF ";V1$(N);
1000 INPUT V0
1010 V=V0*V3(N)
1020 PRINT V0;V1$(N);"=";V;V2$(N)
1030 GOTO 950
1040 PRINT
1050 REM ****** PROGRAM TERMINATION POINT ******
1060 PRINT
1070 PRINT
1080 STOP
1090 REM **********
1100 PRINT
1110 PRINT
1120 DATA INCHES,MILLIMETERS,25.4,FEET,METERS,.3048
1130 DATA YARDS,METERS,.9144,MILES,KILOMETERS,1.6093
1140 DATA MILLIMETERS,INCHES,.0394,METERS,FEET,3.2808
1150 DATA METERS,YARDS,1.0936,KILOMETERS,MILES,.6214
1160 PRINT
1170 DATA SQ INCHES, SQ CENTIMETERS,6.4516,SQ FEET,SQ METERS,.0929
1180 DATA SQ YARDS,SQ METERS,.8361,SQ MILES,SQ KILOMETERS,2.59
1190 DATA ACRES,SQ HECTOMETERS (HECTARES),.4047
1200 DATA SQ CENTIMETERS,SQ INCHES,.155,SQ METERS,SQ YARDS,1.196
1210 DATA SQ KILOMETERS,SQ MILES,.3861
1220 DATA SQ HECTOMETERS(HECTARES),ACRES,2.471
1230 PRINT
1240 DATA OUNCES,GRAMS,28.3495,POUNDS,KILOGRAMS,.4536
1250 DATA SHORT TONS,MEGAGRAMS,.9,GRAMS,OUNCES,.0353
1260 DATA KILOGRAMS,POUNDS,2.2046,MEGAGRAMS,SHORT TONS,1.1
1270 PRINT
1280 DATA OUNCE,MILLILITERS,30,PINTS,LITERS,.4732
1290 DATA QUARTS,LITERS,.9464,GALLONS,LITERS,3.7856
1300 DATA MILLILITERS,OUNCES,.03,LITERS,PINTS,2.1134
1310 DATA LITERS,QUARTS,1.0567,LITERS,GALLONS,.2642
1320 DATA END
```

Figure 2-2   (*continued*)

```
10 OPEN "COM1:300,E,7,1" FOR OUTPUT AS #1
20 FOR X=1 TO 24
30 FOR Y=1 TO 80
40 L=SCREEN(X,Y)
50 L$=CHR$(L)
60 PRINT #1,L$;
70 G=G+1:IF G=80 THEN PRINT #1,CHR$(10):G=0
80 NEXT:NEXT
90 CLOSE
```

CONVERSION TABLES

NBR	FROM	TO
1	INCHES	MILLIMETERS
2	FEET	METERS
3	YARDS	METERS
4	MILES	KILOMETERS
5	MILLIMETERS	INCHES
6	METERS	FEET
7	METERS	YEARS
8	KILOMETERS	MILES

```
ENTER NUMBER OF CONVERSION TO BE USED (0 WHEN FINISHED)? 1
ENTER THE NUMBER OF  INCHES
? 6
 6 INCHES= 152.4 MILLIMETERS
NEXT without FOR in 470
Ok
RUN "PRNSCRN
```

Figure 2-2 (*continued*)

questions asked on the monitor. The converted temperature (in the opposite scale) may then be viewed on the monitor screen.

The program in Fig. 2–2 produces conversions between standard measurements and metric units. The conversion can be either to or from the metric units. Once this program has been entered into the computer, via disk or other media, the program is run and the questions are answered as the computer prompts for them. Modification of this program is possible (and very practical) to include other conversions.

3

HVAC DRAWINGS

Mechanical drawings, as applied to the HVAC trades, are basically accurate, neat, clear line representations of the entire system, including all related controls. Most of these drawings are highly diagrammatical and are used to locate ductwork, equipment, and other necessary details of the HVAC system.

The exact method of showing mechanical layouts on HVAC drawings for building construction varies with the engineer and consulting firm commissioned to design the system. However, the following description is typical.

In general, HVAC drawings indicate the location of all equipment; the supply, makeup, and return air ducts; the fans for ventilation; the size and location of grilles, registers, and diffusers; and any other items falling under the HVAC specifications. The drawings also include equipment schedules and large-scale construction details when they are required.

On very small projects, the architect may merely show a one-line diagram of the ductwork on the architectural floor plans with the volume of air and British thermal units of heat required for each area. The ductwork is often sized, in cases like this, by the mechanical contractor installing the job. Such a drawing appears in Fig. 3-1.

In larger buildings, where the mechanical systems are more extensive and complex, architects normally hire consulting engineers to handle the details of the mechanical (HVAC) construction from the time the design and layout of the work are started, through the bidding and construction sequences, to the final approval and acceptance of the finished job.

The HVAC engineer or designer uses the architect's drawings as a reference when designing a suitable HVAC system for the building in question. This design

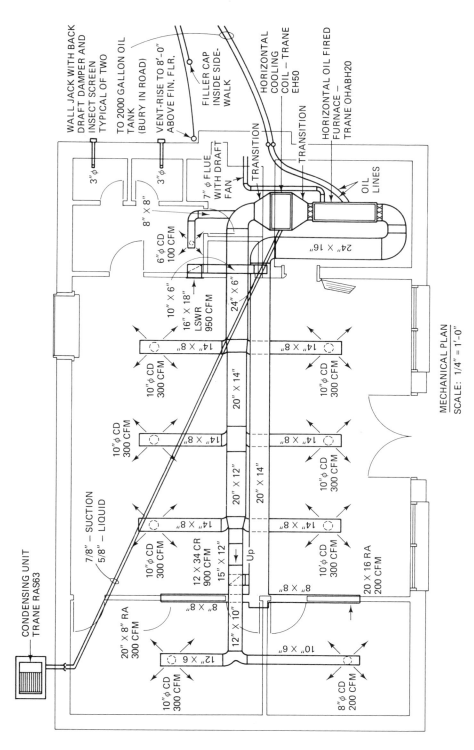

Figure 3-1 Typical simplified HVAC working drawing.

MECHANICAL PLAN
SCALE: 1/4" = 1'-0"

CONDENSING UNIT
TRANE RAS63

7/8" – SUCTION
5/8" – LIQUID

20" X 8" RA
300 CFM

10" φ CD
300 CFM

10" φ CD
300 CFM

10" φ CD
300 CFM

10" φ CD
300 CFM

12 X 34 CR
900 CFM

10" φ CD
300 CFM

8" φ CD
200 CFM

20 X 16 RA
200 CFM

16" X 18"
LSWR
950 CFM

6" φ CD
100 CFM

WALL JACK WITH BACK
DRAFT DAMPER AND
INSECT SCREEN
TYPICAL OF TWO

TO 2000 GALLON OIL
TANK (BURY IN ROAD)

VENT-RISE TO 8'-0"
ABOVE FIN. FLR.

FILLER CAP
INSIDE SIDE-
WALK

HORIZONTAL
COOLING
COIL – TRANE
EH50

HORIZONTAL OIL FIRED
FURNACE –
TRANE OHABH20

OIL
LINES

TRANSITION

TRANSITION

7" φ FLUE
WITH DRAFT
FAN

3"φ

3"φ

8" X 8"

10" X 6"

24" X 6"

14" X 8"

14" X 8"

14" X 8"

14" X 8"

14" X 8"

14" X 8"

20" X 14"

20" X 12"

20" X 14"

24" X 16"

8" X 8"

15" X 12"

Up

12" X 10"

8" X 8"

10" X 6"

12" X 6"

19

usually involves calculating the heat gain for air conditioning, the heat loss for heating, the required air changes per hour for ventilation, the size and shape of duct to deliver the required volume of air to the various areas, control wiring, and similar details.

Draftsmen, in turn, are responsible for translating the engineer's design into neat, detailed, and accurate working drawings that will indicate, beyond any question of a doubt, exactly what is required to install a correct HVAC system in a building. In doing so, the draftsman uses lines, symbols, dimensions, and notations to convey the engineer's design to the workers on the job. Usually, a set of written specifications describing in detail the requirements of the design accompanies these drawings. Together with the working drawings, it forms the basis of the contract requirements for the construction of the project.

SCALE DRAWINGS

Drawings of buildings, and the systems they contain, cannot be made to full size because of the size of buildings as compared to the size of the drawing paper. Therefore, the drawing is reduced in size so that all the distances on the drawing are drawn smaller than the actual dimensions of the building, all dimensions being reduced in the same proportion. The ratio, or relation, between the size of the drawing and the size of the building is indicated on the drawing ($\frac{1}{8}$ inch = 1 foot, for example), and the dimensions are the actual dimensions of the building, not the distance that is measured on the drawing.

The most common method of reducing all the dimensions in the same proportion is to choose a certain distance and let that distance represent 1 foot (ft). This distance is then divided into 12 parts, and each of these parts represents 1 inch (in.). If $\frac{1}{2}$-inch divisions are required, these twelfths are further subdivided into halves. We now have a scale that represents the common foot rule with its subdivisions in inches. When a measurement is layed off on the drawing, it is made with the reduced foot rule known as the architect's scale; when a measurement is taken on the building itself, it is made with the standard foot rule.

Architect's scale.   Architect's scales are available in many different degrees, that is, 1 in. = 1 ft, $\frac{1}{4}$ in. = 1 ft, $\frac{1}{8}$ in. = 1 ft, and so on. (See Fig. 3-2.) However, the most common scales for architectural plans are $\frac{1}{16}$ in. = 1 ft, $\frac{1}{8}$ in. = 1 ft, $\frac{1}{4}$ in. = 1 ft, $\frac{1}{2}$ in. = 1 ft, and $\frac{3}{4}$ in. = 1 ft.

The dimensions in question are found by placing the proper scale on the drawings and reading the figures. The example in Fig. 3-3 shows the dimension to read 24 feet 6 inches.

Figure 3-4 shows a portion of an architect's scale with the 1 in. = 1 ft scale in use. The dimensions of the various lines in this illustration are A equals 5 in., B equals 2 ft 4 in., C equals 6 ft 9 in., and D equals $4\frac{1}{2}$ in.

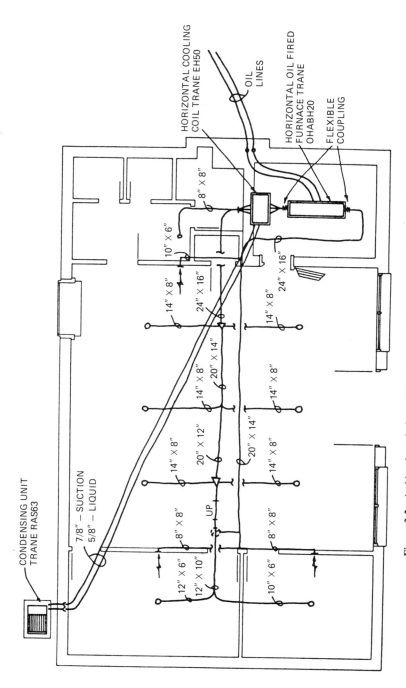

Figure 3-2 Architect's scale is used by engineers, draftsmen, and workers on the job to obtain accurate dimensions when working with scaled drawings.

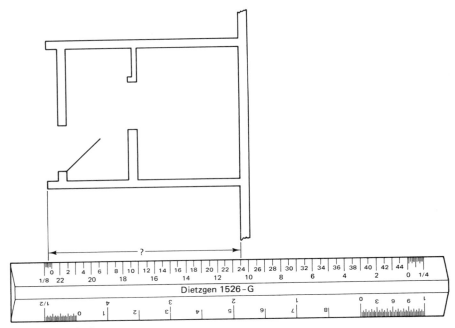

Scale: 1/8″ = 1′-0″

Figure 3-3   Practical use of the architect's scale.

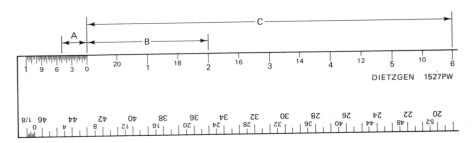

Figure 3-4   Architect's scale in use with the 1″ = 1′ scale.

FIRST FLOOR PLAN

SCALE: 1/4″ = 1′-0″

Figure 3-5   To identify the scale to which the drawing is made, the scale should be plainly marked on the drawing.

The scale should be plainly marked on every drawing as a part of the drawing title, as shown in Fig. 3-5.

SCHEDULES

A working drawing schedule is a systematic method of presenting notes or lists of equipment on a drawing in tabular form. When properly organized and thoroughly understood, schedules are not only powerful time-saving devices for the draftsman, but they can also save the specification writer and the workers on the job much valuable time. A typical diffuser schedule is shown in Fig. 3-6.

SUPPLY DIFFUSER SCHEDULE LOWER LEVEL			
GUEST B.R.	2 - CARNES MODEL 7292-A x 4'0" LONG	157-CFM EACH	
GAME RM.	BASE BOARD ELECTRIC		
BATH #1	1 - CARNES MODEL 200 - 12 x 4 REG.	NO VOLUME CONTROL 50-CFM EACH	STACK HEAD DAMPER
BAR	1 - CARNES MODEL 200 - 12 x 4 REG.	NO VOLUME CONTROL 121-CFM EACH	STACK HEAD DAMPER
KITCHENETTE	1 - CARNES MODEL 200 - 12 x 4 REG.	NO VOLUME CONTROL 64-CFM EACH	STACK HEAD DAMPER
GALLERY	1 - CARNES MODEL C-40 FLOOR 3" x 5'0" / 2 - CARNES MODEL 7261-A x 3'0" LONG	200-CFM EACH / 100-CFM EACH	
STUDY	1 - CARNES MODEL 7292-A x 6'0" LONG	282-CFM EACH	
BED RM. #1	1 - CARNES MODEL 7261-A x 6'0" LONG	188-CFM EACH	
BED RM. #2	1 - CARNES MODEL 7261-A x 6'0" LONG	188-CFM EACH	
BATH #2	1 - CARNES MODEL 200 - 12 x 4 REG.	NO VOLUME CONTROL 50-CFM EACH	STACK HEAD DAMPER
LAV. #1	1 - CARNES MODEL 200 - 12 x 4 REG.	NO VOLUME CONTROL 50-CFM EACH	STACK HEAD DAMPER
LAV. #2	1 - CARNES MODEL 200 - 12 x 4 REG.	NO VOLUME CONTROL 50-CFM EACH	STACK HEAD DAMPER
RETURN AIR DIFFUSER SCHEDULE			
GAME RM.	BASE BOARD ELECTRIC		
GUEST B.R.	CARNES MODEL 7295 x 4'0"	250-CFM EACH	
GALLERY	CARNES MODEL 7295 x 4'0"	400-CFM EACH	
BED RM. #1	CARNES MODEL 7295 x 4'0"	238-CFM EACH	
BED RM. #2	CARNES MODEL 7295 x 4'0"	238-CFM EACH	
STUDY	CARNES MODEL 7295 x 4'0"	332-CFM EACH	

Figure 3-6 Typical diffuser schedule identifying the various types of diffusers used on a particular project.

NOTES

At times it may be desirable to use a few general notes on the working drawings rather than a schedule or elaborate written specifications, especially on projects where only a few special items must be described. Figure 3-7 shows a few such notes as they appeared on an actual HVAC working drawing.

NOTES

THERMOSTAT:
    TRANE (1 STAGE HEATING & 1 STAGE COOLING) W/ON, OFF,
    AUTO. & HEAT-COOL SUB BASE

DIFFUSERS:
    CARNES TYPE DFE W/No. 4 DAMPER & WE FINISH

WALL GRILLES:
    CARNES TYPE CRE-51Q

CLG. GRILLES:
    CARNES TYPE A-CT W/WHITE No. 8-377 FINISH

HOSE BIBBS:
    FREEZE PROOF, REMOVABLE HANDLE, RECESSED
    WITH COVER. BRASS, JOSAM

CONDENSATE DRAIN:
    RUN TO NEAREST D.S.

Figure 3-7 Notes are often used on HVAC drawings to describe certain minor details that usually do not warrant a full schedule.

SYMBOLS

Symbols are used on HVAC working drawings to simplify the draftsman's work and to save time. To briefly illustrate how this is accomplished, the pictorial drawing in Fig. 3-8 clearly indicates how a hot-water heating system is to be installed. A simplified version of this same drawing appears in Fig. 3-9, using symbols (to a certain degree) rather than detailing each item.

In drawing HVAC plans, most engineers and designers use symbols adopted by the ANSI (American National Standards Institute). However, consulting engineering firms, as well as contracting-design firms, frequently modify these standard symbols to better fit their own needs. When these standard symbols are modified, it becomes necessary to provide a symbol list, or legend, on the drawings to facilitate the workers' interpretation.

Figure 3-10 shows a list of HVAC symbols that have been used by a consulting engineering firm with good results since they are:

1. Easy to draw
2. Easily interpreted by workers
3. Sufficient for most applications

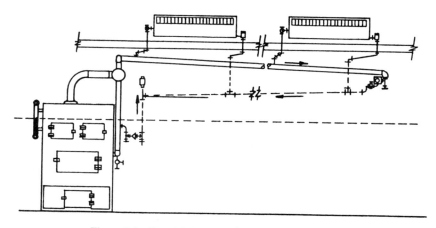

Figure 3-8 Pictorial drawing of a hot water heating system.

It is evident from the symbols in Fig. 3-10 that many have the same basic form but different meanings because of some slight difference. For example, note that each of the valve symbols in Fig. 3-9 has the same basic form (a circle), but that the addition of a line or dot to the circle gives each symbol an individual meaning. It is also apparent that the difference in meaning can be indicated by the addition of either letters or an abbreviation to the symbol. A good procedure to follow in learning symbols is to first learn the basic form and then apply the variations for obtaining different meanings. A complete list of HVAC symbols is given in Chapter 11, along with practical applications of each.

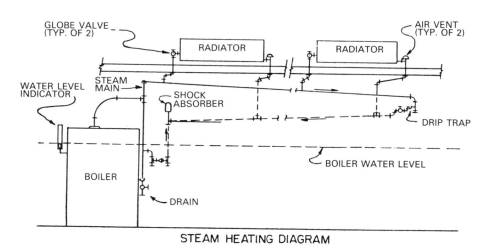

STEAM HEATING DIAGRAM

Figure 3-9 Simplified version of the drawing in Fig. 3-8.

NOTE: THESE ARE STANDARD SYMBOLS AND MAY NOT ALL APPEAR ON THE PROJECT DRAWINGS; HOWEVER,
WHEREVER THE SYMBOL ON THE PROJECT DRAWINGS OCCURS, THE ITEM SHALL BE PROVIDED AND INSTALLED.

Figure 3-10 Typical HVAC drawing symbols.

SECTIONS

If any object, such as an air duct, were sliced or sawed into two parts, the cross section is what would be seen at the point where the section was taken.

During the design of an HVAC system, it is sometimes difficult to adequately show all necessary details in a conventional projection view. If too many dotted or broken lines are used to show hidden objects, the views become confusing and difficult to read. A more practical method is to show the internal construction of an object by imagining its being cut into two sections, as if with a saw.

In dealing with sections, considerable visualization must be used. Some sections are very easy to visualize, but others are not, and there are really no given rules for determining what a particular section will look like. For example, a piece of round duct cut vertically will be in the shape of a rectangle as shown in Fig. 3-11; cut horizontally will be in the shape of a circle as shown in Fig. 3-12; and cut on the slant will be in the shape of an ellipse as shown in Fig. 3-13. The more common sections are described below:

Figure 3-11 A piece of round duct work cut vertically will be drawn in the shape of a rectangle.

Figure 3-12 A piece of round duct cut horizontally will form a circle.

Figure 3-13 A piece of round duct cut on the slant will form an ellipse.

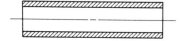

Figure 3-14 Full section.

Full Section: A full section is a sectional view in which the cutting plane is assumed to pass entirely through the object. The view shown in Fig. 3-14 is a full section.

Half Section: A half section is a sectional view in which the cutting plane passes halfway through the object. One-half of the view is shown in section and the other half is shown from the exterior. Figure 3-15 shows a cutting plane passing halfway through a steel shaft and Fig. 3-16 shows the section removed.

Revolved Section: A revolved section (Fig. 3-17) is a cross section that has been revolved through 90°. It is used to show the true shape of the cross section of bars and other elongated parts.

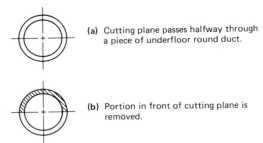

(a) Cutting plane passes halfway through a piece of underfloor round duct.

(b) Portion in front of cutting plane is removed.

Figure 3-15   Half section.

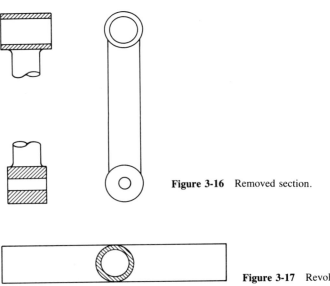

Figure 3-16   Removed section.

Figure 3-17   Revolved section.

4

HEATING AND COOLING
CALCULATIONS

HEATING CALCULATIONS

The HVAC engineer or designer must make certain heat-loss calculations to ascertain that heating equipment of proper capacity will be specified. Heat loss is expressed either in British thermal units (Btu) per hour (which is abbreviated Btuh) or in watts. Both are measures of the rate at which heat is transferred and are easily converted from one to the other by means of the following equations:

$$\text{Watts} = \frac{\text{Btuh}}{3.4}$$

$$\text{Btuh} = \text{watts} \times 3.4$$

Basically, the calculation of heat loss through walls, floors, roof, ceiling, and windows requires three simple steps:

1. Determine the net area in square feet.
2. Find the correct heat-loss factor from a table.
3. Multiply the area by the factor; the product will be expressed in Btuh. However, when electric heating equipment is used, it is normally expressed in watts (W) or kilowatts (kW).

Calculations of heat loss for the average type of residential or commercial building may be made more quickly and efficiently by using the program shown in Fig. 4-1. Once the program has been loaded into the computer and is run, all that is necessary is for the operator to answer the questions as the computer prompts

```
10 REM **SIMPLIFIED HEAT-LOSS PROGRAM**
20 PRINT "HEAT LOSS IS GENERALLY EXPRESSED EITHER IN BTU PER HOUR (BTUH)"
30 PRINT "OR IN WATTS.  BOTH ARE MEASURES OF THE RATE AT WHICH HEAT IS"
40 PRINT "TRANSFERRED AND ARE EASILY CONVERTED FROM ONE TO THE OTHER"
50 PRINT
60 PRINT "THE FOLLOWING PROGRAM ENABLES THE DESIGNER TO EASILY AND QUICKLY"
70 PRINT "DETERMINE THE APPROXIMATE HEAT LOSS FOR A GIVEN AREA.  IT IS"
80 PRINT "SUFFICIENT FOR MOST RESIDENTIAL AND COMMERICIAL APPLICATIONS"
90 PRINT
100 PRINT "MERELY ANSWER THE QUESTIONS AS THEY ARE ASKED"
110 PRINT
120 PRINT "TYPE IN THE STATE IN WHICH THE SYSTEM IS TO BE INSTALLED"
121 PRINT "IF YOU ARE NOT SURE OF THE EXACT ABBREVIATION, DO YOU WANT TO"
122 INPUT "SEE A LIST OF STATES AND THEIR ABBREVIATIONS (Y OR N)";L$
123 IF L$="Y" THEN 8120
130 INPUT "USE STANDARD ABBREVIATION FOR STATE SUCH AS AL, AK, ETC.";S$
140 IF S$="AL" THEN 1000
150 IF S$="AK" THEN 1100
160 IF S$="AZ" THEN 1200
170 IF S$="AR" THEN 1300
180 IF S$="CA" THEN 1400
190 IF S$="CO" THEN 2500
200 IF S$="CT" THEN 1600
210 IF S$="DE" THEN 1600
220 IF S$="DC" THEN 1600
230 IF S$="FL" THEN 1900
240 IF S$="GA" THEN 2000
250 IF S$="HI" THEN 2100
260 IF S$="ID" THEN 2300
270 IF S$="IL" THEN 2300
280 IF S$="IN" THEN 2300
290 IF S$="IA" THEN 2500
300 IF S$="KS" THEN 2300
310 IF S$="KY" THEN 1600
320 IF S$="LA" THEN 1900
330 IF S$="ME" THEN 2500
340 IF S$="MD" THEN 1600
350 IF S$="MA" THEN 1600
360 IF S$="MI" THEN 2300
370 IF S$="MN" THEN 2500
380 IF S$="MS" THEN 2000
390 IF S$="MO" THEN 2300
400 IF S$="MT" THEN 1100
410 IF S$="NE" THEN 2300
420 IF S$="NV" THEN 2300
430 IF S$="NH" THEN 2500
440 IF S$="NJ" THEN 1600
450 IF S$="NM" THEN 1600
460 IF S$="NY" THEN 2300
470 IF S$="NC" THEN 1600
480 IF S$="ND" THEN 2500
490 IF S$="OH" THEN 2300
500 IF S$="OK" THEN 1600
510 IF S$="OR" THEN 1600
520 IF S$="PA" THEN 1600
530 IF S$="RI" THEN 1600
540 IF S$="SC" THEN 2000
550 IF S$="SD" THEN 2500
560 IF S$="TN" THEN 1600
570 IF S$="TX" THEN 1600
580 IF S$="UT" THEN 2300
590 IF S$="VT" THEN 2300
600 IF S$="VA" THEN 1600
610 IF S$="WA" THEN 2300
620 IF S$="WV" THEN 2300
630 IF S$="WI" THEN 2500
640 IF S$="WY" THEN 2500
```

Figure 4-1

```
1000 PRINT "WHICH OF THE TWO LOCATIONS IN AL IS CLOSEST,(1)BIRMINGHAM OR (2)"
1001 INPUT "MOBILE (TYPE EITHER  1 OR 2)";L$
1010 IF L$="1" THEN 1030
1020 IF L$="2" THEN 1040
1030 TD=60:GOTO 5040
1040 TD=55:GOTO 5040
1100 TD=110:GOTO 5040
1200 PRINT "WHICH OF THE THREE LOCATIONS IN AZ IS CLOEST (1)FLAGSTAFF,"
1201 INPUT "(2)PHONIX, OR (3) YUMA";L$
1240 IF L$="1" THEN 5000
1250 IF L$="2" THEN 5001
1260 IF L$="3" THEN 5002
1300 TD=65:GOTO 5040
1400 PRINT "WHICH OF THE LOCATIONS IS CLOSEST, (1)NORTHERN CA OR"
1401 INPUT "(2)SOUTHERN CA";L$
1410 IF L$="1" THEN 1430
1420 IF L$="2" THEN 1440
1430 TD=45:GOTO 5040
1440 TD=35:GOTO 5040
1600 TD=70:GOTO 5040
1900 TD=45:GOTO 5040
2000 TD=60:GOTO 5040
2100 TD=35:GOTO 5040
2300 TD=80:GOTO 5040
2500 TD=90:GOTO 5040
2600 TD=
5000 TD=80:GOTO 5040
5001 TD=45:GOTO 5040
5002 TD=40:GOTO 5040
5010 TD=45:GOTO 5040
5020 TD=40:GOTO 5040
5030 GOTO 6000
5040 PRINT "ENTER THE FOLLOWING DIMENSIONS"
5050 INPUT "TOTAL SQ. FT. OF WINDOWS OR GLASS DOORS";W
5060 INPUT "TOTAL SQ. FT. OF OUTSIDE WALLS";O
5070 INPUT "TOTAL SQ. FT. OF ROOF";R
5080 INPUT "TOTAL SQ. FT. OF FLOOR";F
5081 INPUT "WHAT IS THE LENGTH OF THE ROOM OR AREA";L
5082 INPUT "WHAT IS THE WIDTH OF THE ROOM OR AREA";W2
5083 INPUT "WHAT IS THE HEIGHT OF THE ROOM OR AREA";H2
5084 CFM=((L*W2*H2)/60)
8000 H=(W*.55*TD)+(O*.13*TD)+(R*9.000001E-02*TD)+(F*.2*TD)+(CFM*1.08*TD)
8001 PRINT
8002 PRINT
8010 PRINT "TOTAL HEAT LOAD FOR AREA IS";H;"BUTH"
8020 PRINT
8030 INPUT "DO YOU WANT THE RATING IN WATTS (Y OR N)";E$
8040 IF E$="N" THEN 10
8050 EW=H/3.4
8051 PRINT
8052 PRINT
8060 PRINT "THE TOTAL LOAD IN WATTS IS";EW;"WATTS"
8070 PRINT
8080 PRINT
8090 INPUT "DO YOU WANT TO MAKE ANOTHER CALCULATION (Y OR N)?";C$
8100 IF C$="Y" THEN 10
8110 IF C$="N" THEN STOP
8120 CLS
8130 PRINT "**************************************************************"
8140 PRINT "*    STATE        ABBREVIATION      STATE        ABBREVIATION *"
8150 PRINT "*  Alabama........AL                Montana..........MT        *"
8160 PRINT "*  Alaska.........AK                Nebraska.........NE        *"
8170 PRINT "*  Arizona........AZ                Nevada...........NV        *"
8180 PRINT "*  Arkansas.......AR                New Hampshire.....NH       *"
8190 PRINT "*  California.....CA                New Jersey........NJ       *"
8200 PRINT "*  Colorado.......CO                New Mexico.......NM        *"
8210 PRINT "*  Connecticut....CT                New York..........NY       *"
8220 PRINT "*  Delaware.......DE                North Carolina....NC       *"
8230 PRINT "*  District of Col DC               North Dakota......ND       *"
```

Figure 4-1   (*continued*)

```
8240 PRINT "*  Florida.........FL          Ohio..............OH      *"
8250 PRINT "*  Georgia.........GA          Oklahoma..........OK      *"
8260 PRINT "*  Hawaii..........HI          Oregon............OR      *"
8270 PRINT "*  Idaho...........ID          Pennsylvania......PA      *"
8280 PRINT "*  Illinois........IL          Rhode Island......RI      *"
8290 PRINT "*  Indiana.........IN          South Carolina....SC      *"
8300 PRINT "*  Iowa............IA          South Dakota......SD      *"
8310 PRINT "*  Kansas..........KS          Tennessee.........TN      *"
8320 PRINT "*  Kentucky........KY          Texas.............TX      *"
8330 PRINT "*  Louisiana.......LA          Utah..............UT      *"
8340 PRINT "*  Maine...........ME          Vermont...........VT      *"
8350 PRINT "*  Maryland........MD          Virginia..........VA      *"
8360 PRINT "*  Massachusetts...MA          Washington........WA      *"
8370 PRINT "*  Michigan........MI          West Virginia.....WV      *"
8380 PRINT "*  Minnesota.......MN          Wisconsin.........WI      *"
8390 PRINT "*  Mississippi.....MS          Wyoming...........WY      *"
8400 PRINT "*  Missouri........MO                                    *"
8410 PRINT "******************************************************************"
8420 PRINT
8430 INPUT "ARE YOU NOW READY TO MAKE YOUR CALCULATION (Y OR N)";R$
8440 IF R$="Y" THEN 130
8450 IF R$="N" THEN 10
```

Figure 4-1 (continued)

for them. All calculations are made automatically by the computer, and the heat loss for any area is expressed in both Btuh and watts.

The load estimates used in this program are based on design conditions inside the building and outside in the atmosphere surrounding the building. Outside design conditions are based on the maximum extremes of temperature occurring in a specific locality, which must be stated prior to running the program. The inside design condition is based on a temperature of 70°F, which should give optimum comfort in most situations.

The program in Fig. 4-1 is already provided with the outside design dry-bulb temperatures to calculate the heating loads required for various areas in various locations. This program assumes an 80% relative humidity for the outside design humidity. For more exact data, refer to the *ASHRAE Handbook** and obtain specific humidity from a psychrometric chart.

To use the program, after it is loaded into the computer, first calculate the area (in square feet) of all outside windows in the area under consideration. Continue with the outside walls, roof, and so on, until all dimensions are accounted for. The computer does the rest. Even the infiltration is automatically calculated in this program. Merely answer the questions as the computer asks for them, and the computer does the rest. It will even give a printout of the results if you desire.

When the program is run, the monitor screen first appears as shown in Fig. 4-2. Let's assume that a heating calculation must be made in the state of Virginia. When the first prompt or question mark appears on the screen, the letters "VA" are typed, and the RETURN key is pressed. Then the computer asks for the various dimensions as shown in Fig. 4-3. After the last question, "WHAT IS THE HEIGHT OF THE ROOM OR AREA?", the RETURN KEY is pressed, and the computer

*ASHRAE stands for American Society of Heating, Refrigeration, and Air Conditioning Engineers.

```
LOAD"HEAT
Ok
RUN
HEAT LOSS IS GENERALLY EXPRESSED EITHER IN BTU PER HOUR (BTUH)
OR IN WATTS.  BOTH ARE MEASURES OF THE RATE AT WHICH HEAT IS
TRANSFERRED AND ARE EASILY CONVERTED FROM ONE TO THE OTHER

THE FOLLOWING PROGRAM ENABLES THE DESIGNER TO EASILY AND QUICKLY
DETERMINE THE APPROXIMATE HEAT LOSS FOR A GIVEN AREA.  IT IS
SUFFICIENT FOR MOST RESIDENTIAL AND COMMERICIAL APPLICATIONS

MERELY ANSWER THE QUESTIONS AS THEY ARE ASKED

TYPE IN THE STATE IN WHICH THE SYSTEM IS TO BE INSTALLED
USE STANDARD ABBREVIATION FOR STATE SUCH AS AL, AK, ETC.?
©C
Break in 130
Ok
RUN "PRNSCRN
```

Figure 4-2

almost instantly comes up with the heat loss for the area in question, that is, 12,619.04 Btuh.

The computer then asks if you want this figure converted to watts. If the "Y" key is pressed, the computer prints the following:

"THE TOTAL LOAD IN WATTS IS 3711.483 WATTS"

Another option is provided at the beginning of this program to let the operator review the abbreviations for the various states, since the computer must be provided the exact two letters in order to proceed with the program. It will not work if one letter is out of place. Therefore, since the exact abbreviation as the computer knows it may not be known by the operator, this legend can be invaluable.

```
MERELY ANSWER THE QUESTIONS AS THEY ARE ASKED

TYPE IN THE STATE IN WHICH THE SYSTEM IS TO BE INSTALLED
USE STANDARD ABBREVIATION FOR STATE SUCH AS AL, AK, ETC.? VA
ENTER THE FOLLOWING DIMENSIONS
TOTAL SQ. FT. OF WINDOWS OR GLASS DOORS? 49
TOTAL SQ. FT. OF OUTSIDE WALLS? 268
TOTAL SQ. FT. OF ROOF? 273
TOTAL SQ. FT. OF FLOOR? 273
WHAT IS THE LENGTH OF THE ROOM OR AREA? 10
WHAT IS THE WIDTH OF THE ROOM OR AREA? 27.3
WHAT IS THE HEIGHT OF THE ROOM OR AREA? 8

TOTAL HEAT LOAD FOR AREA IS 12619.04 BUTH

DO YOU WANT THE RATING IN WATTS (Y OR N)? Y

THE TOTAL LOAD IN WATTS IS 3711.483 WATTS
Ok
RUN "PRNSCRN
```

Figure 4-3

Once the computer operator becomes more familiar with basic BASIC programming, more elaborate programs can be performed on even the simplest computers. Such elaborate programs take considerably more time to type into the computer, and errors are therefore more prevalent.

ADVANCED DESIGN

The goals of any HVAC system are to obtain:

1. Adequate, dependable, and trouble-free installation
2. Year-round comfort
3. Reasonable annual operating cost
4. Reasonable installation cost
5. Systems that are easy to maintain

```
10 REM **COMMERCIAL AIR CONDITIONING PROGRAM**
20 PRINT "THIS PROGRAM IS DESIGNED TO CALCULATE THE COOLING LOAD FOR"
30 PRINT "ANY GIVEN BUILDING.  BEFORE USING, HOWEVER, A SURVEY OF THE"
40 PRINT "BUILDING MUST BE TAKEN TO DETERMINE CERTAIN CHARACTERISTICS"
50 PRINT "SUCH AS ROOM DIMENSIONS, TYPE OF CONSTRUCTION, WINDOWS, ETC."
60 PRINT "THE FORM SUPPLIED IN A NEARBY ILLUSTRATION WILL HELP IN"
70 PRINT "OBTAINING THIS INFORMATION.  THEN, WHEN THE PROGRAM IS RUN,"
80 PRINT "THE COMPUTER WILL ASK FOR THIS INFORMATION.  AFTER THE"
90 PRINT "COMPUTER HAS THE NECESSARY INFORMATION, IT WILL THEN AUTOMATICALLY"
91 PRINT "MAKE THE NECESSARY CALCULATIONS TO OBTAIN THE COOLING LOAD FOR"
92 PRINT "THE BUILDING IN QUESTION.  IT WILL ALSO GIVE THE COOLING LOAD FOR"
93 PRINT "EACH INDIVIDUAL AREA WHICH MAY BE USED IN SIZING DUCTS, DIFFUSERS,"
94 PRINT "AND THE LIKE."
95 PRINT
96 PRINT
100 PRINT "ENTER TIME OF PEAK LOAD FROM THE FOLLOWING LIST (1,2,3,OR 4)"
110 PRINT "                    (1) 8 TO 11 AM"
120 PRINT "                    (2) 11AM TO 2 PM"
130 PRINT "                    (3) 2 TO 5 PM"
140 PRINT "                    (4) 8 TO 11 PM"
150 INPUT A
160 PRINT "ENTER DIMENSIONS (IN SQ. FT.) OF OUTSIDE WALLS FACING THE FOLLOWING"
170 PRINT "DIRECTIONS.  ENTER '0' FOR NONE)"
180 INPUT "SQ. FT. OF OUTSIDE WALL FACING NORTH";B
190 INPUT "SQ. FT. OF OUTSIDE WALL FACING NE, E, OR SE";C
200 INPUT "SQ. FT. OF OUTSIDE WALL FACING SOUTH";D
210 INPUT "SQ. FT. OF OUTSIDE WALL FACING SW, W, OR NW";E
220 PRINT
230 PRINT
240 INPUT "ENTER SQ. FT. OF ROOF OR CEILING";F
250 PRINT
260 PRINT
270 INPUT "ENTER SQ. FT. OF FLOOR";G
280 PRINT
290 INPUT "IS THERE A HIGH TEMPERATURE SPACE BELOW ROOM IN QUESTION (Y OR N)";A$
300 IF A$="Y" THEN H=G*16
310 IF A$="N" THEN H=G*0
320 PRINT
```

Figure 4-4

```
330 INPUT "ENTER NUMBER OF OCCUPANTS";I
340 PRINT
350 PRINT "ENTER DIMENSIONS (IN SQ. FT.) OF WINDOWNS FACING IN THE FOLLOWING"
360 PRINT "DIRECTIONS"
370 INPUT "SQ. FT. OF WINDOWS FACING NORTH";J
380 INPUT "SQ. FT. OF WINDOWS FACING NE,E, OR SE";K
390 INPUT "SQ. FT. OF WINDOWS FACING SOUTH";L
400 INPUT "SQ. FT. OF WINDOWS FACING SW, W, OR NW";M
410 PRINT
420 INPUT "GIVE TOTAL WATTAGE OF LIGHTING FIXTURES IN AREA";N
430 IF A=1 THEN 1000
440 IF A=2 THEN 2000
450 IF A=3 THEN 3000
460 IF A= 4 THEN 4000
500 ZZ=AA+BB+CC+DD+EE+FF+GG+HH
510 XX=(I*10)
520 YY=(O/60)
530 IF XX>YY THEN 550
540 IF XX<YY THEN 560
550 WW=(XX*15)+(XX*22)
560 WW=(YY*15)+(YY*22)
570 VV=(N*4.25)
580 UU=(I*200+VV+WW)
581 RR=((ZZ+UU)/12000)
582 QQ=ZZ+UU
600 PRINT "THE TOTAL SENSIBLE COOLING LOAD IS";ZZ;"BTUH"
601 PRINT "                                   ---------"
602 PRINT "THE TOTAL LATENT COOLING LOAD IS";UU;"BTUH"
603 PRINT "                                 ---------"
604 PRINT "THE TOTAL COOLING LOAD IS THEREFORE";QQ;"BTUH, REQUIRING"
605 PRINT "APPROXIMATELY";RR;"TONS OF AIR CONDITIONING"
610 INPUT "DO YOU WANT TO MAKE ANOTHER CALCULATION (Y OR N)";Q$
620 IF Q$="Y" THEN CLS:GOTO 20
630 STOP
1000 MM=B*0
1010 NN=C*2
1020 OO=D*0
1030 PP=E*1
1031 SS=J*25
1032 TT=K*46
1033 U=L*25
1034 V=M*25
1040 AA=(MM+NN+OO+PP)
1090 HH=(SS+TT+U+V)
1100 CC=B*4
1110 EE=I*15
1120 FF=I*200
1130 GG=N*4.25
1140 GOTO 500
2000 MM=B*2
2010 NN=C*4
2020 OO=D*1
2030 PP=E*1
2040 SS=J*25
2050 TT=K*25
2060 U=L*52
2070 V=M*42
2080 GOTO 1040
3000 MM=B*1
3010 NN=C*4
3020 OO=D*3
3030 PP=E*2
3040 SS=J*25
3050 TT=K*25
3060 U=L*37
3070 V=M*70
3080 GOTO 1040
4000 MM=B*2
```

Figure 4-4 (*continued*)

```
4010 NN=C*3
4020 OO=D*3
4030 PP=E*5
4040 SS=J*20
4050 TT=K*20
4060 U=L*20
4070 V=M*20
4080 GOTO 1040
```

```
ENTER TIME OF PEAK LOAD FROM THE FOLLOWING LIST (1,2,3,OR 4)
                    (1) 8 TO 11 AM
                    (2) 11AM TO 2 PM
                    (3) 2 TO 5 PM
? 1                 (4) 8 TO 11 PM
ENTER DIMENSIONS (IN SQ. FT.) OF OUTSIDE WALLS FACING THE FOLLOWING
DIRECTIONS.  ENTER '0' FOR NONE)
SQ. FT. OF OUTSIDE WALL FACING NORTH? 120
SQ. FT. OF OUTSIDE WALL FACING NE, E, OR SE? 360
SQ. FT. OF OUTSIDE WALL FACING SOUTH? 120
SQ. FT. OF OUTSIDE WALL FACING SW, W, OR NW? 360


ENTER SQ. FT. OF ROOF OR CEILING? 800


ENTER SQ. FT. OF FLOOR? 800

IS THERE A HIGH TEMPERATURE SPACE BELOW ROOM IN QUESTION (Y OR N)? N

ENTER NUMBER OF OCCUPANTS?
©C
Break in 330
Ok
RUN "PRNSCRN

IS THERE A HIGH TEMPERATURE SPACE BELOW ROOM IN QUESTION (Y OR N)? N

ENTER NUMBER OF OCCUPANTS? 4

ENTER DIMENSIONS (IN SQ. FT.) OF WINDOWNS FACING IN THE FOLLOWING
DIRECTIONS
SQ. FT. OF WINDOWS FACING NORTH? 6
SQ. FT. OF WINDOWS FACING NE,E, OR SE? 6
SQ. FT. OF WINDOWS FACING SOUTH? 6
SQ. FT. OF WINDOWS FACING SW, W, OR NW? 6

GIVE TOTAL WATTAGE OF LIGHTING FIXTURES IN AREA? 2400
THE TOTAL SENSIBLE COOLING LOAD IS 13346 BTUH
                                   ---------
THE TOTAL LATENT COOLING LOAD IS 11000 BTUH
                                 ---------
THE TOTAL COOLING LOAD IS THEREFORE 24346 BTUH, REQUIRING
APPROXIMATELY 2.028833 TONS OF AIR CONDITIONING
DO YOU WANT TO MAKE ANOTHER CALCULATION (Y OR N)?
©C
Break in 610
Ok
RUN "PRNSCRN
```

Figure 4-4 (*continued*

To provide adequate heat to a given area or space, the existing air (and some makeup in some cases) within the space is heated to a temperature somewhat higher than the desired room temperature; that is, if the desired room temperature is, say, 72°F, the air might be heated to a temperature of 90°F. Once this heated air enters the room to be conditioned, it immediately begins to cool down. In doing so, it surrenders sufficient heat to the area to offset the heat losses from the area.

The program in Fig. 4-4 is designed to give the approximate heat-gain figures for either a residential or relatively small commercial building. Experience has proved that this particular program is a good average for the United States when a degree difference of 15°F is desired and when specialty buildings—such as hospitals or restaurant kitchens—are not considered.

5

DUCT FABRICATION

Air-distribution systems carry the air from the blower unit to the space to be conditioned, and then back to the blower unit for redistribution. In designing such a system, the engineer usually decides on the combination of fans, duct routes, outlets, and controls that results in the best system within the allotted budget.

Ducts are installed in a variety of shapes and sizes, but those most commonly seen in building construction systems are circular, rectangular, or square. The size of the ducts depends on the amount of air to be delivered. The shape often depends on the available space to install the ductwork in any given area.

Duct systems are divided into two general categories: (1) those designed for areas in which the cold season is the major consideration, such as northern climates, and (2) those designed for areas in which the hot season is the major consideration. Generally, duct systems that supply air at or near floor level are best where heat is the major concern. Overhead systems, on the other hand, are usually best for areas where the cooling system is the major concern. Of course, there are exceptions to the preceding statements. Many times it is not practical to install ductwork from below because of the building construction, economy reasons, and the like.

SUPPLY-AIR OUTLETS

Supply-air outlets are a major part of any air-distribution system because they provide a means of distributing properly controlled air to a room or area. Such outlets should deflect or diffuse the air, be adjustable for changing the airflow rate, avoid air noise, and be able to throw the conditioned air no less than three-quarters the distance from the outlet to the opposite wall in most cases.

Many types of supply-air outlets are available, some of which follow:

Supply-air outlet: Floor, ceiling, or wall opening through which conditioned air is delivered to a room or area.

Ceiling diffuser: A square, oval, circular, or semicircular facing device that covers the supply-air opening (usually in the ceiling) of a room or area. Most diffusers are adjustable for airflow direction and rate.

Grille: A covering for any opening through which air passes.

Register: A covering for any opening through which air passes. It usually has a built-in damper for controlling the air passing through it.

Supply-air outlets in the area to be conditioned must be located so that sufficient air is supplied to establish and maintain comfort conditions within the area, that is, a uniform air pattern that is free from hot or cold drafts.

RETURN-AIR OUTLETS

The location of the return-air outlets is not as critical as the location of the supply-air outlets. As a rule of thumb, return-air outlets should be in the opposite location from supply-air outlets. For example, if the supply-air outlets are located in the ceiling or high sidewall, the return-air outlets should be located in the floor or low sidewall. If the supply-air outlets are located on an outside wall, the return-air outlets should be located on an inside wall of the room.

SHEET-METAL PROGRAMS

The fabrication of ductwork for an HVAC system utilizes geometry to a great extent since flat sheets of metal are made into geometrical shapes. The working drawings normally supply the required dimensions, but the worker must also make various calculations to ensure that when the flat metal is cut and bent the result will be the desired shape. Moreover, a knowledge of air volume is necessary to ensure that the size of the ducts will allow adequate airflow at the proper speed or velocity. Often the working drawings may show one size and type of duct, but the structural members in the building make it necessary to change the shape of the duct, while still maintaining the specified air volume, in order to fit the ductwork into the building. Calculations such as this, and many others, can easily and quickly be performed on almost any computer.

In the examples that follow, almost every conceivable shape has been taken

```
0 REM **PROGRAM DESIGNED TO CALCULATE MAIN PIPE WHOSE CAPACITY WILL EQUAL THE COMB
DIAMETER**
20 CLS
30 INPUT"DIAMETER OF ONE BRANCH PIPE";A
40 CLS
50 INPUT"DIAMETER OF SECOND BRANCH PIPE";B
60 CLS
70 INPUT"DIAMETER OF THIRD BRANCH PIPE (IF NO THIRD PIPE EXISTS ENTER 0)";C
80 CLS
90 ZZ=SQR(A↓2+B↓2+C↓2)
100 PRINT ZZ "INCHES"
110 END
```

Figure 5-1

into consideration and put to practical use, utilizing the computer to help solve the problems. The experienced designer or worker will soon see how valuable such programs (and their modifications) can be in everyday applications.

CALCULATING MAIN DUCT OR PIPE

The BASIC program in Fig. 5-1 enables the operator to calculate a main duct or pipe with an air volume equivalent to up to three branch ducts. To use, the program is first entered into the computer keyboard exactly as shown in Fig. 5-1. When the program is run, the monitor screen appears as shown in Fig. 5-2. In Fig. 5-2(a), three duct sizes of 6, 8, and 10 in., respectively, are used. It is desired to know the equivalent main duct with the capacity of the three combined ducts. When the program is run on the computer, the computer prompts for the dimension of the first duct, then the second duct, and so on. After the last dimension is entered and the RETURN key is pressed, the answer immediately appears on the screen. In this case, the equivalent main duct would be 14.14214 in. or, for all practical purposes, 14 in.

```
Ok
RUN
DIAMETER OF ONE BRANCH PIPE? 6
DIAMETER OF SECOND BRANCH PIPE? 8
DIAMETER OF THIRD BRANCH PIPE (IF NO THIRD PIPE EXISTS ENTER 0)? 10      (a)
 14.14214 INCHES
Ok
RUN
DIAMETER OF ONE BRANCH PIPE? 4
DIAMETER OF SECOND BRANCH PIPE? 4
DIAMETER OF THIRD BRANCH PIPE (IF NO THIRD PIPE EXISTS ENTER 0)? 8       (b)
 9.797959 INCHES
Ok
RUN
DIAMETER OF ONE BRANCH PIPE? 4
DIAMETER OF SECOND BRANCH PIPE? 4
DIAMETER OF THIRD BRANCH PIPE (IF NO THIRD PIPE EXISTS ENTER 0)? 4       (c)
 6.928203 INCHES
Ok
```

Figure 5-2

Figure 5-3   Conical ventilator top.

Two other examples are shown in Fig. 5-2(b) and (c).

CONICAL VENTILATOR TOP

Conical ventilator tops (Fig. 5-3) are common in many HVAC systems. To find the slant height of a given cone, use the program in Fig. 5-4. The program in Fig. 5-5 calculates the arc or the amount to be removed from the circumference of the circle.

```
Ok
LOAD "ON
Ok
LIST
10 REM **CONICAL VENTILATOR**
20 INPUT "DIAMETER OF CONE";D
30 INPUT "HEIGHT OF CONE";H
40 R=.5*D
50 S=SQR(H 2+R 2)
60 C=3.1416*D+1.5
65 CLS
70 PRINT "THE SLANT HEIGHT OF THE CONE IS";S;"INCHES"
80 PRINT "THE CIRCUMFERENCE OF THE BASE IS";C;"INCHES"
Ok
RUN "PRNSCRN

                         Ok
RUN
DIAMETER OF CONE? 12
HEIGHT OF CONE? 8


THE SLANT HEIGHT OF THE CONE IS 10 INCHES
THE CIRCUMFERENCE OF THE BASE IS 39.1992 INCHES
Ok
RUN
DIAMETER OF CONE? 10
HEIGHT OF CONE? 4


THE SLANT HEIGHT OF THE CONE IS 6.403125 INCHES
THE CIRCUMFERENCE OF THE BASE IS 32.916 INCHES
Ok
RUN "PRNSCRN
```

Figure 5-4

Ok
RUN
THIS PROGRAM CALCULATES THE ARC OR AMOUNT FROM CIRCUMFERENCE
OF CIRCLE TO BE REMOVED TO FORM THE CONE IN THE PREVIOUS
PROGRAM. ALLOWING .0198 FACTOR TO BE MULTIPLIED TIMES THE
CIRCUMFERENCE FOR LAP.
ENTER DIAMETER OF CONE BASE? 24
ENTER HEIGHT OF CONE? 6

LAP REQUIRED IS 1.492888 INCHES

CIRCUMFERENCE OF FLAT CIRCLE TO BE CUT OUT IS 84.29797 INCHES

THE AMOUNT TO MEASURE ALONG CIRCUMFERENCE IS 7.406677 INCHES

AND IS TO BE REMOVED IN THE FORM OF A TRIANGLE TO ALLOW
THE CONE TO BE FORMED
Ok
SAVE"MULTI.BAS
Ok
RUN "PRNSCRN


```
10 REM **ARC TO BE REMOVED FROM CIRCLE**
20 PRINT "THIS PROGRAM CALCULATES THE ARC OR AMOUNT FROM CIRCUMFERENCE"
30 PRINT "OF CIRCLE TO BE REMOVED TO FORM THE CONE IN THE PREVIOUS"
40 PRINT "PROGRAM.  ALLOWING .0198 FACTOR TO BE MULTIPLIED TIMES THE"
50 PRINT "CIRCUMFERENCE FOR LAP."
60 INPUT "ENTER DIAMETER OF CONE BASE";C
61 INPUT "ENTER HEIGHT OF CONE";H
62 A=C/2
63 S=SQR(H©2+A©2)
64 B=3.1416*C
65 F=S*2*3.1416
66 D=B*.0198
67 E=F-(B+D)
68 PRINT
100 PRINT "LAP REQUIRED IS";D;"INCHES"
101 PRINT "       --------"
105 PRINT "CIRCUMFERENCE OF FLAT CIRCLE TO BE CUT OUT IS";F;"INCHES"
106 PRINT "                                            --------"
110 PRINT "THE AMOUNT TO MEASURE ALONG CIRCUMFERENCE IS";E;"INCHES"
111 PRINT "                                            --------"
120 PRINT "AND IS TO BE REMOVED IN THE FORM OF A TRIANGLE TO ALLOW"
130 PRINT "THE CONE TO BE FORMED"
```


Ok
RUN
THIS PROGRAM CALCULATES THE ARC OR AMOUNT FROM CIRCUMFERENCE
OF CIRCLE TO BE REMOVED TO FORM THE CONE IN THE PREVIOUS
PROGRAM. ALLOWING .0198 FACTOR TO BE MULTIPLIED TIMES THE
CIRCUMFERENCE FOR LAP.
ENTER DIAMETER OF CONE BASE? 8
ENTER HEIGHT OF CONE? 12

LAP REQUIRED IS .4976294 INCHES

CIRCUMFERENCE OF FLAT CIRCLE TO BE CUT OUT IS 79.47689 INCHES

THE AMOUNT TO MEASURE ALONG CIRCUMFERENCE IS 53.84646 INCHES

AND IS TO BE REMOVED IN THE FORM OF A TRIANGLE TO ALLOW

Figure 5-5

```
THE CONE TO BE FORMED
Ok
RUN "PRNSCRN
```

```
Ok
NOTICE IN THE ABOVE CALCULATIONS THAT THE ANSWERS ARE SOMETIMES GIVEN
TO SEVEN DECIMAL PLACES WHICH IS REALLY NOT PRACTICAL FOR AN ACTUAL
APPLICATION.  FOR EXAMPLE, IN "LAP REQUIRED", THE FIGURE IS .4976294.
IN ACTUAL PRACTICE, THE SHEET METAL WORKER WOULD MAKE THE LAP 1/2 OR
0.5 INCH.

RUN "PRNSCRN
```

Figure 5-5 (*continued*)

PROGRAM FOR FINDING MAIN DUCT WHEN
SMALL DUCTS ARE SQUARE OR RECTANGULAR

The program shown in Fig. 5-6, along with printouts of three examples, calculates
the size of a main duct equivalent to up to three small ducts.


```
0 REM METHOD OF FINDING MAIN DUCT WHEN SMALL DUCTS ARE SQUARE OR RECTANGULAR
20 CLS
30 INPUT"AREA OF SQ. OR RD. DUCT";A
40 CLS
50 INPUT"AREA OF SECOND SQ. OR RD. DUCT";B
60 CLS
70 INPUT"AREA OF THIRD SQ. OR RD. DUCT (ENTER 0 IF NONE)";C
80 CLS
90 ZZ=SQR(A+B+C)
100 PRINT ZZ "INCHES"
110 END
Ok
RUN
AREA OF SQ. OR RD. DUCT? 36
AREA OF SECOND SQ. OR RD. DUCT? 74
AREA OF THIRD SQ. OR RD. DUCT (ENTER 0 IF NONE)? 0
 10.48809 INCHES
Ok
RUN
AREA OF SQ. OR RD. DUCT? 72
AREA OF SECOND SQ. OR RD. DUCT? 36
AREA OF THIRD SQ. OR RD. DUCT (ENTER 0 IF NONE)? 12
 10.95445 INCHES
Ok
RUN
AREA OF SQ. OR RD. DUCT? 72
AREA OF SECOND SQ. OR RD. DUCT? 36
AREA OF THIRD SQ. OR RD. DUCT (ENTER 0 IF NONE)? 36
 12 INCHES
Ok
RUN "PRNSCRN
```

Figure 5-6

```
 15.7 CUBIC INCHES
Ok
LIST
0   REM **VOLUME OF METAL RING**
20  CLS
30  INPUT"DIAMETER OF RING IN INCHES";A
40  CLS
50  INPUT"CROSS-SECTION OF RING IN INCHES";B
60  CLS
70  INPUT"HEIGHT OF RING IN INCHES";C
80  CLS
81  D=A*.5
82  E=(D-B)
90  ZZ=3.14*C*((D©2)-E©2)
100 PRINT ZZ "CUBIC INCHES"
110 END
Ok
RUN "PRNSCRN


Ok
RUN
DIAMETER OF RING IN INCHES? 6
CROSS-SECTION OF RING IN INCHES? 1
HEIGHT OF RING IN INCHES? 1
 15.708 CUBIC INCHES
Ok
RUN
DIAMETER OF RING IN INCHES? 10
CROSS-SECTION OF RING IN INCHES? 1
HEIGHT OF RING IN INCHES? 2
 56.5488 CUBIC INCHES
Ok
RUN
DIAMETER OF RING IN INCHES? 12
CROSS-SECTION OF RING IN INCHES? 2
HEIGHT OF RING IN INCHES? 2
 125.664 CUBIC INCHES
Ok
RUN "PRNSCRN
```

Figure 5-7

VOLUME OF A METAL RING

A program for finding the volume of a metal ring is shown in Fig. 5-7; three examples are given to show how the program appears on the monitor screen when run.

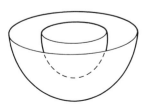

Figure 5-8   Hemispherical bowl.

```
Ok
LIST
0  REM **VOLUME OF HEMISPHERICAL BOWL**
20 CLS
30 INPUT"OUTSIDE DIAMETER OF BOWL";A
40 CLS
50 INPUT"INSIDE DIAMETER OF BOWL";B
60 CLS
70 ZZ=((.5236*A©3)-.5236*B©3)/2
80 PRINT ZZ "CUBIC INCHES"
90 END
Ok
RUN "PRNSCRN




Ok
RUN
OUTSIDE DIAMETER OF BOWL? 12
INSIDE DIAMETER OF BOWL? 9
 261.5382 CUBIC INCHES
Ok
RUN
OUTSIDE DIAMETER OF BOWL? 11
INSIDE DIAMETER OF BOWL? 4.5
 324.5993 CUBIC INCHES
Ok
RUN
OUTSIDE DIAMETER OF BOWL? 14
INSIDE DIAMETER OF BOWL? 2
 716.2848 CUBIC INCHES
Ok
RUN "PRNSCRN
```
Figure 5-9

VOLUME OF AN HEMISPHERICAL BOWL

A drawing of an hemispherical bowl is shown in Fig. 5-8. To find the volume of this shape, both the outside and inside diameter must be known; then the program in Fig. 5-9 may be used to make the calculations.

VOLUME OF A FRUSTUM

Since duct reductions are common in the fabrication of ductwork systems (often performed with the use of a frustum), the area of a frustum (see Fig. 5-10) may be found by using the program shown in Fig. 5-11. In using this program, note

Figure 5-10   Frustum.

```
SAVE"OFFSET",A
Ok
RUN
OFFSET PIECES OF DUCT ARE QUITE COMMON IN THE HVAC TRADES
FURTHERMORE MANY OFFSET BOOTS FORM A TRANSITION FROM THE
ROUND MAIN SUPPLY DUCT TO A RECTANGULAR DUCT TO FIT THE
FLANGE OF A GRILLE OR DIFFUSER.  A TYPICAL EXAMPLE IS SHOWN
IN A NEARBY ILLUSTRATION.  HERE A 10-INCH ROUND DUCT IS FEEDING
A FLOOR DIFFUSER WITH A 4-INCH WIDE FLANGE.  THIS BASIC PROGRAM
CALCULATES THE LENGTH OF THE RECTANGULAR DUCT SO ITS DIMENSION
WILL EQUAL THE AREA OF THE ROUND DUCT.  IN USE, ANY DIMENSIONS
CAN BE SUBSTITUED IN THE PROGRAM--AS THEY ARE CALLED FOR--SO ITS
USE CAN BE APPLIED TO MANY APPLICATIONS IN THE SHEET METAL OR
HVAC TRADES.
DIAMETER OF ROUND DUCT? 10
WIDTH OF RECTANGULAR DUCT? 4


A ROUND DUCT WITH A DIAMETER OF 10 IS EQUAL TO A RECTANGULAR
DUCT WITH A WIDTH OF 4  AND A LENGTH OF 19.625 INCHES.
Ok
RUN "PRNSCRN
```

Figure 5-11

that three dimensions are required: the circumference of the upper and lower base and the height of the frustum. Once the computer prompts for these three dimensions, and they are given, the rather lengthy calculation is handled quickly. Three examples are provided in Fig. 5-12 to show how this program appears on the monitor screen.

```
10 REM **RECTANGULAR MAIN DUCT-SIZING PROGRAM**
20 PRINT "THIS PROGRAM CALCULATES THE DUCT SIZE REQUIRED TO DELIVER"
30 PRINT "A GIVEN VOLUME OF AIR AT A VELOCITY OF 800 FPM.  TO RUN, "
40 PRINT "ANSWER THE QUESTIONS AS THE COMPUTER ASKED FOR THEM."
50 PRINT
60 PRINT "THIS PROGRAM CALCULATES THE DUCT SIZES AT FOUR DIFFERENT"
70 PRINT "DEPTHS: (1) 6-INCH, (2) 8-INCH, (3) 10-INCH, AND (4) 12-INCH"
80 INPUT "ENTER THE DEPTH YOU WANT TO USE (1,2,3 OR 4)";D
91 PRINT
92 PRINT
100 IF D=1 THEN 700
110 IF D=2 THEN 800
120 IF D=3 THEN 900
121 INPUT "ENTER CFM REQUIREMENT";C
130 IF C<241 THEN 500
140 IF C<371 THEN 505
150 IF C<501 THEN 510
160 IF C<631 THEN 515
170 IF C<721 THEN 520
180 IF C<881 THEN 525
190 IF C<10001 THEN 530
200 IF C<1151 THEN 535
210 IF C<1251 THEN 540
220 IF C<1351 THEN 545
230 IF C<1451 THEN 550
240 IF C<1601 THEN 555
250 IF C<1701 THEN 560
```

Figure 5-12

```
260 IF C<1801 THEN 565
270 IF C<1901 THEN 570
280 IF C<2001 THEN 575
290 IF C<2101 THEN 580
300 IF C<2301 THEN 585
310 IF C<2501 THEN 590
320 IF C<2801 THEN 595
330 IF C<3101 THEN 600
340 IF C<3401 THEN 605
350 PRINT "A 12-INCH X";W;"-INCH DUCT WILL HANDLE";C;"CFM OF AIR AT A VELOCITY"
355 PRINT "OF APPROXIMATELY 800 FPM.  THE STATIC PRESSURE IN THIS CASE WILL BE"
360 PRINT ;SP;"INCHES PER 100 EQUIVALENT FEET OF DUCTWORK.
365 PRINT
370 INPUT "DO YOU WISH TO MAKE ANOTHER CALCULATION (Y OR N)";Q$
375 IF Q$="N" THEN STOP
380 CLS: GOTO 10
381 PRINT "A 6-INCH X";W;"-INCH DUCT WILL HANDLE";C;"CFM OF AIR AT A VELOCITY"
382 PRINT "OF APPROXIMATELY 800 FPM.  THE STATIC PRESSURE IN THIS CASE WILL BE"
383 PRINT ;SP;"INCHES PER 100 EQUIVALENT FEET OF DUCT.
384 GOTO 365
385 PRINT "AN 8-INCH X";W;"-INCH DUCT WILL HANDLE";C;"CFM OF AIR AT A VELOCITY"
386 PRINT "OF APPROXIMATELY 800 FPM.  THE STATIC PRESSURE IN THIS CASE WILL BE"
387 PRINT ;SP;"INCHES PER 100 EQUIVALENT FEET OF DUCT."
388 GOTO 365
389 PRINT "A 10-INCH X";W;"-INCH DUCT WILL HANDLE";C;"CFM OF AIR AT A VELOCITY"
390 PRINT "OF APPROXIMATELY 800 FPM.  THE STATIC PRESSURE IN THIS CASE WILL BE"
391 PRINT ;SP;"INCHES PER 100 EQUIVALENT FEET OF DUCT."
392 GOTO 365
500 LET W=4: LET SP=.15: GOTO 350
505 LET W=6: LET SP=.12: GOTO 350
510 LET W=8: LET SP=.095:GOTO 350
515 LET W=10:LET SP=.081:GOTO 350
520 LET W=12:LET SP=.075:GOTO 350
530 LET W=16:LET SP=.062:GOTO 350
535 LET W=18:LET SP=.058:GOTO 350
540 LET W=20:LET SP=.055:GOTO 350
545 LET W=22:LET SP=.052:GOTO 350
550 LET W=24:LET SP=.049:GOTO 350
555 LET W=26:LET SP=.048:GOTO 350
560 LET W=28:LET SP=.046:GOTO 350
565 LET W=30:LET SP=.044:GOTO 350
570 LET W=32:LET SP=.042:GOTO 350
575 LET W=34:LET SP=.041:GOTO 350
580 LET W=36:LET SP=.039:GOTO 350
585 LET W=40:LET SP=.037:GOTO 350
590 LET W=44:LET SP=.036:GOTO 350
595 LET W=48:LET SP=.033:GOTO 350
600 LET W=54:LET SP=.032:GOTO 350
605 LET W=60:LET SP=.03:GOTO 350
700 INPUT "ENTER CRM REQUIREMENT";C
701 IF C<121 THEN 750
702 IF C<161 THEN 751
703 IF C<201 THEN 752
704 IF C<251 THEN 753
705 IF C<311 THEN 754
706 IF C<361 THEN 755
707 IF C<421 THEN 756
708 IF C<461 THEN 757
709 IF C<531 THEN 758
710 IF C<591 THEN 759
711 IF C<631 THEN 760
712 IF C<681 THEN 761
713 IF C<711 THEN 762
714 IF C<751 THEN 763
715 IF C<801 THEN 764
716 IF C<851 THEN 765
717 IF C<901 THEN 766
718 IF C<941 THEN 767
719 IF C>941 THEN PRINT "CFM REQUIREMENT TOO LARGE, GO TO DEEPER DUCT SIZE"
```

Figure 5-12 (*continued*)

```
720 GOTO 20
750 LET W=4:LET SP=.25: GOTO 381
751 LET W=5:LET SP=.2:GOTO 381
752 LET W=6:LET SP=.17:GOTO 381
753 LET W=8:LET SP=.15: GOTO 381
754 LET W=10:LET SP=.13:GOTO 381
755 LET W=12:LET SP=.12:GOTO 381
756 LET W=14:LET SP=.11:GOTO 381
757 LET W=16:LET SP=.105:GOTO 381
758 LET W=18:LET SP=9.399999E-02:GOTO 381
759 LET W=20:LET SP=.089:GOTO 381
760 LET W=22:LET SP=.084:GOTO 381
761 LET W=24:LET SP=.08:GOTO 381
762 LET W=26:LET SP=.076:GOTO 381
763 LET W=28:LET SP=.073:GOTO 381
764 LET W=30:LET SP=.071:GOTO 381
765 LET W=32:LET SP=.069:GOTO 381
766 LET W=34:LET SP=.067:GOTO 381
767 LET W=36:LET SP=.065:GOTO 381
800 INPUT "ENTER CFM REQUIREMENT";C
801 IF C<161 THEN 850
802 IF C<211 THEN 851
803 IF C<251 THEN 852
804 IF C<341 THEN 853
805 IF C<421 THEN 854
806 IF C<501 THEN 855
807 IF C<581 THEN 856
808 IF C<651 THEN 857
809 IF C<716 THEN 858
810 IF C<791 THEN 859
811 IF C<871 THEN 860
812 IF C<931 THEN 861
813 IF C<1001 THEN 862
814 IF C<1081 THEN 863
815 IF C<1151 THEN 864
816 IF C<1201 THEN 865
817 IF C<1251 THEN 866
818 IF C<1321 THEN 867
819 IF C>1321 THEN PRINT "CFM RANGE TOO LARGE, GO TO DEEPER SIZE DUCT"
820 GOTO 20
850 LET W=4:LET SP=.19:GOTO 385
851 LET W=5:LET SP=.165:GOTO 385
852 LET W=6:LET SP=.15:GOTO 385
853 LET W=8:LET SP=.13:GOTO 385
854 LET W=10:LET SP=.11:GOTO 385
855 LET W=12:LET SP=.095:GOTO 385
856 LET W=14:LET SP=.089:GOTO 385
857 LET W=16:LET SP=.083:GOTO 385
858 LET W=18:LET SP=.078:GOTO 385
859 LET W=20:LET SP=.073:GOTO 385
860 LET W=22:LET SP=.069:GOTO 385
861 LET W=24:LET SP=.066:GOTO 385
862 LET W=26:LET SP=.063:GOTO 385
863 LET W=28:LET SP=.06:GOTO 385
864 LET W=30:LET SP=.058:GOTO 385
865 LET W=32:LET SP=.056:GOTO 385
866 LET W=34:LET SP=.055:GOTO 385
867 LET W=36:LET SP=.054:GOTO 385
900 INPUT "ENTER CFM REQUIREMENT";C
901 IF C<201 THEN 950
902 IF C<311 THEN 951
903 IF C<421 THEN 952
904 IF C<521 THEN 953
905 IF C<631 THEN 954
906 IF C<731 THEN 955
907 IF C<821 THEN 956
908 IF C<941 THEN 957
```

Figure 5-12 (*continued*)

```
909 IF C<1051 THEN 958
910 IF C<1151 THEN 959
911 IF C<1251 THEN 960
912 IF C<1351 THEN 961
913 IF C<1426 THEN 962
914 IF C<1501 THEN 963
915 IF C<1576 THEN 964
916 IF C<1651 THEN 965
917 IF C<1726 THEN 966
918 IF C<1901 THEN 967
919 IF C<2101 THEN 968
920 IF C<2251 THEN 969
921 IF C<2401 THEN 970
922 IF C<2801 THEN 971
923 IF C>2801 THEN PRINT "CFM RANGE TOO GREAT, USE A DEEPER DUCT SIZE"
924 GOTO 20
950 LET W=4:LET SP=.17:GOTO 389
951 LET W=6:LET SP=.13:GOTO 389
952 LET W=8:LET SP=.11:GOTO 389
953 LET W=10:LET SP=.093:GOTO 389
954 LET W=12:LET SP=.081:GOTO 389
955 LET W=14:LET SP=.075:GOTO 389
956 LET W=16:LET SP=.071:GOTO 389
957 LET W=18:LET SP=.064:GOTO 389
958 LET W=20:LET SP=.061:GOTO 389
959 LET W=22:LET SP=.058:GOTO 389
960 LET W=24:LET SP=.055:GOTO 389
961 LET W=26:LET SP=.053:GOTO 389
962 LET W=28:LET SP=.052:GOTO 389
963 LET W=30:LET SP=.049:GOTO 389
964 LET W=32:LET SP=.048:GOTO 389
965 LET W=34:LET SP=.046:GOTO 389
966 LET W=36:LET SP=.044:GOTO 389
967 LET W=40:LET SP=.042:GOTO 389
968 LET W=44:LET SP=.04:GOTO 389
969 LET W=48:LET SP=.038:GOTO 389
970 LET W=54:LET SP=.036:GOTO 389
971 LET W=60:LET SP=.034:GOTO 389
```

Figure 5-12 (*continued*)

```
Ok
LOAD"MAIN
Ok
RUN
THIS PROGRAM CALCULATES THE DUCT SIZE REQUIRED TO DELIVER
A GIVEN VOLUME OF AIR AT A VELOCITY OF 800 FPM.  TO RUN,
ANSWER THE QUESTIONS AS THE COMPUTER ASKED FOR THEM.

THIS PROGRAM CALCULATES THE DUCT SIZES AT FOUR DIFFERENT
DEPTHS: (1) 6-INCH, (2) 8-INCH, (3) 10-INCH, AND (4) 12-INCH
ENTER THE DEPTH YOU WANT TO USE (1,2,3 OR 4)? 1


ENTER CRM REQUIREMENT? 400
A 6-INCH X 14 -INCH DUCT WILL HANDLE 400 CFM OF AIR AT A VELOCITY
OF APPROXIMATELY 800 CFM.  THE STATIC PRESSURE IN THIS CASE WILL BE
 .11 INCHES PER 100 EQUIVALENT FEET OF DUCT.

DO YOU WISH TO MAKE ANOTHER CALCULATION (Y OR N)?
cC
Break in 370
Ok
RUN "PRNSCRN

Ok
RUN
```

Figure 5-13

THIS PROGRAM CALCULATES THE DUCT SIZE REQUIRED TO DELIVER
A GIVEN VOLUME OF AIR AT A VELOCITY OF 800 FPM. TO RUN,
ANSWER THE QUESTIONS AS THE COMPUTER ASKED FOR THEM.

THIS PROGRAM CALCULATES THE DUCT SIZES AT FOUR DIFFERENT
DEPTHS: (1) 6-INCH, (2) 8-INCH, (3) 10-INCH, AND (4) 12-INCH
ENTER THE DEPTH YOU WANT TO USE (1,2,3 OR 4)? 1

ENTER CRM REQUIREMENT? 400
A 6-INCH X 14 -INCH DUCT WILL HANDLE 400 CFM OF AIR AT A VELOCITY
OF APPROXIMATELY 800 FPM. THE STATIC PRESSURE IN THIS CASE WILL BE
.11 INCHES PER 100 EQUIVALENT FEET OF DUCT.

DO YOU WISH TO MAKE ANOTHER CALCULATION (Y OR N)?
¢C
Break in 370
Ok
RUN "PRNSCRN

Ok
RUN
THIS PROGRAM CALCULATES THE DUCT SIZE REQUIRED TO DELIVER
A GIVEN VOLUME OF AIR AT A VELOCITY OF 800 FPM. TO RUN,
ANSWER THE QUESTIONS AS THE COMPUTER ASKED FOR THEM.

THIS PROGRAM CALCULATES THE DUCT SIZES AT FOUR DIFFERENT
DEPTHS: (1) 6-INCH, (2) 8-INCH, (3) 10-INCH, AND (4) 12-INCH
ENTER THE DEPTH YOU WANT TO USE (1,2,3 OR 4)? 2

ENTER CFM REQUIREMENT? 285
AN 8-INCH X 8 -INCH DUCT WILL HANDLE 285 CFM OF AIR AT A VELOCITY
OF APPROXIMATELY 800 FPM. THE STATIC PRESSURE IN THIS CASE WILL BE
.13 INCHES PER 100 EQUIVALENT FEET OF DUCT.

DO YOU WISH TO MAKE ANOTHER CALCULATION (Y OR N)?
¢C
Break in 370
Ok
RUN "PRNSCRN

Ok
RUN
THIS PROGRAM CALCULATES THE DUCT SIZE REQUIRED TO DELIVER
A GIVEN VOLUME OF AIR AT A VELOCITY OF 800 FPM. TO RUN,
ANSWER THE QUESTIONS AS THE COMPUTER ASKED FOR THEM.

THIS PROGRAM CALCULATES THE DUCT SIZES AT FOUR DIFFERENT
DEPTHS: (1) 6-INCH, (2) 8-INCH, (3) 10-INCH, AND (4) 12-INCH
ENTER THE DEPTH YOU WANT TO USE (1,2,3 OR 4)? 3

ENTER CFM REQUIREMENT? 1000
A 10-INCH X 20 -INCH DUCT WILL HANDLE 1000 CFM OF AIR AT A VELOCITY
OF APPROXIMATELY 800 FPM. THE STATIC PRESSURE IN THIS CASE WILL BE
.061 INCHES PER 100 EQUIVALENT FEET OF DUCT.

DO YOU WISH TO MAKE ANOTHER CALCULATION (Y OR N)?
¢C
Break in 370
Ok
RUN "PRNSCRN

Figure 5-13 (*continued*)

```
10 REM **SUPPLY AND RETURN AIR OUTLET PROGRAM**
19 CLS
20 PRINT "WHICH OF THE FOLLOWING DO YOU WISH TO SELECT(1,2,3 OR 4)?"
30 PRINT "          (1)SIDE WALL REGISTERS
40 PRINT "          (2)ROUND CEILING DIFFUSERS
50 PRINT "          (3)FLOOR OUTLETS
60 PRINT "          (4)RETURN AIR GRILLES
70 INPUT Q$
80 IF Q$="1" THEN 200
90 IF Q$="2" THEN 300
100 IF Q$="3" THEN 400
110 IF Q$="4" THEN 600
200 PRINT "YOU HAVE CHOSEN TO SELECT SIDE WALL REGISTERS, PLEASE ENTER THE"
210 INPUT "CFM REQUIREMENTS AT THE OUTLET";C
211 CLS
220 IF C<61 THEN 521
225 IF C<81 THEN 526
227 IF C<101 THEN 528
229 IF C<121 THEN 530
231 IF C<141 THEN 532
233 IF C<161 THEN 534
235 IF C<181 THEN 536
237 IF C<201 THEN 538
239 IF C<221 THEN 540
240 IF C<241 THEN 541
242 IF C<261 THEN 543
244 IF C<281 THEN 545
246 IF C<301 THEN 547
248 IF C>301 THEN PRINT "THE CFM RANGE IS BEYOND THIS PROGRAM.  PLEASE CONSULT"
249 PRINT "A HVAC MANUAL OR HANDBOOK.
250 INPUT "DO YOU WISH TO SELECT ANOTHER SIDE WALL REGISTERS (Y OR N)";Q3$
251 IF Q3$="Y" THEN 200
289 PRINT
290 INPUT "DO YOU WISH TO SELECT ANOTHER SIDE WALL REGISTER (Y OR N)";Q1$
291 IF Q1$="Y" THEN 200
300 PRINT "YOU HAVE SELECTED ROUND CEILING DIFFUSERS"
310 INPUT "HOW MANY CFM ARE REQUIRED AT THE OUTLET";C
320 IF C<101 THEN PRINT "A 6-INCH DIAMETER DIFFUSER IS REQUIRED" : GOTO 370
330 IF C<180 THEN PRINT "AN 8-INCH DIAMETER DIFFUSER IS REQUIRED": GOTO 370
340 IF C<240 THEN PRINT "A 10-INCH DIAMETER DIFFUSER IS REQUIRED": GOTO 370
350 IF C>240 THEN PRINT "THE CFM IS TOO GREAT FOR THIS PROGRAM, PLEASE"
360 PRINT "CONSULT A HVAC MANUAL OR HANDBOOK FOR YOUR REQUIREMENTS"
365 PRINT
370 INPUT "DO YOU WISH TO CONTINUE WITH MORE CALCULATIONS (Y OR N)";Q1$
380 IF Q1$="Y" THEN 19
390 STOP
400 PRINT "YOU HAVE CHOSEN TO SELECT FLOOR OUTLETS"
405 INPUT "WHAT IS THE CFM REQUIREMENT FOR THE OUTLET";C
410 IF C<61 THEN 450
415 IF C<81 THEN 455
420 IF C<101 THEN 460
425 IF C<121 THEN 465
430 IF C<141 THEN 470
435 IF C<161 THEN 475
440 IF C>161 THEN 480
441 PRINT "A FLOOR OUTLET";W;"INCHES WIDE AND";L;"INCHES IN LENGTH"
442 PRINT "IS REQUIRED TO HANDLE";C;"CFM OF AIR WITH A THROW OF";T;"FEET"
443 INPUT "DO YOU WISH TO SELECT ANOTHER FLOOR OUTE (Y OR N)";Q4$
444 IF Q4$="Y" THEN 405
450 LET W=2.25: LET L=10: LET T=7: GOTO 441
455 LET W=2.25: LET L=12: LET T=11: GOTO 441
460 LET W=2.25: LET L=14: LET T=11: GOTO 441
465 LET W=4: LET L=10: LET T=11: GOTO 441
470 LET W=4: LET L=10: LET T=13: GOTO 441
475 LET W=4: LET L=12: LET T=13: GOTO 441
480 PRINT "THE CFM IS OUT OF RANGE FOR THIS PROGRAM, PLEASE CONSULT A"
481 PRINT "HVAC MANUAL FOR YOUR REQUIREMENTS"
```

Figure 5-14

```
482 GOTO 443
521 LET L=10: LET W=4: LET T=12: GOTO 822
526 LET L=10: LET W=6: LET T=12: GOTO 822
528 LET L=14: LET W=6: LET T=14: GOTO 822
530 LET L=14: LET W=6: LET T=16: GOTO 822
532 LET L=16: LET W=6: LET T=16: GOTO 822
534 LET L=16: LET W=6: LET T=18: GOTO 822
536 LET L=20: LET W=6: LET T=14: GOTO 822
538 LET L=20: LET W=6: LET T=16: GOTO 822
540 LET L=20: LET W=6: LET T=18: GOTO 822
541 LET L=20: LET W=6: LET T=20: GOTO 822
543 LET L=24: LET W=6: LET T=20: GOTO 822
545 LET L=30: LET W=6: LET T=18:GOTO 822
547 LET L=30: LET W=6: LET T= 20 :GOTO 822
600 PRINT "YOU HAVE CHOSEN TO SELECT A RETURN AIR GRILLE"
610 PRINT
620 INPUT "ENTER THE CFM REQUIREMENTS (60 TO 3020 CFM)";C
630 INPUT "DO YOU WANT A SIDE WALL RETURN (S) OR FLOOR GRILLE (F)";Q$
650 IF C<141 THEN 700
651 IF C<171 THEN 705
652 IF C<191 THEN 710
653 IF C<236 THEN 715
654 IF C<261 THEN 720
655 IF C<371 THEN 725
656 IF C<561 THEN 730
657 IF C<761 THEN 735
658 IF C<871 THEN 740
659 IF C<961 THEN 745
660 IF C<1171 THEN 750
661 IF C<1471 THEN 755
662 IF C<1581 THEN 760
663 IF C<1771 THEN 765
664 IF C<1991 THEN 770
665 IF C<2401 THEN 775
666 IF C<3021 THEN 780
667 IF C>3021 THEN 785
668 PRINT
669 PRINT "THE FREE AREA OF THE RETURN AIR GRILL IS";FA;"SQ. INCHES"
670 IF Q$="F" THEN 676
671 PRINT "THE SIDE WALL RETURN GRILLE IS";SW;"INCHES WIDE BY";SL;"INCHES"
672 PRINT "IN LENGTH.
673 PRINT
674 INPUT "DO YOU WISH TO SELECT ANOTHER RETURN AIR GRILLE (Y OR N)";Q5$
675 IF Q5$="Y" THEN 600
676 PRINT "THE FLOOR GRILLE IS";FW;"INCHES WIDE BY";FL;"INCHES IN LENGTH"
677 GOTO 674
700 LET FA=40: LET SW=6: LET SL=10:LET FW=4: LET FL=14: GOTO 669
705 LET FA=48: LET SW=6: LET SL=12:LET FW=4:LET FL=18: GOTO 669
710 LET FA=55: LET SW=8:LET SL=10:LET FW=4:LET FL=14: GOTO 669
715 LET FA=67: LET SW=8: LET SL=12:LET FW=6:LET FL=14: GOTO 669
720 LET FA=74:LET SW=6:LET SL=18:LET FW=8:LET FL=14: GOTO 669
725 LET FA=106:LET SW=12:LET SL=12:LET FW=8:LET FL=20: GOTO 669
730 LET FA=162:LET SW=12:LET SL=18:LET FW=8:LET FL=30: GOTO 669
735 LET FA=218:LET SW=12:LET SL=24:LET FW=12:LET FL=24: GOTO 669
740 LET FA=252:LET SW=18:LET SL=18:LET FW=12:LET FL=30: GOTO 669
745 LET FA=276:LET SW=12:LET SL=30:LET FW=12:LET FL=30: GOTO 669
750 LET FA=340:LET SW=18:LET SL=24:LET FW=14:LET FL=30: GOTO 669
755 LET FA=423:LET SW=18:LET SL=30:LET FW=18:LET FL=30: GOTO 669
760 LET FA=455:LET SW=24:LET SL=24:LET FW=20:LET FL=30: GOTO 669
765 LET FA=510:LET SW=18:LET SL=36:LET FW=22:LET FL=30: GOTO 669
770 LET FA=572:LET SW=24:LET SL=30:LET FW=24:LET FL=30: GOTO 669
775 LET FA=690:LET SW=24:LET SL=36:LET FW=24:LET FL=36: GOTO 669
780 LET FA=870:LET SW=30:LET SL=36:LET FW=30:LET FL=36: GOTO 669
785 PRINT "THE CFM REQUIREMENT IS OUT OF RANGE FOR THIS PROGRAM"
786 PRINT "PLEASE CONSULT A HVAC HANDBOOK FOR LARGER SYSTEMS"
787 GOTO 600
822 PRINT "A";L;"INCH BY";W;"INCH WALL REGISTER WILL BE REQUIRED TO"
823 PRINT "HANDLE";C;"CFM WITH AN AIR THROW OF";T;"FEET."
824 GOTO 289
832 PRINT "HANDLE";C;"CFM WITH AN AIR THROW OF";T;"FEET."
842 GOTO 289
```

Figure 5-14 (*continued*)

```
WHICH OF THE FOLLOWING DO YOU WISH TO SELECT(1,2,3 OR 4)?
          (1)SIDE WALL REGISTERS
          (2)ROUND CEILING DIFFUSERS
          (3)FLOOR OUTLETS
          (4)RETURN AIR GRILLES
?
cC
Break in 70
Ok
RUN "PRNSCRN




WHICH OF THE FOLLOWING DO YOU WISH TO SELECT(1,2,3 OR 4)?
          (1)SIDE WALL REGISTERS
          (2)ROUND CEILING DIFFUSERS
          (3)FLOOR OUTLETS
          (4)RETURN AIR GRILLES
? 1
YOU HAVE CHOSEN TO SELECT SIDE WALL REGISTERS, PLEASE ENTER THE
CFM REQUIREMENTS AT THE OUTLET?
cC
Break in 210
Ok
RUN "PRNSCRN



A 20 INCH BY 6 INCH WALL REGISTER WILL BE REQUIRED TO
HANDLE 200 CFM WITH AN AIR THROW OF 16 FEET.

DO YOU WISH TO SELECT ANOTHER SIDE WALL REGISTER (Y OR N)? Y
YOU HAVE CHOSEN TO SELECT SIDE WALL REGISTERS, PLEASE ENTER THE
CFM REQUIREMENTS AT THE OUTLET?
cC
Break in 210
Ok
RUN "PRNSCRN

WHICH OF THE FOLLOWING DO YOU WISH TO SELECT(1,2,3 OR 4)?
          (1)SIDE WALL REGISTERS
          (2)ROUND CEILING DIFFUSERS
          (3)FLOOR OUTLETS
          (4)RETURN AIR GRILLES
? 2
YOU HAVE SELECTED ROUND CEILING DIFFUSERS
HOW MANY CFM ARE REQUIRED AT THE OUTLET? 75
A 6-INCH DIAMETER DIFFUSER IS REQUIRED
DO YOU WISH TO CONTINUE WITH MORE CALCULATIONS (Y OR N)?
cC
Break in 370
Ok
RUN "PRNSCRN

WHICH OF THE FOLLOWING DO YOU WISH TO SELECT(1,2,3 OR 4)?
          (1)SIDE WALL REGISTERS
          (2)ROUND CEILING DIFFUSERS
          (3)FLOOR OUTLETS
          (4)RETURN AIR GRILLES
? 3
YOU HAVE CHOSEN TO SELECT FLOOR OUTLETS
WHAT IS THE CFM REQUIREMENT FOR THE OUTLET? 225
THE CFM IS OUT OF RANGE FOR THIS PROGRAM, PLEASE CONSULT A
HVAC MANUAL FOR YOUR REQUIREMENTS
```

Figure 5-15

```
DO YOU WISH TO SELECT ANOTHER FLOOR OUTE (Y OR N)?
cC
Break in 443
Ok
RUN "PRNSCRN

WHICH OF THE FOLLOWING DO YOU WISH TO SELECT(1,2,3 OR 4)?
               (1)SIDE WALL REGISTERS
               (2)ROUND CEILING DIFFUSERS
               (3)FLOOR OUTLETS
               (4)RETURN AIR GRILLES
? 4
YOU HAVE CHOSEN TO SELECT A RETURN AIR GRILLE

ENTER THE CFM REQUIREMENTS (60 TO 3020 CFM)? 3000
DO YOU WANT A SIDE WALL RETURN (S) OR FLOOR GRILLE (F)? F
THE FREE AREA OF THE RETURN AIR GRILL IS 870 SQ. INCHES
THE FLOOR GRILLE IS 30 INCHES WIDE BY 36 INCHES IN LENGTH
DO YOU WISH TO SELECT ANOTHER RETURN AIR GRILLE (Y OR N)?
cC
Break in 674
Ok
RUN "PRNSCRN
```

Figure 5-15   (*continued*)

RECTANGULAR MAIN DUCT SIZING

The program in Fig. 5-12 calculates the duct size required to deliver a given volume of air at a velocity of 800 feet per minute. Figure 5-13 shows examples of the program in use. Another supply and return outlet program is shown in Fig. 5-14, and Fig. 5-15 shows this program in use.

6

HOT-WATER SYSTEMS

In all types of water-heating applications, the engineer or designer must make heat-loss calculations to ascertain that the heating equipment and related components are of sufficient capacity to obtain the desired results. Heat loss is expressed either in Btu per hour (Btuh) or watts (W). Both are measures of the rate at which heat is transferred and are easily converted from one to the other by the following equations:

$$\text{Watts} = \text{Btuh}/3.4$$

$$\text{Btuh} = \text{watts} \times 3.4$$

Basically, the calculation of heat loss through walls, roof, ceilings, windows, and floors requires three simple steps:

1. Determine the net area in square feet.
2. Find the proper heat-loss factor from a table.
3. Multiply the area by the factor; the product will be expressed in Btuh.

The basic heat-loss factors shown in Table 6-1 are for most widely used types of building construction. To use, select the proper factor in Table 6-1. Then locate this factor in the left column of Table 6-2; follow horizontally until the correct area or volume is reached. Then read the Btuh heat loss at the top of this column. Table 6-2 is based on a 70° temperature difference. If a higher or lower temperature difference is required, refer to Table 6-3. Locate total Btuh under the 70° column

TABLE 6-1 Basic Heat Loss Factors

FRAME WALLS			INTERIOR PLAS. OR ½" DRYWALL				CEILINGS	ATTIC-SPACE ABOVE					
								NO FLOOR			1" PINE FLOOR		
EXTERIOR		SHEATHING	NO INSULATION	½" INSUL. LATH	2" INSULATION	4" INSULATION	INSULATION BETWEEN CEILING JOISTS	LATH & PLAS. OR DRYWALL	½" INSUL. LATH	½" INS. BOARD TOP OF JOISTS	LATH & PLAS. OR DRYWALL	½" INSUL. LATH	1" INS. BOARD TOP OF JOISTS
CLAPBOARDS WOOD SIDING OR WOOD SHINGLES		NONE	.33	.24	.15	.11	NONE	.30	.22	.19	.21	.16	.12
		WOOD 1"	.25	.20	.11	.08	1" BLANKET	.17	.14		.14	.10	
		RIGID INSL. ¾"	.21	.16	.09	.07	2" ROCKWOOL OR EQUAL	.13			.13		
BRICK OR STONE VENEER		WOOD 1"	.27	.21	.11	.08	4" ROCKWOOL OR EQUAL	.09			.09		
		RIGID INSL. ¾"	.21	.18	.09	.07		NO CEILING			PLASTER CEILING		
BARE CORRUGATED SHEET METAL SIDING						1.7	FLAT BUILT-UP	RIGID INSL.				RIGID INSL.	

MASONRY WALLS				INTERIOR PLASTER OR ½" DRYWALL					NO INS.	½"	1"	1½"	2"	NO INS.	½"	1"	1½"	2"

(DECKING, IN.)

MASONRY WALLS EXTERIOR		NO FINISH	½" THICK	FURRING	ON ½" RIGID INSL. FURRED	ON 1" RIGID INSL. FURRED	FURRED PLUS 1" BLANKET INS.
BACKING, IN.							
CINDER BLOCK	4	.42	.40	.27	.21	.16	.15
	8	.33	.33	.24	.18	.16	.14
	12	.31	.30	.23	.18	.14	.14
CONCRETE BLOCK	4	.50	.47	.31	.22	.17	.15
	8	.44	.40	.28	.21	.16	.15
	12	.40	.38	.27	.20	.15	.14
HOLLOW TILE	4	.41	.39	.28	.21	.18	.15
	8	.36	.34	.26	.19	.16	.14
	10	.35	.33	.25	.18	.14	.14
CINDER BLOCK	8	.42	.39	.28	.20	.16	.15
	12	.37	.35	.26	.19	.15	.14
CONCRETE BLOCK	8	.56	.52	.34	.23	.17	.15
	12	.49	.46	.32	.22	.16	.15
SOLID BRICK	8	.50	.46	.32	.22	.16	.15
	12	.36	.34	.25	.19	.14	.14
	16	.28	.27	.21	.16	.13	.13
HOLLOW TILE STUCCO EXTERIOR	8	.40	.39	.27	.20	.15	.14
	10	.36	.35	.25	.18	.15	.14
	12	.30	.29	.23	.17	.14	.14
LIMESTONE OR SANDSTONE	8	.70	.64	.39	.25	.18	.15
	12	.58	.53	.34	.23	.17	.15
	16	.49	.45	.31	.21	.16	.14
POURED CONCRETE	ABOVE GRADE 8	.70					
	12	.58					
	BELOW GRADE 8	.06					
	12	.06					

CEILINGS / FLAT BUILT-UP		NO INS.	½"	1"	1½"	2"	NO INS.	½"	1"	1½"	2"
WOOD	1	.49	.28	.20	.14	.12	.32	.21	.16	.12	.10
	1½	.37	.24	.18	.13	.11	.26	.19	.15	.11	.10
	2	.30	.22	.16	.12	.10	.24	.17	.14	.11	.09
	3	.22	.18	.16							
	4	.17	.13								
CONCRETE SLAB	2	.82	.37	.24	.16	.13	.42	.26	.19	.14	.11
	4	.72	.34	.23	.16	.12	.40	.25	.18	.13	.11
	6	.64	.33	.22	.15	.12	.37	.24	.18	.13	.11
FLAT METAL		.95	.39	.25	.17	.13	.46	.27	.19	.14	.11

MASONRY PARTITIONS		PLAIN	ONE SIDE	BOTH SIDES
4" GYPSUM TILE		.30	.28	.27
4" CLAY TILE		.45	.42	.40
4" COMMON BRICK		.50	.46	.43

FRAME PARTITIONS	PLASTER ON		
		ONE SIDE	BOTH SIDES
LATH & PLASTER OR ½" DRYWALL			.31	.17
STUDDING & ½" INSULATING BOARD		.18	.10
STUDDING & 2" BAT INSULATION		.07	.06

INFILTRATION	WINDOWS & DOORS		
	NOT WEATHER-STRIPPED NO STORM SASH	WITH WEATHER-STRIPPING OR STORM SASH	BLOCK WALLS ABOVE GRADE NO FINISH
NO. OF SIDES EXPOSED	AIR CHANGE PER HOUR	FACTOR		
1	1	.018	.012	.027
2	1½	.027	.018	.036
3	2	.036	.027	.054
ENTRANCE HALLS		.036	.027	
SUN ROOMS 3 walls exp.		.054		

CONCRETE FLOORS			
ON GROUND OR FILL	EDGE INSULATION	NONE	60 BTU	PER LINEAL FOOT
		1"	45 BTU	OF EXPOSED EDGE
		2"	40 BTU	
ON GROUND BELOW GRADE			.06

WINDOWS & DOORS

FIGURE EXTERIOR DOORS WITH OR WITHOUT GLASS, SAME AS WINDOWS

SINGLE GLASS	1.14
WITH STORM SASH	.55
DOUBLE GLAZED - WITH ¼" AIR SPACE	.63

WOOD FLOORS

OVER ENCLOSED UNHEATED CRAWL SPACE	DOUBLE WOOD FLOORING ON JOISTS	.15
	WITH ½" INSL. BOARD ON BOTTOM OF JOISTS	.10
	WITH 2" INSL. BETWEEN JOISTS	.06
OVER EXPOSED SPACE	DOUBLE WOOD FLOORING ON JOISTS	.36
	WITH ½" INSL. BOARD ON BOTTOM OF JOISTS	.21
	WITH 2" INSL. BETWEEN JOISTS	.10
OVER UNHEATED BASEMENT		.06

NOTE - FIGURE RADIATION FOR BATHROOM SAME AS OTHER ROOMS AND THEN INCREASE BY AT LEAST 25%

on the left side. On the same line, read the equivalent heat loss in the desired temperature-difference column.

DESIGNING A ONE-PIPE HOT-WATER HEATING SYSTEM

A typical one-pipe hot-water heating system is shown in Fig. 6-1. Basically, such a system is designed by using the following steps.

1. Determine the heat loss of building
2. Make a piping layout

3. Determine the gallons of water required per minute
4. Select a circulator
5. Size the main
6. Size the radiator branches
7. Select the boiler
8. Select the pressure tank
9. Select the flow control valve.

TABLE 6-2 Total Btu Heat Loss of Areas and Volumes at Various Factors

FACTORS	HEAT LOSS THRU WINDOWS, DOORS, CEILINGS, FLOORS & WALLS, BTU'S																			
	100	200	300	400	500	600	700	800	900	1000	1100	1200	1300	1400	1500	1600	1700	1800	1900	2000
	AREAS, SQ. FT.																			
0.06	24.0	48.0	71.0	95.0	119.0	143.0	167.0	191.0	214.0	238.0	262.0	286.0	310.0	333.0	357.0	381.0	405.0	428.0	453.0	477.0
0.07	20.0	41.0	61.0	82.0	102.0	122.0	143.0	163.0	184.0	204.0	224.0	245.0	265.0	286.0	306.0	327.0	347.0	368.0	388.0	409.0
0.09	16.0	32.0	48.0	63.0	79.0	95.0	111.0	127.0	143.0	159.0	175.0	191.0	206.0	222.0	238.0	254.0	270.0	286.0	302.0	318.0
0.10	14.0	29.0	43.0	57.0	72.0	86.0	100.0	114.0	129.0	143.0	157.0	172.0	186.0	200.0	214.0	228.0	243.0	257.0	271.0	286.0
0.11	13.0	26.0	39.0	52.0	65.0	78.0	91.0	104.0	117.0	130.0	143.0	156.0	169.0	182.0	195.0	208.0	221.0	234.0	247.0	260.0
0.12	12.0	24.0	36.0	48.0	60.0	72.0	83.0	95.0	107.0	119.0	131.0	143.0	155.0	167.0	179.0	190.0	202.0	214.0	226.0	238.0
0.13	11.0	22.0	33.0	44.0	55.0	66.0	77.0	88.0	99.0	110.0	121.0	132.0	143.0	154.0	165.0	176.0	187.0	198.0	209.0	220.0
0.14	10.0	20.0	31.0	41.0	51.0	61.0	71.0	82.0	92.0	102.0	112.0	123.0	133.0	143.0	153.0	163.0	173.0	184.0	194.0	204.0
0.15	9.5	19.0	28.0	38.0	48.0	57.0	67.0	76.0	86.0	95.0	105.0	114.0	124.0	133.0	143.0	152.0	162.0	171.0	181.0	191.0
0.16	9.0	18.0	27.0	36.0	45.0	54.0	62.0	71.0	80.0	89.0	98.0	107.0	116.0	125.0	134.0	143.0	152.0	161.0	170.0	179.0
0.17	8.5	17.0	25.0	34.0	42.0	50.0	59.0	67.0	76.0	84.0	92.0	101.0	109.0	118.0	126.0	134.0	143.0	151.0	160.0	168.0
0.18	8.0	16.0	24.0	32.0	40.0	48.0	56.0	64.0	72.0	79.0	87.0	95.0	103.0	111.0	119.0	127.0	135.0	143.0	151.0	159.0
0.19	7.5	15.0	23.0	30.0	38.0	45.0	53.0	60.0	68.0	75.0	83.0	90.0	98.0	105.0	113.0	120.0	128.0	135.0	143.0	150.0
0.20	7.2	14.0	22.0	29.0	36.0	43.0	50.0	57.0	60.0	72.0	79.0	86.0	93.0	100.0	107.0	114.0	121.0	129.0	136.0	143.0
0.21	6.8	13.6	21.0	27.0	34.0	41.0	48.0	54.0	61.0	68.0	75.0	82.0	89.0	95.0	102.0	109.0	115.0	122.0	129.0	136.0
0.22	6.5	13.0	20.0	26.0	32.0	39.0	45.0	52.0	58.0	65.0	71.0	78.0	84.0	91.0	97.0	108.0	110.0	117.0	123.0	130.0
0.23	6.2	12.4	19.0	25.0	31.0	37.0	44.0	50.0	56.0	62.0	68.0	75.0	81.0	87.0	93.0	99.0	105.0	112.0	118.0	124.0
0.24	6.0	11.9	18.0	24.0	30.0	36.0	42.0	48.0	54.0	60.0	66.0	72.0	77.0	83.0	89.0	95.0	101.0	107.0	113.0	119.0
0.25	5.7	11.4	17.0	23.0	29.0	34.0	40.0	46.0	51.0	57.0	63.0	69.0	74.0	80.0	86.0	91.0	97.0	103.0	109.0	114.0
0.26	5.5	11.0	16.0	22.0	27.0	33.0	38.0	44.0	49.0	55.0	60.0	66.0	71.0	77.0	83.0	88.0	94.0	99.0	105.0	110.0
0.27	5.3	10.6	15.8	21.0	26.0	32.0	37.0	42.0	47.0	53.0	58.0	63.0	69.0	74.0	79.0	84.0	90.0	95.0	100.0	105.0
0.28	5.1	10.2	15.3	20.0	25.0	31.0	36.0	41.0	46.0	51.0	56.0	61.0	67.0	72.0	77.0	82.0	87.0	92.0	97.0	102.0
0.30	4.8	9.5	14.3	19.0	24.0	28.0	33.0	38.0	43.0	48.0	53.0	57.0	62.0	67.0	72.0	76.0	81.0	86.0	91.0	92.0
0.31	4.6	9.2	13.8	18.4	23.0	28.0	32.0	37.0	42.0	46.0	51.0	55.0	60.0	65.0	69.0	74.0	76.0	81.0	86.0	92.0
0.32	4.5	8.9	13.4	17.8	22.0	27.0	31.0	36.0	41.0	45.0	49.0	54.0	58.0	63.0	67.0	72.0	76.0	81.0	85.0	89.0
0.33	4.3	8.7	13.0	17.3	21.6	26.0	30.0	35.0	39.0	43.0	48.0	52.0	56.0	61.0	65.0	70.0	74.0	78.0	82.0	87.0
0.34	4.2	8.4	12.6	16.8	21.0	25.0	29.0	34.0	38.0	42.0	46.0	50.0	55.0	59.0	63.0	67.0	71.0	76.0	80.0	84.0
0.35	4.1	8.2	12.2	16.3	20.4	24.5	28.6	33.0	37.0	41.0	45.0	49.0	53.0	57.0	61.0	65.0	70.0	74.0	78.0	82.0
0.36	4.0	7.9	11.9	15.9	19.9	23.8	27.8	32.0	36.0	40.0	44.0	48.0	52.0	56.0	60.0	64.0	68.0	72.0	76.0	80.0
0.37	3.9	7.7	11.6	15.6	19.3	23.1	27.0	31.0	35.0	39.0	43.0	47.0	50.0	54.0	58.0	62.0	66.0	70.0	73.0	77.0
0.38	3.8	7.5	11.3	15.0	18.8	22.6	26.3	30.0	34.0	38.0	42.0	45.0	49.0	53.0	57.0	60.0	64.0	68.0	72.0	75.0
0.39	3.7	7.3	11.0	14.6	18.3	22.0	25.6	29.0	33.0	37.0	40.0	44.0	48.0	51.0	55.0	59.0	62.0	66.0	70.0	73.0
0.40	3.6	7.2	10.7	14.3	17.9	21.4	25.0	28.6	32.0	36.0	39.0	43.0	47.0	50.0	54.0	57.0	61.0	64.0	68.0	72.0
0.42	3.4	6.8	10.2	13.6	17.0	20.4	23.8	27.4	31.0	34.0	38.0	41.0	44.0	48.0	51.0	55.0	58.0	61.0	65.0	68.0
0.45	3.2	6.4	9.5	12.7	15.9	19.1	22.0	25.7	28.6	32.0	35.0	38.0	41.0	44.0	48.0	51.0	54.0	57.0	60.0	64.0
0.46	3.1	6.2	9.3	12.3	15.5	18.6	21.7	24.8	28.0	31.0	34.0	37.0	40.0	43.0	47.0	50.0	53.0	56.0	59.0	62.0
0.48	3.0	5.9	8.9	11.9	14.9	17.9	20.8	23.8	27.0	30.0	33.0	36.0	39.0	42.0	45.0	48.0	51.0	54.0	57.0	60.0
0.49	2.9	5.8	8.7	11.7	14.6	17.5	20.4	23.3	26.0	29.0	32.0	35.0	38.0	41.0	43.0	46.0	49.0	52.0	55.0	58.0
0.50	2.8	5.7	8.6	11.4	14.3	17.1	20.0	22.9	25.7	28.6	31.0	34.0	37.0	40.0	42.0	45.0	49.0	51.0	54.0	57.0
0.52	2.7	5.5	8.2	11.0	13.7	16.5	19.2	22.0	24.7	27.5	30.0	33.0	36.0	38.0	41.0	44.0	47.0	49.0	52.0	55.0
0.55	2.6	5.2	7.8	10.4	13.0	15.6	18.2	20.8	23.4	26.0	29.0	31.0	34.0	36.0	39.0	42.0	44.0	47.0	49.0	52.0
0.56	2.5	5.1	7.7	10.2	12.8	15.3	17.9	20.4	23.0	25.5	28.0	30.0	33.0	35.0	38.0	41.0	43.0	46.0	48.0	51.0
0.58	2.4	4.8	7.2	9.6	12.0	14.4	16.8	19.3	21.7	24.0	27.0	29.0	31.0	34.0	36.0	39.0	41.0	43.0	46.0	48.0
0.63	2.3	4.6	6.8	9.1	11.4	13.6	15.9	18.2	20.4	22.7	25.0	27.0	30.0	32.0	34.0	36.0	39.0	41.0	43.0	45.0
0.64	2.2	4.5	6.7	8.9	11.2	13.4	15.6	17.8	20.1	22.3	24.5	26.0	29.0	31.0	33.0	35.0	38.0	40.0	42.0	44.0
0.70	2.0	4.1	6.1	8.2	10.4	12.3	14.3	16.4	18.4	20.4	22.5	25.0	27.0	29.0	31.0	33.0	35.0	37.0	39.0	41.0
0.72	1.9	4.0	6.0	8.0	9.9	11.9	13.9	15.9	17.9	19.9	21.8	24.0	26.0	28.0	30.0	32.0	34.0	36.0	38.0	40.0
0.82	1.7	3.5	5.2	7.0	8.7	10.4	12.2	14.0	15.7	17.4	19.2	21.0	23.0	24.0	26.0	28.0	30.0	31.0	33.0	35.0
0.95	1.5	3.0	4.5	6.0	7.5	9.0	10.5	12.0	13.5	15.1	16.6	18.0	20.0	21.0	23.0	24.0	26.0	27.0	29.0	30.0
1.14	1.3	2.5	3.8	5.0	6.3	7.5	8.8	10.0	11.3	12.5	13.8	15.0	16.0	18.0	19.0	20.0	21.0	23.0	24.0	25.0

FACTORS	HEAT LOSS THRU AIR CHANGES, BTU'S																			
	100	200	300	400	500	600	700	800	900	1000	1100	1200	1300	1400	1500	1600	1700	1800	1900	2000
	ROOM VOLUME, CU. FT.																			
0.012	119	238	357	476	595	714	833	952	1071	1190	1310	1429	1548	1667	1786	1905	2024	2143	2262	2381
0.018	79	159	238	318	398	477	555	635	715	794	875	951	1030	1110	1190	1270	1350	1430	1510	1590
0.027	53	106	159	212	264	317	370	423	476	530	582	635	688	741	794	846	900	953	1005	1060
0.036	40	80	119	159	198	238	278	318	357	397	437	476	516	555	595	635	675	715	755	795
0.054	26	53	79	106	132	159	185	212	238	265	291	317	344	370	397	423	450	476	503	529

TABLE 6-2   (continued)

FACTORS	HEAT LOSS THRU WINDOWS, DOORS, CEILINGS, FLOORS & WALLS, BTU'S																			
	2100	2200	2300	2400	2500	2600	2700	2800	2900	3000	3100	3200	3300	3400	3500	3600	3700	3800	3900	4000
	AREAS, SQ. FT.																			
0.06	500	524	548	571	595	619	643	667	690	714	738	762	786	810	833	857	881	905	929	952
0.07	429	449	469	490	510	531	551	571	592	612	633	653	674	694	714	734	755	775	796	816
0.09	333	349	365	381	398	413	429	445	461	476	492	508	524	540	556	572	586	603	619	635
0.10	300	314	329	343	357	371	386	400	414	428	443	457	472	486	500	514	528	543	557	571
0.11	273	286	299	312	325	338	351	364	377	390	403	416	429	442	455	468	481	494	507	520
0.12	250	262	274	286	298	310	322	334	346	358	369	381	393	405	417	429	441	452	464	476
0.13	231	242	253	264	275	286	297	308	319	330	341	352	363	374	385	396	407	418	429	440
0.14	214	224	235	245	255	265	275	286	296	306	316	326	336	347	357	367	378	388	398	408
0.15	200	209	219	229	238	248	257	267	276	286	295	305	314	324	333	343	352	362	371	381
0.16	187	196	205	214	223	232	241	250	259	268	277	286	295	303	312	321	330	339	348	357
0.17	176	185	193	202	210	218	227	235	244	252	260	269	277	286	294	302	311	319	328	336
0.18	167	175	183	190	198	206	214	222	230	238	246	254	262	270	278	286	294	302	309	318
0.19	158	165	173	180	188	195	203	210	218	225	233	240	248	255	263	270	278	286	293	301
0.20	150	157	164	172	179	186	193	200	207	214	221	228	236	243	250	257	264	271	279	286
0.21	143	150	156	163	170	177	184	190	197	204	211	218	224	231	238	245	252	259	265	272
0.22	136	143	149	156	162	169	175	182	188	195	201	208	214	221	227	234	240	246	253	260
0.23	130	137	143	149	155	161	167	174	180	186	192	198	205	211	217	223	230	236	242	248
0.24	125	131	137	143	149	155	161	167	173	179	185	190	196	202	208	214	220	226	232	238
0.25	120	126	132	137	143	149	154	160	166	172	177	183	188	194	200	206	212	217	223	229
0.26	115	121	126	132	137	143	148	154	159	165	170	176	181	187	192	198	203	209	214	220
0.27	111	116	122	127	132	137	143	148	153	159	164	169	175	180	185	191	196	201	206	212
0.28	107	112	117	122	127	133	138	143	148	153	158	163	168	173	179	184	189	194	199	204
0.30	100	105	110	114	119	124	129	133	138	143	148	152	157	162	167	171	176	181	186	191
0.31	97	101	106	110	115	120	124	129	133	138	143	147	152	157	161	166	171	175	180	184
0.32	94	98	102	107	111	116	120	125	129	134	138	143	147	152	156	161	165	170	174	179
0.33	91	95	100	104	108	112	117	121	125	130	134	138	143	147	152	156	160	165	169	173
0.34	88	92	96	101	105	109	112	117	122	126	130	135	139	143	147	151	156	160	164	168
0.35	86	90	94	98	102	106	110	115	119	123	126	131	135	139	143	147	151	155	159	163
0.36	83	87	91	95	99	103	107	111	115	120	124	127	131	135	139	143	147	151	155	159
0.37	81	85	89	93	97	100	104	108	112	116	120	124	127	131	135	139	143	147	151	154
0.38	79	83	87	90	94	98	102	105	109	113	117	120	124	128	132	135	139	143	146	150
0.39	77	80	84	88	92	95	99	103	106	110	113	117	121	124	125	129	132	136	139	143
0.40	75	78	82	86	89	93	96	100	103	107	111	114	118	121	125	129	133	136	139	143
0.42	71	75	78	82	85	88	92	95	99	102	105	109	112	116	119	123	128	129	133	138
0.45	67	70	73	76	79	82	86	89	92	95	98	101	105	108	111	114	117	121	124	127
0.46	65	68	71	74	78	81	84	87	90	93	96	99	102	105	109	112	115	118	121	124
0.48	63	66	69	72	75	78	81	84	87	90	92	95	98	101	104	107	110	113	116	117
0.49	61	64	67	70	73	76	79	82	85	88	88	91	94	97	99	102	105	108	109	114
0.50	60	63	66	69	72	74	77	80	83	86	88	91	94	96	99	102	104	107	110	
0.52	58	60	63	66	68	71	74	77	80	83	86	88	91	94	96	99	102	104	107	110
0.55	55	57	60	62	65	67	70	73	75	78	80	83	86	88	91	93	96	99	102	104
0.56	54	56	59	61	64	66	69	71	74	77	79	82	84	87	89	92	94	97	99	102
0.58	52	54	57	59	62	64	67	69	72	74	77	79	81	84	86	89	91	94	96	99
0.63	48	50	52	54	57	59	61	63	65	67	70	72	74	77	79	81	83	85	87	89
0.64	47	49	51	53	56	58	60	62	65	67	69	71	73	76	78	80	82	85	87	89
0.70	43	45	47	49	51	53	55	57	59	61	63	65	67	69	71	73	75	78	80	82
0.72	42	44	46	48	50	52	54	56	58	60	62	64	66	67	69	71	73	75	77	79
0.82	37	38	40	42	44	45	47	49	51	52	54	56	58	59	61	63	64	66	68	70
0.95	32	33	35	36	38	39	41	42	44	45	47	48	50	51	53	54	56	57	59	60
1.14	26	27	29	30	31	32	34	35	36	38	39	40	41	43	44	45	46	48	49	50

FACTORS	HEAT LOSS THRU AIR CHANGES, BTU'S																			
	2100	2200	2300	2400	2500	2600	2700	2800	2900	3000	3100	3200	3300	3400	3500	3600	3700	3800	3900	4000
	ROOM VOLUME, CU. FT.																			
0.012	2500	2619	2738	2857	2976	3095	3214	3333	3452	3571	3690	3810	3929	4048	4167	4286	4405	4524	4643	4762
0.018	1675	1750	1825	1905	1985	2063	2140	2220	2300	2380	2460	2540	2620	2700	2780	2850	2935	3020	3100	3120
0.027	1110	1160	1220	1270	1320	1370	1430	1480	1530	1590	1640	1690	1750	1800	1850	1910	1960	2010	2060	2120
0.036	835	875	915	955	990	1030	1070	1110	1150	1190	1230	1270	1310	1350	1390	1430	1470	1510	1550	1590
0.054	556	582	608	635	661	688	714	741	767	794	820	847	873	899	926	952	979	1005	1032	1058

Determine the heat loss of the building.   Calculate the heat loss of the structure by any accepted method, but preferably by the Btuh method. Basic heat-loss factors for most types of construction are given in Table 6-1. For the example of Fig. 6-1, a total heat loss of 65,000 Btuh has been figured.

Make a piping layout.   First determine if a one- or two-loop circuit is most adaptable. This depends somewhat on the design of the structure and the number of radiators required. For an average-sized residence, design the system as a single circuit. The circuit should be as short and direct as possible, with horizontal

TABLE 6-2 *(continued)*

	HEAT LOSS THRU WINDOWS, DOORS, CEILINGS, FLOORS & WALLS, BTU'S																			
	4100	4200	4300	4400	4500	4600	4700	4800	4900	5000	5100	5200	5300	5400	5500	5600	5700	5800	5900	6000
									AREAS, SQ. FT.											
0.06	978	1000	1024	1048	1062	1094	1120	1142	1168	1191	1215	1240	1262	1284	1310	1334	1358	1382	1404	1430
0.07	837	858	878	898	919	939	960	980	1000	1020	1040	1061	1081	1101	1121	1142	1162	1183	1203	1223
0.09	651	667	683	699	714	730	746	762	778	794	810	826	842	858	873	889	905	921	937	953
0.10	586	600	614	628	643	657	672	686	700	714	729	743	757	772	786	800	814	829	843	858
0.11	533	545	558	577	584	597	611	624	636	649	662	675	688	702	715	728	740	753	766	779
0.12	488	500	512	524	536	548	560	572	584	596	608	619	631	643	655	667	679	690	702	715
0.13	451	462	473	484	495	506	517	528	539	550	561	572	583	594	605	615	626	637	648	659
0.14	418	428	438	449	460	470	480	490	500	510	520	530	541	551	561	571	581	592	602	612
0.15	390	400	409	419	428	438	448	457	466	476	486	495	505	514	524	533	543	552	562	571
0.16	366	375	384	393	402	411	420	429	438	447	456	464	473	482	491	500	509	518	527	536
0.17	344	353	361	370	378	387	395	404	412	420	428	437	445	453	462	470	479	487	496	504
0.18	326	333	341	349	357	365	373	381	389	397	405	413	421	429	437	445	453	461	469	476
0.19	308	316	323	331	338	346	353	361	369	376	383	391	398	406	413	421	428	436	443	451
0.20	293	300	307	314	321	328	336	343	350	357	364	371	379	386	393	400	407	415	422	429
0.21	279	286	292	299	306	313	320	326	333	340	347	354	360	367	374	381	388	395	402	408
0.22	266	273	279	286	292	299	305	312	318	325	331	338	344	351	357	363	370	377	383	389
0.23	254	261	267	273	280	286	292	298	304	311	317	323	329	335	342	348	354	360	367	373
0.24	244	250	256	262	268	274	280	286	292	298	304	310	315	321	327	333	339	345	351	357
0.25	234	240	246	252	257	263	269	274	280	286	292	297	303	309	314	320	326	331	337	343
0.26	225	231	236	242	247	253	258	264	269	275	280	286	291	297	302	308	313	319	324	330
0.27	217	222	228	233	238	244	249	254	259	264	270	275	280	286	291	296	302	307	312	318
0.28	209	214	219	224	229	234	240	245	250	255	260	265	270	275	280	288	291	296	301	306
0.30	195	200	205	209	214	219	224	228	233	238	244	247	252	257	262	267	271	276	281	286
0.31	189	194	198	203	207	212	216	221	225	230	235	240	244	249	254	258	263	267	272	277
0.32	183	187	192	196	201	205	210	214	219	223	228	232	237	241	246	250	254	259	263	268
0.33	177	182	186	190	195	199	203	208	212	216	221	225	229	234	238	242	247	251	255	260
0.34	172	176	180	185	189	193	197	202	206	210	214	218	222	226	231	235	239	244	248	252
0.35	167	171	175	179	183	188	192	196	200	204	208	212	216	220	224	228	233	237	241	245
0.36	163	167	171	174	178	182	186	190	194	198	202	206	210	214	218	222	226	230	234	238
0.37	158	162	166	170	174	178	182	185	189	193	197	201	205	209	212	216	220	224	228	232
0.38	154	158	162	165	169	173	177	180	184	188	192	195	199	203	207	210	214	218	222	226
0.39	150	154	157	161	165	169	172	176	179	183	187	191	194	198	202	205	209	212	216	220
0.40	146	150	153	157	160	164	168	171	175	178	182	185	189	193	196	200	204	207	211	214
0.42	139	143	146	150	153	156	160	163	166	170	173	177	180	184	187	191	194	197	201	204
0.45	130	133	136	140	143	146	149	152	156	159	162	165	168	171	175	178	181	184	187	191
0.46	127	130	133	137	140	143	146	149	152	155	158	161	164	168	171	174	177	180	183	186
0.48	122	125	128	131	134	137	140	143	146	149	152	155	158	161	164	167	170	173	176	179
0.49	120	122	125	128	131	134	137	140	143	146	149	152	154	157	160	163	166	169	172	175
0.50	117	120	123	126	129	131	134	137	140	143	146	149	152	154	157	160	163	166	169	172
0.52	113	115	118	121	124	126	129	132	135	137	140	143	146	148	151	154	157	159	162	165
0.55	106	109	111	114	117	119	122	124	127	130	132	135	138	140	143	145	148	151	153	156
0.56	105	107	110	112	115	117	120	122	125	127	130	132	135	138	140	143	145	148	150	153
0.58	101	103	106	108	111	113	116	118	121	123	126	128	131	133	136	138	141	143	146	148
0.63	93	95	98	100	102	104	107	109	111	113	116	118	120	122	125	127	129	131	134	136
0.64	91	94	96	98	100	102	105	107	109	111	114	116	118	120	123	125	127	129	132	134
0.70	84	86	88	90	92	94	96	98	100	102	104	106	108	110	112	114	116	118	120	122
0.72	81	83	85	87	89	91	93	95	97	99	101	103	105	107	109	111	113	115	117	119
0.82	71	73	75	77	78	80	82	84	85	87	89	90	92	94	96	98	99	101	103	105
0.95	62	63	65	66	68	69	71	72	74	75	77	78	80	81	83	84	86	87	89	90
1.14	51	53	54	55	56	57	59	60	61	62	64	65	66	67	69	70	71	72	73	75

	HEAT LOSS THRU AIR CHANGES, BTU'S																			
	4100	4200	4300	4400	4500	4600	4700	4800	4900	5000	5100	5200	5300	5400	5500	5600	5700	5800	5900	6000
									ROOM VOLUME, CU. FT.											
0.012	4881	5000	5119	5238	5357	5476	5595	5714	5833	5952	6071	6190	6309	6428	6547	6666	6785	6904	7023	7142
0.018	3255	3335	3415	3495	3570	3650	3730	3805	3890	3970	4050	4130	4215	4285	4370	4450	4525	4605	4685	4765
0.027	2170	2223	2277	2330	2380	2433	2487	2540	2593	2647	2700	2753	2810	2860	2913	2967	3017	3070	3123	3177
0.036	1628	1666	1708	1746	1785	1825	1865	1903	1945	1985	2025	2065	2108	2143	2185	2225	2263	2303	2343	2383
0.054	1085	1111	1138	1164	1190	1217	1243	1270	1296	1323	1349	1375	1401	1428	1454	1481	1507	1534	1560	1587

branches from main to risers not over 3 to 4 ft long. To simplify the use of the following tables, show radiator size in Btuh. This can be changed to square feet of radiation by dividing the Btuh output of each radiator by a Btuh emission corresponding with the type of radiation used and the average water temperature selected for the heating system (see Table 6-4).

Determine the gallons of water required per minute. The gallons of water required per minute for the system must be know so that a proper sized circulator can be selected. The tables in this chapter are based on a 20° temperature

TABLE 6-3   Total Btu Heat Loss Conversion Equivalents

70	50	55	60	65	75	80	85	90
1000	715	790	860	930	1070	1145	1215	1285
1100	790	870	950	1020	1180	1260	1340	1420
1200	860	950	1030	1120	1290	1370	1460	1540
1300	930	1020	1120	1210	1400	1490	1580	1680
1400	1000	1100	1200	1300	1500	1600	1700	1800
1500	1070	1180	1290	1400	1610	1720	1820	1930
1600	1150	1260	1370	1490	1720	1830	1940	2060
1700	1220	1340	1460	1580	1830	1950	2070	2190
1800	1290	1420	1540	1680	1930	2060	2190	2310
1900	1360	1500	1630	1770	2040	2170	2310	2440
2000	1430	1570	1720	1860	2150	2290	2430	2570
2100	1500	1650	1800	1950	2250	2400	2550	2700
2200	1570	1730	1890	2050	2360	2520	2670	2830
2300	1650	1810	1970	2140	2470	2630	2800	2960
2400	1720	1890	2060	2230	2580	2750	2920	3090
2500	1790	1970	2140	2320	2680	2860	3040	3210
2600	1860	2050	2230	2420	2790	2980	3160	3340
2700	1930	2120	2320	2510	2900	3090	3280	3470
2800	2000	2200	2400	2600	3000	3200	3400	3600
2900	2080	2280	2490	2700	3120	3320	3520	3730
3000	2145	2360	2570	2790	3220	3430	3650	3860
3100	2220	2440	2660	2880	3330	3550	3770	3980
3200	2290	2520	2740	2980	3440	3660	3890	4110
3300	2360	2600	2830	3070	3550	3780	4010	4240
3400	2430	2670	2920	3160	3650	3890	4130	4370
3500	2500	2750	3000	3250	3760	4000	4250	4500
3600	2580	2830	3090	3350	3870	4110	4370	4630
3700	2640	2910	3170	3440	3970	4230	4490	4750
3800	2720	2990	3260	3530	4080	4340	4610	4880
3900	2790	3070	3340	3630	4190	4460	4740	5010
4000	2860	3150	3430	3720	4300	4570	4860	5140
4100	2930	3220	3510	3810	4400	4690	4980	5270
4200	3000	3300	3600	3900	4500	4800	5100	5400
4300	3080	3380	3690	4000	4610	4910	5220	5520
4400	3150	3460	3770	4090	4720	5030	5340	5650
4500	3220	3540	3860	4180	4830	5150	5460	5780
4600	3290	3620	3940	4270	4940	5260	5590	5910
4700	3360	3700	4030	4370	5050	5370	5710	6040
4800	3430	3770	4120	4460	5150	5490	5830	6170
4900	3500	3850	4200	4560	5260	5600	5950	6300
5000	3575	3930	4280	4650	5370	5710	6070	6430
5100	3650	4010	4370	4740	5480	5830	6200	6550
5200	3720	4090	4460	4830	5580	5950	6320	6680
5300	3790	4170	4540	4920	5690	6060	6440	6810
5400	3860	4240	4630	5020	5800	6170	6560	6940
5500	3940	4320	4710	5110	5900	6290	6680	7060
5600	4000	4400	4800	5200	6000	6400	6800	7200
5700	4070	4480	4880	5300	6120	6510	6920	7320
5800	4150	4560	4970	5390	6230	6630	7050	7450
5900	4220	4640	5060	5480	6330	6750	7170	7580
6000	4290	4720	5140	5580	6440	6860	7290	7710
6100	4360	4790	5220	5670	6550	6970	7410	7840
6200	4430	4870	5310	5760	6650	7090	7530	7970
6300	4510	4950	5400	5860	6760	7200	7650	8100
6400	4580	5030	5480	5950	6870	7310	7780	8230
6500	4650	5110	5570	6040	6980	7430	7900	8350
6600	4720	5190	5660	6140	7090	7550	8020	8480
6700	4790	5270	5740	6230	7200	7660	8140	8600
6800	4860	5340	5830	6320	7300	7770	8260	8740
6900	4930	5420	5910	6410	7410	7890	8380	8870

70	50	55	60	65	75	80	85	90
7000	5000	5500	6000	6500	7500	8000	8500	9000
7100	5080	5580	6080	6600	7620	8110	8620	9130
7200	5150	5660	6170	6690	7730	8230	8750	9250
7300	5220	5740	6260	6790	7840	8350	8870	9380
7400	5290	5820	6340	6880	7950	8460	8990	9510
7500	5360	5890	6420	6970	8050	8570	9110	9640
7600	5430	5970	6510	7060	8140	8690	9230	9760
7700	5500	6050	6600	7150	8250	8800	9350	9900
7800	5560	6130	6680	7250	8370	8920	9470	10030
7900	5650	6210	6770	7340	8480	9030	9600	10180
8000	5720	6290	6850	7440	8590	9150	9720	10290
8100	5790	6370	6940	7530	8700	9260	9840	10420
8200	5860	6440	7030	7620	8800	9370	9960	10540
8300	5930	6520	7110	7710	8910	9490	10080	10680
8400	6000	6600	7200	7800	9000	9600	10200	10800
8500	6080	6680	7280	7900	9120	9710	10320	10920
8600	6150	6760	7360	7990	9230	9830	10440	11060
8700	6220	6840	7450	8090	9340	9950	10570	11190
8800	6290	6910	7540	8190	9450	10070	10690	11310
8900	6360	6990	7620	8270	9550	10180	10810	11440
9000	6440	7070	7710	8360	9660	10290	10930	11570
9100	6510	7150	7800	8460	9770	10400	11050	11700
9200	6580	7230	7890	8550	9880	10520	11170	11830
9300	6650	7310	7970	8640	9980	10630	11300	11960
9400	6720	7390	8050	8740	10090	10740	11420	12090
9500	6790	7460	8140	8830	10200	10860	11540	12210
9600	6860	7550	8220	8920	10300	10980	11660	12340
9700	6930	7620	8310	9010	10400	11100	11790	12470
9800	7000	7700	8400	9100	10500	11200	11910	12600
9900	7080	7780	8480	9200	10610	11320	12020	12730
10000	7150	7860	8570	9300	10720	11430	12150	12860
10100	7220	7940	8660	9390	10830	11540	12270	12990
10200	7290	8020	8740	9480	10950	11660	12390	13110
10300	7360	8100	8830	9570	11060	11790	12510	13230
10400	7440	8170	8910	9660	11170	11900	12630	13370
10500	7510	8250	9000	9750	11280	12000	12750	13500
10600	7580	8330	9090	9850	11390	12110	12880	13610
10700	7650	8410	9170	9940	11500	12230	13000	13750
10800	7720	8490	9260	10030	11600	12350	13120	13890
10900	7790	8560	9340	10120	11700	12460	13240	14000
11000	7870	8640	9430	10220	11800	12580	13360	14120
11100	7930	8720	9520	10310	11910	12700	13490	14280
11200	8000	8800	9600	10410	12010	12810	13610	14400
11300	8080	8880	9690	10500	12120	12910	13730	14530
11400	8150	8960	9780	10600	12230	13020	13850	14660
11500	8220	9040	9860	10690	12340	13140	13980	14790
11600	8290	9120	9950	10790	12450	13260	14100	14910
11700	8360	9200	10030	10880	12560	13380	14210	15030
11800	8430	9280	10110	10980	12670	13500	14330	15170
11900	8500	9350	10200	11060	12780	13600	14450	15300
12000	8580	9430	10290	11170	12890	13710	14580	15420
12100	8650	9510	10370	11260	13000	13830	14700	15560
12200	8720	9590	10460	11350	13100	13950	14820	15690
12300	8790	9670	10540	11440	13200	14070	14940	15810
12400	8860	9740	10620	11530	13310	14190	15070	15930
12500	8930	9820	10710	11620	13410	14300	15190	16070
12600	9000	9900	10800	11710	13520	14400	15310	16200
12700	9080	9980	10890	11810	13630	14510	15430	16320
12800	9150	10060	10980	11900	13730	14620	15560	16460
12900	9220	10130	11060	11990	13830	14750	15680	16590

drop, as this has been found to be the most economical for this type of system. It is assumed there will be a difference of 20°F between the return and supply outlet water temperature of the boiler. However, this difference occurs only when the system is operating at its maximum design temperature.

To find the gallons per minute (gpm) required for the system, divide the total heat loss of 65,000 Btuh by 9600 and find that approximately 6.8 gpm is required. The 9600 is obtained by multiplying the 20° temperature drop by 60 minutes in

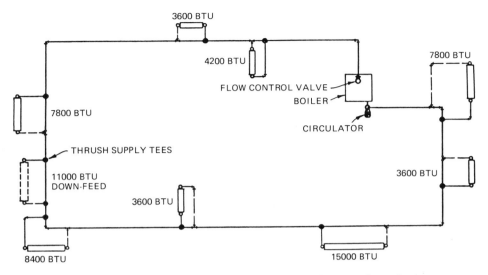

3600 BTU

4200 BTU

FLOW CONTROL VALVE

7800 BTU

BOILER

7800 BTU

CIRCULATOR

THRUSH SUPPLY TEES

11000 BTU
DOWN-FEED

3600 BTU

3600 BTU

8400 BTU

15000 BTU

Figure 6-1 Typical diagrammatic layout of a single-circuit flow control one-pipe hot water heating system.

one hour by 8 lb of water in 1 gallon at 215°F ($20 \times 60 \times 8$). To simplify, divide the total heat loss by 10,000, which is accurate enough for all practical purposes.

Select a circulator.   To select a circulator, refer to the chart in Table 6-5. Read to the right on the bottom line, in the chart for model H, V or B, until 6.8 gpm is found. Draw a line upward until it intersects the first circulator capacity curve. From this point read at the left 7 ft head in feet of water. Therefore, a 3/4-in. H or 3/4-in. V circulator will deliver 6.8 gpm against a head pressure of 7 ft.

For some installations it may be more practical to use a larger-sized circulator or a Hi-Head Circulator because of a possible reduction in pipe sizes. For this example, a 3/4-in. H or V circulator is selected.

TABLE 6-4   Heat Emission Rates

Average Water Temperature (°F)	Approximate BTU Emission per Hour per Square Foot of Radiation at Minimum Design Temperature
160	130
165	140
170	150
180	170
190	190
195	200 Maximum for thrush flow control system

TABLE 6-5

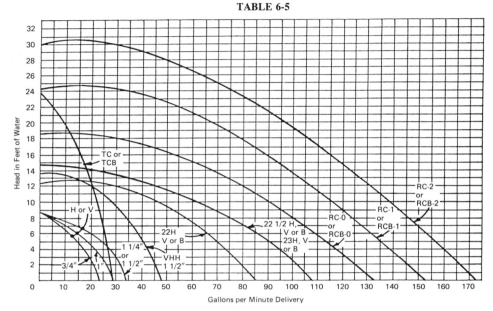

Performance Curves Based on 1750 RPM 60 C 115 V Motors

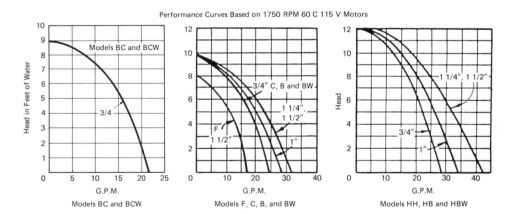

Models BC and BCW

Models F, C, B, and BW

Models HH, HB and HBW

Size the main. In a forced circulating system, the piping design must be such that the head in feet of water created by the circulator forcing the water from the boiler to any radiator is equal to the friction head in the radiator circuit when the system is operating at its maximum design temperature.

The measured length of the main circuit in the example of Fig. 6-1 is 120 ft. To this must be added the resistance of the one-pipe tees. Allow 10 equivalent feet of piping for each one-pipe tee. Thus 10 tees × 10 will be the 100 equivalent feet

TABLE 6-6A

Circulator Head in Feet	Milinches per Foot of Pipe										
	50	100	150	200	250	300	350	400	500	600	700
	Total Equivalent Length of Pipe in Feet: Longest Circuit										
1	240	120	80	60	48	40	34	30	25	20	17
2	480	240	160	120	96	80	69	60	48	40	34
2.5	600	300	200	150	120	100	86	75	60	50	43
3	720	360	240	180	144	120	103	90	72	60	51
3.5	840	420	280	210	168	140	120	105	84	70	60
4	960	480	320	240	192	160	137	120	96	80	68
4.5	1,080	540	360	270	216	180	154	135	108	90	77
5	1,200	600	400	300	240	200	172	150	120	100	85
5.5	1,320	660	440	330	264	220	189	165	132	110	94
6	1,440	720	480	360	288	240	206	180	144	120	102
6.5	1,560	780	520	390	312	260	222	195	156	130	111
7	1,680	840	560	420	336	280	240	210	168	140	119
7.5	1,800	900	600	450	360	300	257	225	180	150	128
8	1,920	960	640	480	384	320	274	240	192	160	136
8.5	2,040	1020	680	510	408	340	292	255	204	170	145
9	2,160	1080	720	540	431	360	308	270	216	180	153
9.5	2,280	1140	760	570	455	380	326	285	228	190	162
10	2,400	1200	800	600	480	400	343	300	240	200	170
10.5	2,520	1260	840	630	505	420	361	315	252	210	180
11	2,640	1320	880	660	529	440	378	330	264	220	187
11.5	2,760	1380	920	690	554	460	396	345	276	230	197
12	2,880	1440	960	720	576	480	412	360	288	240	204
14	3,360	1680	1120	840	672	560	479	420	336	280	240
16	3,840	1920	1280	960	770	640	550	480	384	320	274
18	4,320	2160	1440	1080	864	720	617	540	432	360	309
20	4,800	2400	1600	1200	962	800	688	600	480	400	340
24	5,760	2880	1920	1440	1152	960	825	720	576	480	410
28	6,720	3360	2240	1680	1344	1120	960	840	672	560	480
32	7,680	3840	2560	1920	1536	1280	1097	960	768	640	548
36	8,640	4320	2880	2160	1728	1440	1234	1080	864	720	617
40	9,600	4800	3200	2400	1920	1600	1370	1200	960	800	685
45	10,800	5400	3600	2700	2160	1800	1543	1350	1080	900	771
50	12,000	6000	4000	3000	2400	2000	1715	1500	1200	1000	857
55	13,200	6600	4400	3300	2640	2200	1886	1650	1320	1100	943
60	14,400	7200	4800	3600	2880	2400	2060	1800	1440	1200	1028

of piping to be added to the measured length of 120 ft, making a total equivalent length of 220 ft of piping.

    To size the main, refer to Table 6-6A, and, reading to the right from the 7-ft circulator head, find the closest equivalent length of piping to that required for the system (220 ft), which is 210 ft in the 400-milinch column. In this same column in Table 6-6B, we find that 66,000 Btuh is the closest and next largest to the

TABLE 6-6B

Nominal Pipe Size (in.)	Milinches per Foot of Pipe										
	50	100	150	200	250	300	350	400	500	600	700
	Heat-carrying Capacity of Pipes in Thousands of BTUs*										
½	5.2	7.2	9	10.5	12	13	14	16	17.5	19.5	22
¾	11.1	15.2	19	22.5	25	27.5	30	34	37	40	44
1	21	30	38	44	49	55	60	66	72	80	89
1¼	45	65	82	95	105	120	130	138	155	175	182
1½	68	97	125	148	165	180	190	215	240	270	283
2	132	190	240	280	310	351	370	415	470	508	565
2½	215	312	390	462	508	570	605	655	723	800	860
3	390	565	700	805	900	1010	1140	1250	1350	1505	1710
3½	570	830	1050	1200	1350	1500	1630	1800	2000	2250	2480
4	800	1200	1400	1700	1900	2100	2300	2600	2950	3150	3475
5	1400	2200	2700	3200	3500	4000	4300	4600	3400	5900	6400
6	2500	3700	4600	5400	6000	6700	7000	8000	9000	10000	11000

*Based on 20°F temperature drop.

required 65,000 Btuh. Reading to the left on the same line, a 1-in. pipe is indicated as being required for this circuit.

Size the radiator branches. To size the radiator branches, refer to Table 6-6C, where capacities are indicated for using one or two one-pipe tees for upfeed radiators and include sizes for first-, second-, and third-floor radiators, as well as downfeed radiators. Downfeed radiators require two one-pipe tees.

Using the same 400-milinch column as was used in Table 6-6B and reading to the right on the 400-milinch line in the Nonadjustable Tee section, we find that 1/2-in. pipe will carry up to 11,000 Btuh and 3/4-in. pipe will carry up to 26,000 Btuh.

Select the boiler. Net boiler output should be used for selecting a proper-sized boiler. This may be *net rating* in Btuh or installed square feet of water radiation at 150-Btuh emission. To select a boiler on net installed radiation basis, divide the total heat loss by 150-Btuh emission. In the preceding example, this would be 65,000/150 = 433 ft.^{2} of installed radiation.

Select the pressure tank. To select the correct size of pressure tank, refer to Fig. 6-2.

Select the flow control valve. The flow control valve should be the same size as the trunk or branch main in which it is installed.

To design a two-circuit one-pipe system, follow the same steps as were used to design a single-circuit one-pipe system.

TABLE 6-6C Nonadjustable One-pipe Tees

Riser Capacities in Thousands of BTU Per Hour*

Millinches per Foot of Pipe	One One-pipe Tee						Two One-pipe Tees							
	1st Floor Pipe Size		2nd Floor Pipe Size		3rd Floor Pipe Size		1st Floor Pipe Size		2nd Floor Pipe Size		3rd Floor Pipe Size		Down-feed Pipe Size	
	1/2 in.	3/4 in.	1/2 in.	3/4 in.	1/2 in.	3/4 in.	1/2 in.	3/4 in.	1/2 in.	3/4 in.	1/2 in.	3/4 in.	1/2 in.	3/4 in.
100	5	12	3.5	9	3	7	6	16	5	11	4	9	5	11
150	6	15	4	10	3.5	9	8	20	6	14	5	11	6	14
200	7	18	5	12	4	10	9	23	7	16	6	13	7	16
250	8	20	5.5	14	4.5	12	11	26	7	18	6	15	7	18
300	9	22	6	16	5	13	12	29	8	21	6.5	16	8	21
350	10	25	6.5	17	5.5	14	13	32	9	22	7	18	9	22
400	11	26	7	18	6	15	14	34	9	24	8	19	9	24
500	12	29	8	21	6.5	17	16	38	11	26	9	22	11	26
600	14	32	9	22	7	18	18	43	12	30	10	24	12	30

*Based on 20°F temperature drop.

65

SIZES AND CAPACITIES

No.	Gallons Capacity	Size	*Select Pressure Tank from Total BTU Requirements of System
8	8	12" × 16"	50,000 BTU
12	12	12" × 24"	70,000 BTU
15	15	12" × 30"	85,000 BTU
18	18	12" × 36"	100,000 BTU
24	24	12" × 48"	200,000 BTU
30	30	12" × 60"	400,000 BTU
36	36	12" × 72"	500,000 BTU

Figure 6-2   Sizes and capacities of pressure tanks.

Heat loss.   Assume for this example that the heat loss is 148.8 Mbh or 148,000 Btuh. See Fig. 6-3.

Piping layout.   The system in Fig. 6-3 is a good example of a one-pipe two-circuit installation. Suggestions for design are given in the previous example for a single circuit one-pipe system.

Gallons of water required per minute.   148,800 Btu divided by 9600 equals 15.5 gpm.

Circulator.   Referring to Table 6-6C, a 1-in. C circulator is shown to deliver 15.5 gpm against a head pressure of 6 ft.

Main size.   The measured length of the longest circuit is 115 ft. This includes the trunk main and the longest branch main circuit. (The longest branch main circuit is used because it offers the most resistance, and if the circulator selected will pump through the longest circuit, it will be more than ample to pump through the shorter circuit.)

One hundred fifteen feet measured length plus 100 (10 equivalent ft of pipe for each supply tee on the longest branch main) gives a total equivalent length of 215 ft for the longest circuit (trunk and longest branch main circuit).

From Table 6-6A at 6-ft circulator head, read across to find that the closest equivalent length of piping to that required for the system (215) is 240 ft (closest and next largest). This will be found in the 300-milinch column. In this same column in Table 6-6B, we find 180,000 Btuh to be the closest and next largest to the required 148,000 Btuh. Reading to the left, we find that 1½-in. pipe is required to carry the total radiation. This will be the trunk main size.

Branch mains are sized in a like manner. In the 300-milinch column of Table 6-6B, we find 120,000 Btuh can be carried on 1¼-in. pipe and up to 55,000 Btuh on 1-in. pipe. The longest branch main circuit must carry 89,000 Btuh. Therefore, both circuits for this system require 1¼-in. piping.

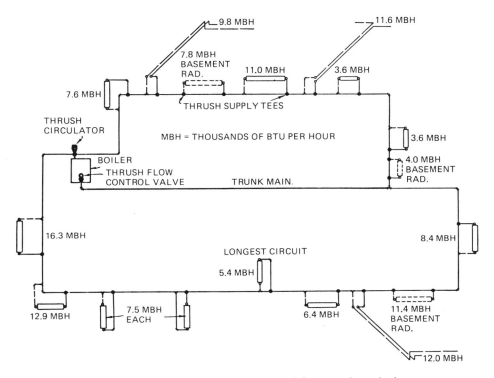

Figure 6-3 Typical diagrammatic layout of a two-circuit flow control one-pipe hot water heating system.

Radiator branches. Radiator branches are sized from Table 6-6C. On the 300-milinch line and using one one-pipe tee, we find that up to 9000 Btuh can be carried by 1/2-in. pipe, and up to 22,000 Btuh on 3/4-in. pipe for first-floor radiators. Up to 6000 Btuh can be carried by 1/2-in. pipe and up to 16,000 Btuh on 3/4-in. pipe for second-floor radiators.

In the same 300-milinch line, we see that downfeed radiators up to 8000 Btuh can be carried on 1/2-in. pipe and up to 21,000 Btuh on 3/4-in. pipe.

When two one-pipe tees are installed, one in the supply and one in the return radiator branch, more water is diverted through the radiator and the carrying capacity of the radiator branches is thereby increased.

To find the Btuh carrying capacity of radiator branches when two one-pipe tees are used, read to right on the same milinch line as was used previously in the column under the heading of two one-pipe tees.

Boiler. Divide the total heat loss of 148,000 Btuh by 150 to arrive at a net boiler rating of 992 ft². Therefore, select a boiler with a net rating or installed radiation load of not less than 992 ft² at 150-Btuh emission.

Pressure tank.   See Fig. 6-2.

Flow control valve.   The flow control valve should be the same size as the trunk main.

Sometimes it will be economical to use a larger-sized circulator, because of a possible reduction in main size and the possible use of smaller one-pipe tees.

Going back to the circulator and referring to the chart of model HH or HB in Table 6-5, we find a 1-in. HH circulator will deliver 15.5 gpm against a head pressure of $9\frac{1}{2}$ ft.

From Table 6-6A, on the line for $9\frac{1}{2}$-ft circulator head, we find 215 ft of equivalent piping in the 500-milinch column. In this same column in Table 6-6B, we find $1\frac{1}{2}$-in. pipe will carry up to 240,000 Btuh, $1\frac{1}{4}$-in. pipe up to 155,000 Btuh, and 1-in. pipe up to 72,000 Btuh. Therefore, the short branch main circuit may be 1-in. pipe if a 1-in. HH circulator is used.

The carrying capacities of one-pipe tees and radiator branches are also increased by using the 350-milinch line in Table 6-6C.

TWO-PIPE DIRECT RETURN SYSTEM

To design a two-pipe direct return flow control system, the following steps are necessary:

1. Determine heat loss
2. Make piping layout
3. Determine gallons of water required per minute
4. Select circulator
5. Size mains
6. Size branches
7. Select boiler
8. Select pressure tank
9. Select flow control valve

Determine heat loss.   The heat loss for the job in Fig. 6-4 is indicated.

Make piping layout.   The layout has been made with radiation divided as evenly as possible.

Determine gallons of water required per minute.   To determine the required gallons per minute to be circulated, total Btuh loss is divided by 9600 for 20°F temperature drop. Total Btuh 96,000/9600 = 10 gpm.

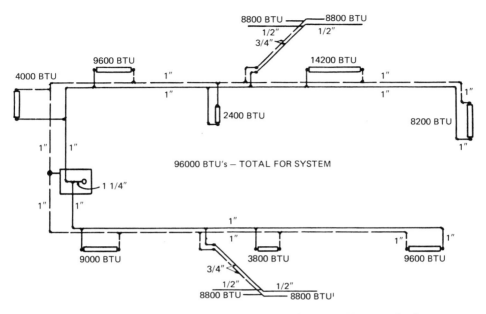

Figure 6-4 Typical diagrammatic layout of a two-pipe flow control hot water heating system.

Select circulator. Referring to the circulator performance charts, Table 6-5, find a regular 1-in. H or V circulator that will deliver 10 gpm at 7-ft head. 7-ft head × 12,000 (milinches in 1 ft) = 84,000 milinches.

Size mains. The main size is based on the milinch resistance of piping in the longest circuit. This includes both the supply and return mains. The measured length of the longest circuit (Fig. 6-4) is 136 ft. To this measured length add 50% (68 ft) for friction loss in the boiler, fittings, and end radiator. The total equivalent length would then be 204 ft (136 + 68). Divide 84,000 milinches (as found in the previous paragraph) by 204 ft and obtain 411 milinches per foot of piping in longest circuit.

Referring to Table 6-6B, use the 400-milinch column (closest and next smallest to the required 411 milinches). The longest circuit supplies a total of 56,000 Btuh; therefore, a 1-in. supply and return will be required (1-in. main in 400-milinch column will carry up to 66,000 Btuh). The shorter circuit having 40,000 Btuh will also require a 1-in. supply and return. The combined total of 96,000 Btuh will require a $1\frac{1}{4}$-in. flow riser and a $1\frac{1}{4}$-in. return drop to the 1-in. circulator.

Size branches. Radiator branches are also sized from the same 400-milinch column in Table 6-6B.

Select boiler.   To select the boiler, divide the total Btuh of the job (96,000) by 150 to obtain 640 ft^2 net boiler load.

Select pressure tank.   Select the pressure tank from Fig. 6-2.

Select flow control valve.   The flow control valve is the same size as the flow riser ($1\frac{1}{4}$ in.).

TWO-PIPE REVERSE RETURN SYSTEM

To design a two-pipe reverse return flow control system, the following steps are necessary:

1. Determine heat loss
2. Make piping layout
3. Determine gallons of water required per minute
4. Select circulator
5. Size mains
6. Size branches
7. Select boiler
8. Select pressure tank
9. Select flow control valve

Determine heat loss.   The heat loss for the job in Fig. 6-5 is indicated.

Make piping layout.   The layout has been made with radiation divided as evenly as possible.

Determine gallons of water required per minute.   To determine the required gallons per minute to be circulated, total Btuh loss is divided by 9600 for 20°F temperature drop. Total Btuh 96,000/9600 = 10 gpm.

Select circulator.   Referring to the circulator performance chart, Table 6-5, we find a regular 1-in. H or V circulator will deliver 10 gpm at 7-ft head. 7 ft × 12,000 (milinches in 1 ft) = 84,000 milinches.

Size mains.   Main size is based on the milinch resistance of the piping in the longest circuit. This includes both the supply and return mains. The measured length of the longest circuit (Fig. 6-5) is 136 ft. To this measured length add 50% (68 ft) for friction loss in the boiler, fittings, and end radiator. The total equivalent length would then be 204 ft (136 + 68). Divide 84,000 milinches (as found in the previous paragraph) by 204 ft and obtain 411 milinches per foot of piping in the

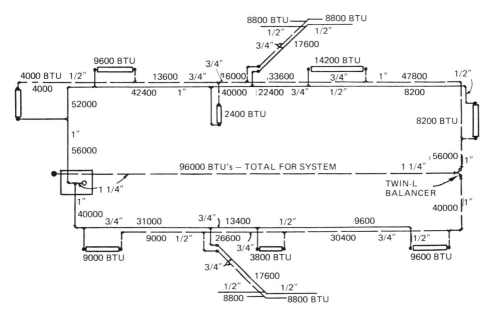

Figure 6-5 Typical diagrammatic layout for a two-pipe reverse return system.

longest circuit. Referring to Table 6-6B, use the 400-milinch column (closest and next smallest to the required 411 milinches) to find that 1/2-in. pipe will supply up to 16,000 Btuh, 3/4-in. pipe up to 34,000 Btuh, 1-in. pipe up to 66,000 Btuh, and $1\frac{1}{4}$-in. pipe up to 138,000 Btuh.

Size branches.   Radiator branches are also sized from the same 400-milinch column of Table 6-6B.

Select boiler.   To select the boiler, divide the total Btuh of the job, 96,000, by 150 to obtain 640 ft² net boiler load.

Select pressure tank.   Select the pressure tank from Fig. 6-2.

Select flow control valve.   The flow control valve is the same size as the flow riser, $1\frac{1}{4}$ in.

TWO-PIPE FLOW CONTROL SYSTEM: QUICK DESIGN METHOD

Tables 6-7 and 6-8 are suitable for sizing the average two-pipe forced circulating installation in residences and other buildings. When two circuits are to be installed, the radiation load should be as equally divided as possible. A system with a total

TABLE 6-7

Square Feet of Radiation	Main Size Steel or Copper Pipe (in.)
Up to 150	$\frac{3}{4}$
150–350	1
350–600	$1-1\frac{1}{4}$ or 2–1
600–1000	$1-1\frac{1}{2}$ or $2-1\frac{1}{4}$
1000–1500	1–2 or $2-1\frac{1}{2}$
1500–2500	$1-2\frac{1}{2}$ or 2–2
2500–3500	1–3 or $2-2\frac{1}{2}$
3500–5000	$1-3\frac{1}{2}$ or $2-2\frac{1}{2}$
5000–7000	1–4 or 2–3

of 900 ft^2 of radiation equally divided would require two $1\frac{1}{4}$-in. supply and return mains. If the job was unbalanced, one circuit might have 575 ft^2 and the other circuit 325 ft^2. In this case, $1\frac{1}{4}$-in. mains would be used for 575 ft^2 and 1-in. mains for 325 ft^2. Mains smaller than $1\frac{1}{2}$ in. should run full size to the end radiator. One and a half inch mains can be reduced to $1\frac{1}{4}$ in. at proper intervals. Larger mains may be reduced at proper points but should terminate at the end radiator at $1\frac{1}{2}$ in. It is not good practice to reduce mains drastically through the run on a direct return system.

Figure 6-6 illustrates a two-pipe direct return system with two circuits. In this system the first radiator supplied is also returned first.

Figure 6-7 shows a two-loop reverse return system. The flow main is run across the building and split. Returns start at the first radiators supplied and flows end in radiators near the boiler.

Figure 6-8 shows a single-circuit two-pipe reverse return system. Here again the return starts at the first radiator supplied and the flow ends in a radiator near the boiler.

TABLE 6-8

Riser Size (in.)		First Floor (square feet of radiation)	Second Floor (square feet of radiation)	Third Floor (square feet of radiation)
Steel	Copper			
	$\frac{3}{8}$	Up to 40		
$\frac{1}{2}$	$\frac{1}{2}$	Up to 80	Up to 75	Up to 70
$\frac{3}{4}$	$\frac{3}{4}$	Up to 150	Up to 140	Up to 130
1	1	Up to 300	Up to 250	Up to 200

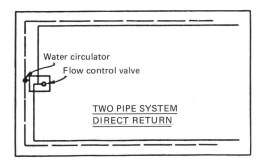

Figure 6-6 Diagram of a two-pipe direct return system with two circuits.

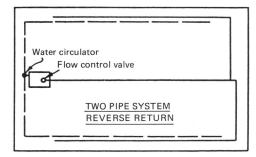

Figure 6-7 Diagram of a two-loop reverse return system.

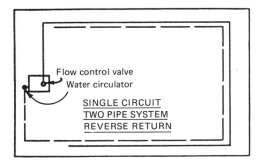

Figure 6-8 Diagram of a single-circuit two-pipe reverse return system.

MAINLESS HOT-WATER HEATING SYSTEMS

On some jobs it may be necessary to install a mainless baseboard system to keep the cost down. A mainless system will operate satisfactorily if engineered and installed properly. On small jobs it is possible to install a one-loop mainless system; however, on larger jobs it is advisable to install a two-loop system. The example

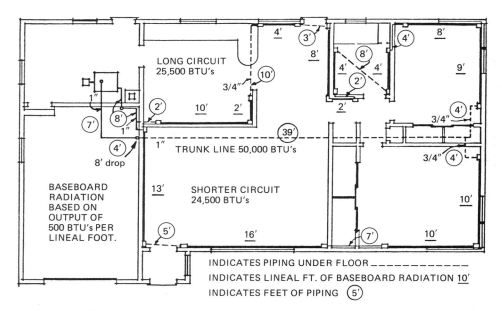

Figure 6-9 Typical diagrammatic layout of a mainless hot water heating system.

in Figure 6-9 outlines in detail the method of designing a two-loop mainless system. For a one-loop mainless system the procedure is the same.

To design a mainless hot-water heating system, the following steps are necessary.

1. Determine heat loss of the building
2. Make piping layout
3. Size piping
4. Select proper-sized flow control valve
5. Determine equivalent length of piping
6. Determine gallons of water required per minute
7. Determine resistance of circuit and head
8. Select circulator
9. Select pressure tank
10. Select boiler

Determine heat loss.   Calculate heat loss the same as for any other job. Heat loss of this job is 50,000 Btuh, 25,500 Btuh for the long circuit and 24,500 Btuh for the short circuit.

Make piping layout.   First determine is a one- or two-loop circuit is most desirable. This will depend somewhat on the design of the building and the amount of radiation. If a two-loop system is chosen, divide the radiation as evenly as possible. The example is that of a two-loop system.

Piping between baseboards should be run along the walls as much as possible and should be on the same level with the baseboard. The piping should be dropped under the floor where there are doorways or where the piping is not along a wall. Dashed lines show piping that runs under the floor. All pipes should be level except those that run under the floor. Under-the-floor piping should be pitched to avoid troublesome air problems. Drains should be installed at all low points and air vents on all baseboards and high points of piping.

Size piping.   All piping between baseboards should be the same size as the baseboard connection size. The trunk line should be one size larger than the baseboard connection size. In Fig. 6-9, the baseboard is 3/4-in. size. Therefore, all piping between baseboard is 3/4 in. and the trunk line is 1 in.

Select flow control valve.   The flow control valve should be the same size as the trunk line.

Determine equivalent length of piping.   The equivalent length of piping is necessary to find the resistance of the job. In a two-loop system, only the longest loop including the trunk line should be considered.

51	lineal feet of baseboard (considered as $\frac{3}{4}$-in. pipe) (consult manufacturer's specification)
33	lineal feet of $\frac{3}{4}$-in. piping
36	equivalent feet for twenty-four $\frac{3}{4}$-in. 90° elbows; see Table 6–9
120	equivalent feet of $\frac{3}{4}$-in. piping

66	lineal feet of 1-in. piping
6.2	equivalent feet for 1 boiler: 1 in; see Table 6–9
20.8	equivalent feet for 1 FCV: 1 in.; see Table 6–9
16	equivalent feet for eight 1-in. 90° elbows; see Table 6–9
109	equivalent feet of 1-in. piping

Determine gallons of water required per minute.   Total Btuh divided by 9600 equals gallons per minute for 20°F temperature drop.

50,000 divided by 9600 = 5.2 gpm required in the 1-in. trunk line

25,500 divided by 9600 = 2.7 gpm required in the 3/4-in. longest circuit

TABLE 6-9   Equivalent Lengths of Pipe (ft)

Pipe Size (in.)	Boiler	Flow Control Valve	Rad. or Conv.	Angle Rad. Valve	Open Gate Valve	Open Globe Valve	Elbow 90°	Elbow 45°	Tee Percent through Branch 50	25
$\frac{3}{4}$			4.7	3.1	0.8	18.7	1.5	1.1	6.2	24.8
1	6.2	20.8	6.2	4.2	1.0	25.0	2.0	1.5	8.3	33.2
$1\frac{1}{4}$	7.8	26.0	7.8	5.2	1.3	31.2	2.6	1.8	10.4	41.6
$1\frac{1}{2}$	9.4	31.3	9.4	6.2	1.6	37.5	3.1	2.2	12.5	50.0
2	12.5	41.7	12.5	8.3	2.1	50.0	4.2	2.9	16.7	66.8
$2\frac{1}{2}$	15.6	52.0	15.6	10.4	2.6	62.5	5.2	3.6	20.8	83.2
3	18.8	62.5	18.8	12.5	3.1	75.0	6.2	4.4	25.0	100.0
$3\frac{1}{2}$	21.8		21.8	14.6	3.7	87.5	7.3	5.1	29.2	116.8
4	25.0		25.0	17.5	4.2	100.0	8.3	5.8	33.4	133.6

Determine resistance in circuit and head.   Table 6-10 shows 250 milinches per foot resistance in 1-in. pipe at 5 gpm and 225 milinches per foot resistance in 3/4-in. pipe at 2.5 gpm.

$$\text{Total resistance in 1-in. pipe: } 250 \times 109 = 27{,}250 \text{ milinches}$$

$$\text{Total resistance in 3/4-in. pipe: } 225 \times 120 = \underline{27{,}000} \text{ milinches}$$

$$\text{Total resistance in system } 54{,}250 \text{ milinches}$$

$$\frac{\text{Total resistance}}{12{,}000} = \text{head in feet}$$

$$\frac{54{,}250}{12{,}000} = 4.5 \text{ head required in this job}$$

Select circulator.   From Table 6-5, select the circulator nearest to 5.2 gpm at a 4.5-ft head. A model 3/4-in. H or V circulator is selected for this job.

Select pressure tank.   The pressure tank ratings are given in Fig. 6-2.

Select boiler.   Divide the total heat loss of 50,000 Btuh by 150 to arrive at a net boiler rating of 334 ft². Therefore, select a boiler with a net rating or installed radiation load of not less than 334 ft² at 150-Btuh emission.

All calculations given in the preceding example were based on steel pipe. The steps and procedures are identical for copper pipe, except use Table 6-11 in place of Table 6-10 when determining the resistance of the pipe, fitting, and the like, in question.

TABLE 6-10   Friction Heads for Standard Black Iron Pipe

Flow of Water — Gallons per Minute

Heat Conveyed per Hour in 1000 Btu Based on Temperature Difference
of 20°F Between Supply and Return Water

COMPUTER APPLICATIONS

The BASIC program in Fig. 6-10 is one approach to computer use in designing hot-water heating systems. Once the program is keyed into the computer, exactly as shown, it may be run. All that is required of the operator is to supply the data as the computer asks for them. Other BASIC programs should readily occur to the operator as he or she becomes more familiar with programs and the design of HVAC systems.

TABLE 6-11   Friction Heads for Copper Pipe

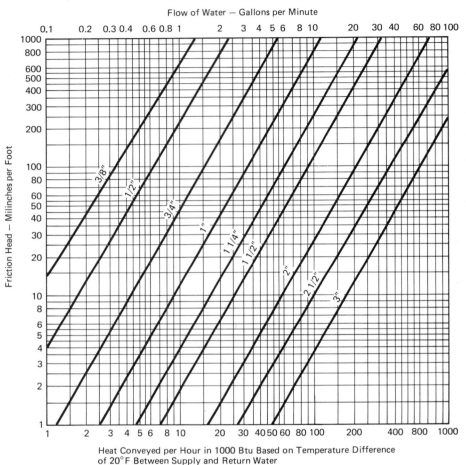

Heat Conveyed per Hour in 1000 Btu Based on Temperature Difference
of 20°F Between Supply and Return Water

Figure 6-11 shows the monitor screen as the program is run. In this example, the total heat loss is 50,000 Btuh, and the heat loss for the longest circuit in the system is 25,500 Btuh. These figures are entered into the computer, and it then asks the size of the baseboard heater connections. In this case, the connections are 3/4 in., or .75 in. computer language. This figure is entered along with the other fitting in this circuit.

The computer then automatically calculates the size of the main pipe coming from the boiler and feeding the two branches. It then asks the operator some information about this pipe, which happens to be 1 in. diameter. When these figures are entered, the computer calculates and prints the total equivalent feet for both the 3/4- and 1-in. pipes. Furthermore, the computer calculates the gallons per minute

```
10 REM **PROGRAM TO AID IN THE DESIGN OF A MAINLESS HOT WATER SYSTEM**
12 PRINT "THIS PROGRAM IS DESIGNED TO FIND THE EQUIVALENT FEET OF PIPE"
20 PRINT "BASEBOARD HEATERS, VALVES, BOILERS, AND THE LIKE.  WHEN RUN,"
30 PRINT "THIS PROGRAM WILL ALSO DETERMINE THE GALLON OF WATER PER MINUTE"
40 PRINT "REQUIRED TO OBTAIN THE PROPER TEMPERATURE IN THE SYSTEM."
50 PRINT "THIS PROGRAM WILL ALSO SIZE THE NET BOILER RATING REQUIRED"
70 PRINT
110 PRINT "YOU HAVE CHOSEN TO USE A MAINLESS HOT WATER SYSTEM,"
120 PRINT "PLEASE ANSWER THE FOLLOWING QUESTIONS"
130 PRINT
140 PRINT
149 INPUT "ENTER TOTAL HEAT LOSS FOR LONGEST CIRCUIT IN SYSTEM";H1
150 INPUT "ENTER TOTAL HEAT LOSS FOR AREA IN BTU'S";H
151 INPUT "ENTER SIZE OF BASEBOARD CONNECTION";C
152 IF C=.75 THEN 500
153 IF C=1 THEN 510
154 IF C=1.25 THEN 520
155 IF C=1.5 THEN 530
156 IF C=2 THEN 540
157 IF C=2.5 THEN 550
158 IF C=3 THEN 560
159 IF C=3.5 THEN 570
160 PRINT "ALL PIPING BETWEEN BASEBOARD TO BE SAME SIZE AS THE BASEBOARD"
161 PRINT "CONNECTION"
162 PRINT "ENTER LINEAL FEET OF";C;"-INCH PIPE":INPUT P
163 INPUT "ENTER TOTAL LENGTH OF BASEBOARD HEATERS";B
165 PRINT "ARE THERE ANY OTHER VALVES, ELBOWS, ETC. THE SAME SIZE AS"
166 INPUT "THE CONNECTIONS (Y OR N)";Q$
167 IF Q$="Y" THEN 1000
168 GOTO 300
169 T1=(P+B+T)
170 PRINT
171 PRINT
172 GOTO 2000
174 CLS
175 PRINT "THE TOTAL EQUIVALENT FEET OF";C;"-INCH PIPE IS";T1;"FEET"
212 PRINT "                       -----            -----"
213 PRINT
230 PRINT "THE TOTAL EQUIVALENT FEET OF";L;"-INCH PIPE IS";T3;"FEET"
250 PRINT "                       -----            ------"
260 GPM=H/9600
261 GPM1=H1/9600
262 PRINT
263 PRINT "THE WATER REQUIRED FOR THE";L;"-INCH LINE IS";GPM;"GPM"
264 PRINT
265 PRINT "THE WATER REQUIRED FOR THE LONGEST";C;"INCH CIRCUIT IS";GPM1;"GPM"
266 PRINT
267 R=H/150
268 PRINT "THE NET BOILER RATING FOR THIS PROJECT IS";R;"SQ. FT. SELECT A"
269 PRINT "BOILER FROM MANUFACTURER'S SPECS WITH A RADIATION LOAD OF NOT"
270 PRINT "LESS THAN";R;"SQ. FT. AT 150 BTU IMMISSION.
280 STOP
300 Z=1.5: GOTO 169
500 C=.75
501 L=1: GOTO 160
502 FCV=20.8
503 R=6.2
504 ARV=4.2
505 OGV=.8
506 GV=25!
507 EL1=2
```

Figure 6-10

```
508 EL2=1.5
510 C=1
511 L=1.25: GOTO 160
520 C=1.25
521 L=1.5: GOTO 160
530 C=1.5
531 L=2: GOTO 160
540 C=2
541 L=2.5: GOTO 160
550 C=2.5
551 L=3: GOTO 160
560 C=3
561 L=3.5: GOTO 160
570 C=3.5
571 L=4: GOTO 160
1000 PRINT "PLEASE ANSWER THE FOLLOWING QUESTIONS"
1010 PRINT
1020 INPUT "NUMBER OF ANGLE RAD VALVES (0 FOR NONE)";ARV
1030 INPUT "NUMBER OF OPEN GATE VALVES (0 FOR NONE)";OGV
1040 INPUT "NUMBER OF GLOBE VALVES (0 FOR NONE)";GV
1050 INPUT "NUMBER OF 90-DEGREES ELS (0 FOR NONE)";E
1060 INPUT "NUMBER OF 45-DEGREE ELS (0 FOR NONE)";E1
1061 IF C=.75 THEN 1070
1062 IF C=1 THEN 1071
1063 IF C=1.25 THEN 1072
1064 IF C=1.5 THEN 1073
1065 IF C=2.5 THEN 1075
1066 IF C=3 THEN 1076
1067 IF C=3.5 THEN 1077
1070 T=(ARV*3.1)+(OGV*.8)+(GV*18.7)+(E*1.5)+(E1*1.1):GOTO 169
1071 T=(ARV*4.2)+(OGV*1)+(GV*25)+(E*2)+(E1*1.5): GOTO 169
1072 T=(ARV*5.2)+(OGV*1.3)+(GV*31.1)+(E*2.6)+(E1*1.8): GOTO 169
1073 T=(ARV*6.2)+(OGV*1.6)+(GV*37.5)+(E*3.1)+(E1*2.2): GOTO 169
1074 T=(ARV*8.3)+(OGV*2.1)+(GV*50)+(E*4.2)+(E1*2.9): GOTO 169
1075 T=(ARV*10.4)+(OGV*2.6)+(GV*62.5)+(E*5.2)+(E1*3.6): GOTO 169
1076 T=(ARV*12.5)+(OGV*3.1)+(GV*75)+(E*6.2)+(E1*4.4): GOTO 169
1077 T= (ARV*14.6)+(OGV*3.7)+(GV*87.5)+(E*7.3)+(E1*5.1)" GOTO 169
1080 GOTO 168
2000 PRINT "ENTER LINEAL FEET OF";L;"-INCH PIPE": INPUT P1
2010 PRINT "ARE THERE ANY OTHER BOILERS, VALVES, ETC. ON THE";L;"-INCH"
2020 INPUT "LINE (Y OR N)"; Q2$
2030 IF Q2$="Y" THEN 3000
2040 T3=P1+T2: GOTO 174
3000 PRINT "PLEASE ANSWER THE FOLLOWING QUESTIONS"
3010 INPUT "ENTER NUMBER OF BOILERS (0 FOR NONE";BO
3020 INPUT "ENTER NUMBER OF FLOW CONTROL VALVES";FCV
3030 INPUT "ENTER NUMBER OF ANGLE RAD VALVES";ARV
3040 INPUT "ENTER NUMBER OF OPEN GATE VALVES (0 FOR NONE)";OGV
3050 INPUT "ENTER NUMBER OF OPEN GLOBE VALVES (0 FOR NONE)";GV
3060 INPUT "ENTER NUMBER OF 90-DEGREE ELS (0 FOR NONE)";E
3070 INPUT "ENTER NUMBER OF 45-DEGREE ELS (0 FOR NONE)";E2
3071 IF L=1 THEN 3080
3072 IF L=1.25 THEN 3082
3073 IF L=1.5 THEN 3084
3074 IF L=2 THEN 3086
3075 IF L=2.5 THEN 3088
3076 IF L=3 THEN 3090
3077 GOTO 2040
3078 IF L=4 THEN 3094
3080 T2=(BO*6.2)+(FCV*20.8)+(ARV*4.2)+(OGV*1)+(GV*25!)+(E*2)+(E2*1.5)
3081 GOTO 2040
```

Figure 6-10   *(continued)*

```
3082 T2=(BO*7.8)+(FCV*26)+(ARV*5.2)+(OGV*1.3)+(GV*31.2)+(E*2.6)+(E1*1.8)
3083 GOTO 2040
3084 T2=(BO*9.399999)+(FCV*31.3)+(ARV*6.2)+(OGV*1.6)+(GV*37.5)+(E*3.1)+(E1*2.2)
3085 GOTO 2040
3086 T2=(BO*12.5)+(FCV*41.7)+(ARV*8.3)+(OGV*2.1)+(GV*50)+(E*4.2)+(E1*2.9)
3087 GOTO 2040
3088 T2=(BO*15.6)+(FCV*52)+(ARV*10.4)+(OGV*2.6)+(GV*62.5)+(E*5.2)+(E1*3.6)
3089 GOTO 2040
3090 T2=(BO*18.8)+(FCV*62.5)+(ARV*12.5)+(OGV*3.1)+(GV*75)+(E*6.2)+(E1*4.4)
3091 GOTO 2040
3092 T2=(BO*21.8)+(FCV*0)+(ARV*14.6)+(OGV*3.7)+(GV*87.5)+(D*7.3)+(E1*5.1)
3093 GOTO 2040
3094 T2=(BO*25)+(FCV*0)+(ARV*17.5)+(OGV*4.2)+(GV*100)+(E*8.3)+(E1*5.8)
3095 GOTO 2040
```

Figure 6-10 (*continued*)

```
Ok
RUN
THIS PROGRAM IS DESIGNED TO FIND THE EQUIVALENT FEET OF PIPE
BASEBOARD HEATERS, VALVES, BOILERS, AND THE LIKE.  WHEN RUN,
THIS PROGRAM WILL ALSO DETERMINE THE GALLON OF WATER PER MINUTE
REQUIRED TO OBTAIN THE PROPER TEMPERATURE IN THE SYSTEM.
THIS PROGRAM WILL ALSO SIZE THE NET BOILER RATING REQUIRED

YOU HAVE CHOSEN TO USE A MAINLESS HOT WATER SYSTEM,
PLEASE ANSWER THE FOLLOWING QUESTIONS


ENTER TOTAL HEAT LOSS FOR LONGEST CIRCUIT IN SYSTEM? 25500
ENTER TOTAL HEAT LOSS FOR AREA IN BTU'S? 50000
ENTER SIZE OF BASEBOARD CONNECTION? .75
ALL PIPING BETWEEN BASEBOARD TO BE SAME SIZE AS THE BASEBOARD
CONNECTION
ENTER LINEAL FEET OF .75 -INCH PIPE
? 33
ENTER TOTAL LENGTH OF BASEBOARD HEATERS? 51
ARE THERE ANY OTHER VALVES, ELBOWS, ETC. THE SAME SIZE AS
THE CONNECTIONS (Y OR N)? Y
PLEASE ANSWER THE FOLLOWING QUESTIONS

NUMBER OF ANGLE RAD VALVES (0 FOR NONE)? 0
NUMBER OF OPEN GATE VALVES (0 FOR NONE)? 0
NUMBER OF GLOBE VALVES (0 FOR NONE)? 0
NUMBER OF 90-DEGREES ELS (0 FOR NONE)? 24
NUMBER OF 45-DEGREE ELS (0 FOR NONE)? 0


ENTER LINEAL FEET OF 1 -INCH PIPE
?
CC
Break in 2000
Ok
RUN "PRNSCRN

NUMBER OF ANGLE RAD VALVES (0 FOR NONE)? 0
NUMBER OF OPEN GATE VALVES (0 FOR NONE)? 0
NUMBER OF GLOBE VALVES (0 FOR NONE)? 0
NUMBER OF 90-DEGREES ELS (0 FOR NONE)? 24
NUMBER OF 45-DEGREE ELS (0 FOR NONE)? 0
```

Figure 6-11

```
ENTER LINEAL FEET OF 1 -INCH PIPE
? 66
ARE THERE ANY OTHER BOILERS, VALVES, ETC. ON THE 1 -INCH
LINE (Y OR N)? Y
PLEASE ANSWER THE FOLLOWING QUESTIONS
ENTER NUMBER OF BOILERS (0 FOR NONE? 1
ENTER NUMBER OF FLOW CONTROL VALVES? 1
ENTER NUMBER OF ANGLE RAD VALVES? 0
ENTER NUMBER OF OPEN GATE VALVES (0 FOR NONE)? 0
ENTER NUMBER OF OPEN GLOBE VALVES (0 FOR NONE)? 0
ENTER NUMBER OF 90-DEGREE ELS (0 FOR NONE)? 8
ENTER NUMBER OF 45-DEGREE ELS (0 FOR NONE)? 0
CC
Break in 3070
Ok
RUN "PRNSCRN


THE TOTAL EQUIVALENT FEET OF .75 -INCH PIPE IS 120 FEET
                                  ----              -----

THE TOTAL EQUIVALENT FEET OF 1 -INCH PIPE IS 109 FEET
                                ----             ------

THE WATER REQUIRED FOR THE 1 -INCH LINE IS 5.208334 GPM

THE WATER REQUIRED FOR THE LONGEST .75 INCH CIRCUIT IS 2.65625 GPM

THE NET BOILER RATING FOR THIS PROJECT IS 333.3334 SQ. FT. SELECT A
BOILER FROM MANUFACTURER'S SPECS WITH A RADIATION LOAD OF NOT
LESS THAN 333.3334 SQ. FT. AT 150 BTU IMMISSION.
Break in 280
Ok
RUN "PRNSCRN
```

Figure 6-11 (*continued*)

of water for each circuit to enable the designer to select a suitable circulator. Finally, the computer automatically calculates the net boiler rater to use for selecting the boiler for the installation.

This program will take some time to type into computer memory and then more time to correct any typos that the operator may make. However, once it is in the computer's memory and ready to run, much calculation time can be saved, as this portion of the design can be completed in 5 minutes or less.

7

ELECTRIC HEATING SYSTEMS

Less than 25 years ago, electric heating units were used only for supplemental heat in small, seldom-used areas of the home, such as a laundry room or workshop, or in vacation homes on chilly autumn nights. Today, however, electric heat is used extensively in both new and renovated homes.

In addition to the fact that electricity is the cleanest fuel available, electric heat is usually the least expensive to install and maintain. Individual room heaters are very inexpensive compared to furnaces and ductwork required in oil or gas forced-air systems, no chimney is required, no utility room is necessary since there is no furnace or boiler, and the installation time and labor are less. Combine all these features and we have a heating system that ranks with the best.

Several types of electric heating units are available (Fig. 7-1) and a description of each will help you decide which will best suit your needs, and also help in the repair and maintenance of such units.

ELECTRIC BASEBOARD HEATERS

Electric baseboard heaters are mounted on the floor along the baseboard, preferably on outside walls under windows for the most efficient operation. It is absolutely noiseless in operation and is the type most often used for heating residential occupancies. The ease with which each room or area may be controlled separately is another great advantage of this heater. Living areas can be heated to, say, 70°F; bedroom heat lowered to, say, 55°F, for sleeping comfort; and unused areas may be turned off completely.

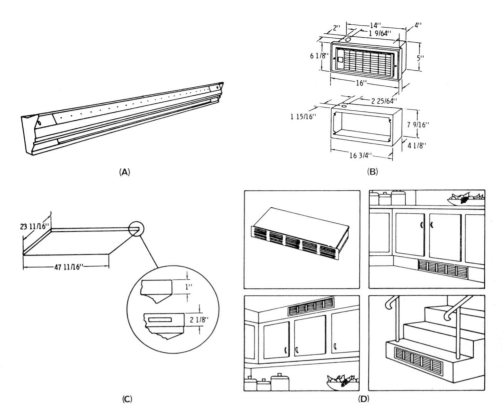

Figure 7-1   Several types of electric heating units: (a) electric baseboard, (b) fan-forced wall units, (c) radiant ceiling panel, and (d) four applications of kick-space heaters. (Courtesy of the author)

Electric baseboard units may be mounted on practically any surface (wood, plaster, drywall, etc.), but if polystyrene foam insulation is used near the unit, a $\frac{3}{4}$-in. (minimum) ventilated spacer strip must be used between the heater and the wall. In such cases, the heater should also be elevated above the floor or rug to allow ventilation to flow from the floor upward over the total heater space.

One complaint received over the years about this type of heater has been wall discoloration directly above the heating units. When this problem occurred, the reason was almost always traced to one or more of the following:

1. High wattage per square foot of heating element
2. Heavy smoking by occupants
3. Poor housekeeping

RADIANT CEILING HEATERS

Radiant ceiling heaters are often used in bathrooms and similar areas so that the entire room does not have to be overheated to meet the need for extra warmth after a bath or shower. They are also used in larger areas, such as a garage or basement, or for spot-warming a person standing at a workbench.

Most of these units are rated from 800 to 1500 watts (W) and normally operate on 120-V circuits. As with most electric heating units, they may be controlled by a remote thermostat, but since they are usually used for supplemental heat, a conventional wall switch is usually used. They are quickly and easily mounted on an outlet box in much the same way as conventional lighting fixtures. In fact, where very low wattage is used, ceiling heaters may often be installed by merely replacing the ceiling lighting fixture with a heater.

RADIANT HEATING PANELS

Radiant heating panels are commonly manufactured in 2-ft. by 4-ft. sizes and are rated at 500 W. They may be located on ceiling or walls to provide radiant heat that spreads evenly through the room. Each room may be controlled by its own thermostat. Since this type of heater may be mounted on the ceiling, its use allows complete freedom for room decor, furniture placement, and drapery arrangement. Most are finished in beige to blend in with nearly any room or furniture color.

Units mounted on the ceiling give the best results when located parallel to, and approximately 2 ft. from, the outside wall. However, this type of unit may also be mounted on walls.

ELECTRIC INFRARED HEATERS

Rays from infrared heaters do not heat the air through which they travel. Rather, they heat only persons and certain objects that they strike. Therefore, infrared heaters are designed to deliver heat into controlled areas for the efficient warming of people and surfaces both indoors and outdoors (such as to heat persons on a patio on a chilly night or around the perimeter of an outdoor swimming pool). This type of heater is excellent for heating a person standing at a workbench without heating the entire room, melting snow from steps or porches, sunlike heat over outdoor areas, and similar applications.

Some of the major advantages of infrared heat are:

1. No warm-up period is required. Heat is immediate.
2. Heat rays are confined to the desired areas.

3. They are easy to install, as no ducts, vents, and so on, are required.

4. The infrared quartz lamps provide some light in addition to heat.

When installing this type of heating unit, never mount the heater closer than 24 in. from vertical walls unless the specific heating unit is designed for closer installation. Read the manufacturer's directions carefully.

FORCED-AIR WALL HEATERS

Forced-air wall heaters are designed to bring quick heat into an area where the sound of a quiet fan will not be disturbing. Some are very noisy. Most of these units are equipped with a built-in thermostat with a sensor mounted in the intake airstream. Some types are available for mounting on high walls or even ceilings, but the additional force required to move the air to a usable area produces even more noise.

FLOOR INSERT CONVECTION HEATERS

Floor insert convection heaters require no wall space, as they fit into the floor. They are best suited for placement beneath conventional or sliding glass doors to form an effective draft barrier. All are equipped with safety devices, such as a thermal cutout to disconnect the heating element automatically in the event that normal operating temperatures are exceeded.

Floor insert convector heaters may be installed in both old and new homes by cutting through the floor, inserting the metal housing, and wiring according to the manufacturer's instructions. A heavy-gauge floor grille then fits over the entire unit.

ELECTRIC KICK-SPACE HEATERS

Modern kitchens contain so many appliances and so much cabinet space for the convenience of the housewife that there often is no room to install electric heaters except on the ceiling. Therefore, a kick-space heater was added to the lines of electric heating manufacturers to overcome this problem.

For the most comfort, kick-space heaters should not be installed in such a manner that warm air blows directly on occupants' feet. Ideally, the air discharge should be directed along the outside wall adjacent to normal working areas, not directly under the sink.

RADIANT HEATING CABLE

Radiant heating cable provides an enormous heating surface over the ceiling or concrete floor so that the system need not be raised to a high temperature. Rather, gentle warmth radiates downward (in the case of ceiling-mounted cable) or upward (in the case of floor-mounted cable), heating the entire room or area evenly.

There is virtually no maintenance with a radiant heating system, as there are no moving parts and the entire heating system is invisible—except for the thermostat.

COMBINATION HEATING AND COOLING UNITS

One way to have individual control of each room or area in your home, as far as heating and cooling are concerned, is to install through-wall heating and cooling units. Such a system gives the occupants complete control of their environment with a room-by-room choice of either heating or cooling at any time of year—at any temperature they desire. Operating costs are lower than for many other systems due to the high efficiency of room-by-room control. Another advantage is that if a unit should fail the defective chassis can be replaced immediately or taken to a shop for repair without shutting down the remaining units in the home.

When selecting any electric heating units, obtain plenty of literature from suppliers and manufacturers before settling on any one type. In most cases you are going to get what you pay for, but shop around at different suppliers before ordering the equipment.

Delivery of any of these units may take some time, so once the brand, size, and supplier have been selected, order in plenty of time before the unit is actually needed.

ELECTRIC FURNACES

Electric furnaces are becoming more popular, although they are somewhat surpassed by the all-electric heat pump. Most are very compact, versatile units designed for either wall, ceiling, or closet mounting. The vertical model can be flush mounted in a wall or shelf mounted in a closet; the horizontal design (Fig. 7-2) can be furred into a ceiling (flush or recessed).

Central heating systems of the electrically energized type distribute heat from a centrally located source by means of circulating air or water. Compact electric boilers can be mounted on the wall of a basement, utility room, or closet with the necessary control and circuit protection, and will furnish hot water to convectors or to embedded pipes. Immersion heaters may be stepped in one at a time to provide heat capacity to match heat loss.

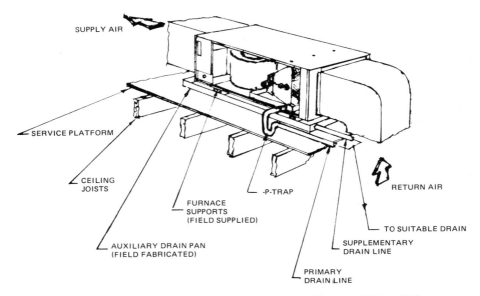

SUPPLY AIR

SERVICE PLATFORM

CEILING
JOISTS

FURNACE
SUPPORTS
(FIELD SUPPLIED)

AUXILIARY DRAIN PAN
(FIELD FABRICATED)

-P-TRAP

RETURN AIR

TO SUITABLE DRAIN

SUPPLEMENTARY
DRAIN LINE

PRIMARY
DRAIN LINE

Figure 7-2 Horizontal application of an electric furnace. (Courtesy of Square D Company)

The majority of electric furnaces are commonly available in sizes up to 24 kilowatts (kW) for residential use. The larger boilers with proper controls can take advantage of lower off-peak electricity rates, where they prevail, by heating water during off-peak periods, storing it in insulated tanks, and circulating it to convectors or radiators to provide heat as needed.

ELECTRIC HEATING CONTROLS

Electric heating units of all types may be effectively controlled by either line-voltage or low-voltage thermostats and related controls. In general, a line-voltage thermostat acts simply as an automatic switch to turn the heater on and off to maintain temperature in the heated space at the level desired as established by the thermostat setting. The line-voltage thermostat makes and breaks the actual operating current flowing to the heater. A low-voltage thermostat has its contacts arranged to make and break the low value of current to a low-voltage, 24-V operating coil of a relay, which in turn has its contacts arranged to make and break actual operating current to the heating load.

Each type of thermostat—line voltage and low voltage—has advantages and disadvantages. The low-voltage type, for example, can be made more sensitive to temperature changes because it only has to make and break the low current of the relay coil. Furthermore, whereas the line-voltage thermostat requires a switch box and standard power wiring for its installation, the low-voltage model can usually be simply screwed to the wall surface and connected with stapled low-voltage cable or bell wire for its low-voltage coil circuit. On the other hand, low-voltage controls are more expensive, and additional labor is involved in installing the relays. There are also more components to cause trouble in a low-voltage system.

Line-voltage thermostats (Fig. 7-3) are used separately to control heater units, but they are also built into heaters, using a sensing bulb in the heater airstream. This is probably the least expensive room control and is effective. However, such thermostats are slow cycling and are not in the best position to sample temperature conditions in a room.

Although single-pole line-voltage thermostats are in common use where the *National Electric Code*® permits, double-pole line-voltage thermostats are normally considered to be the safest, mainly because they completely disconnect both legs of the 240-V power circuit, not just one leg as a single-pole thermostat does. With the two-pole type, the heater, while undergoing repairs, should then be completely free of any live wires.

One application of a special two-pole thermostat is in modulating control hookups for two-stage heaters. One set of contacts is designed to close $\frac{1}{2}$ to $1\frac{1}{2}$ degrees below the other set. Under moderate conditions, the first set of contacts close to bring on the first stage of the heater. If that stage cannot match the heat loss of the space and keep the temperature at the desired level, the falling temperature actuates the second set of contacts to turn on the second stage of the heater to increase the heat input to the heated space.

Low-voltage thermostats (Fig. 7-4) in combination with relays offer a wide range of control arrangements to meet practically any need that might be encountered. Two-stage low-voltage thermostats can be used with two relays to connect a given heating unit from phase to neutral or from phase to phase on 120/240-V one-phase, three-wire circuit. In the 120-V connection, the heater output is only one-fourth that of its output when connected for 240-V operation. Again, this is

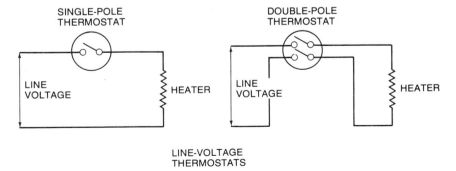

Figure 7-3   Two types of line-voltage thermostats.

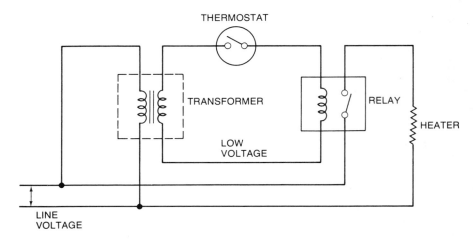

Figure 7-4   Typical low-voltage heating control circuit.

done by having $\frac{1}{2}$ to 1 degree of difference between the operating points of the two sets of contacts in the low-voltage thermostat.

Another control feature that may be used with electric heating systems is *night setback*. Under most conditions it can be advantageous to lower the house temperature during sleeping hours and to bring the thermostat up to a high value about an hour before the family arises so that the house will be relatively warm when they get out of bed. This is accomplished by a double thermostat working in conjunction with an electric timer. The controls, which can be set for any desired night and day periods, are arranged so that the two thermostats are connected in series. The day unit is always in the circuit, but during the day hours the night thermostat is merely short circuited. The timer opens this short circuit and puts the night control into action at night, and then takes it out of the circuit again in the morning. During the night, the furnace or heating units are controlled by the lower setting. Controls are also available that can automatically sense nightfall.

In any case, however, the control circuit of the thermostats is rearranged during night hours to set the thermostat to keep the temperature in the heated space at, say, 55°F or some other low level, instead of 70°F, which is the normal temperature to maintain during the daytime. This provides economy and meets the preference for lower temperature during sleeping hours.

TROUBLESHOOTING

In troubleshooting electrical heating units, it is often necessary to measure various electrical values, such as current, resistance, and voltage. With an inexpensive volt-ohm-ammeter and a basic knowledge of its use, practically anyone can quickly determine the cause of most electrical problems that develop with the heating system. Then, with this knowledge, the person can decide whether repair of the problem is within his or her capabilities or whether a repairperson should be called.

The volt-ohm-ammeter is often referred to as a *multimeter*. These meters are available from electrical supply houses and electronic shops (such as Radio Shack) and sell anywhere from $25 to several hundred dollars depending on the quality. All will give good service if given the care they deserve. By the same token, if mistreated, any of them may fail to function properly.

When using any instrument for testing or measuring electrical circuits, always consider your personal safety first. Know the voltage levels and shock hazards related to all wiring and equipment to be tested. Also be certain that the instrument used for the application has been tested and calibrated properly.

When taking measurements with meters available with different ranges and functions, as in the case of a combination volt-ohm-ammeter, make certain that the meter selector and range switches are in the correct position for the circuit to be tested. For example, if voltage is being measured, make certain that the selector switch is set at VOLTAGE and is at the level of voltage (100, 150, 200, etc.) expected to be encountered. If there is any doubt as to what the exact voltage is, start at the highest voltage setting on the meter and work down as the pointer dictates.

The volt-ohm-ammeter is a great aid in troubleshooting electric heating systems. Troubleshooting covers a wide range of problems, from a small job such as finding a short circuit in, say, a baseboard heater to tracing out troubles in a complex control circuit. In any case, troubleshooting usually requires a basic knowledge of the testing instrument, and then the location of the problem in a systematic and methodical manner by testing one part of the circuit or system at a time until the trouble is located.

In general, there are only three basic electrical faults: a short circuit, an open circuit, or a change in electrical value.

Short circuit.   A short circuit is probably the most common cause of electrical problems. Basically, it is an undesired current path that allows the electrical current to bypass the load on the circuit. Sometimes the short is between two wires due to faulty insulation, or it can occur between a wire and a grounded object such as the metal frame on an electric heater.

When a short circuit is suspected, disconnect all loads from the circuit and then reset the circuit breaker or replace the fuse. If this corrects the problem, it indicates that one of the heating units or devices is at fault. With the heaters still disconnected, connect the test leads of the ohmmeter to the heater leads, one test lead to each heater lead. If there is a full-scale reading on the meter, the short circuit is more than likely in that particular unit. You may, however, get only a partial reading on the ohmmeter scale; this is probably due to the resistance of the heating element. Try another unit until one is found that gives a full-scale reading.

Should the fault be in the circuit wiring itself (indicated by a tripped circuit breaker or blown fuse when all loads are disconnected from the circuit), the next step is to go along the circuit and open up the various outlet and junction boxes, and so on, until the trouble is located. In most cases, the short circuit will be found at one of the heater junction boxes where a terminal has vibrated loose. Perhaps one of the splices has become loose and is rubbing against the grounded heater housing.

At times, however, if repair or remodeling work has recently been done, the trouble may be caused by someone having driven a nail into a piece of nonmetallic cable, surface molding, or even through a piece of thin-wall (EMT) tubing; or the conductors may have accidentally been cut in two with a saw or drill.

Open circuit.   An open circuit is an incomplete circuit path like the broken wires in a circuit. Therefore, if the circuit is supplying an electric wall heater and the circuit is open, the heater will not operate. A light switch or thermostat, for example, purposely opens a circuit supplying a load. If the switch is then turned to the ON position and the light does not burn or the heater does not heat, the first assumption is that perhaps the lamp is bad or else the heating element has burned out. Both can be checked with the ohmmeter to determine if the element is good or bad. If either is good, the ohmmeter should show some resistance reading on the meter. If bad, there will be no reading on the meter. Should the element prove to be good, check for other problems in the circuit in the following order.

1. Blown fuse or a tripped circuit breaker
2. Wire loose at the switch or thermostat or in the fuse box.
3. Faulty switch or thermostat

If the circuit in question is protected by a plug fuse, the nature of the problem can often be determined by the appearance of the fuse window. For example, if the window is clear and the metal strip appears to be intact, the fuse is probably not blown. But it is always best to check the fuse with a voltmeter or test lamp just to make sure. To test a plug fuse, place one lead of the voltmeter on the neutral block in the panelboard or fuse cabinet, and the other on the load side of the fuse. If a reading is obtained between 110 and 120 V, the fuse is all right. If the voltmeter does not show any reading or one that is below 100 V, examine the fuse window more closely. If the window is clear but you notice that the metal strip is in two pieces, it probably blown due to a light overload. Perhaps a portable appliance was plugged in on the same circuit. In any event, check to see what overloaded the fuse before replacing it.

Change in electrical value.   A change in either current, voltage, or resistance from the normal can lead to electrical problems. One of the most common causes of electrical problems is low equipment input voltage. This problem usually occurs for one or more of the following reasons:

1. Undersized conductors
2. Loose connections
3. Overloaded circuit
4. Taps set too low on power company's transformer

To check for low voltage, set the multimeter to the voltage setting of 250 V and take a reading at the main switch or service entrance. In most cases, residential electric services are single-phase, 120/240-V, three-wire. Therefore, the voltage reading taken between any two "hot" wires (usually colored black on one conductor and red on the other) should be around 240 V, and the reading between any of the "hot" wires and the neutral (white) wire should be around 120 V. If the reading is below these figures, the fault lies with the utility company supplying the power, and it should be notified to correct the problem. However, if the reading checks out normal, the next procedure is to check the voltage reading at various outlets throughout the heating system.

When a low-voltage problem is found on a circuit—say, 100 V instead of the normal 120V—leave the voltmeter terminals connected across the line, and begin disconnecting all loads, one at a time. If the problem is corrected after several of the loads have been disconnected, the circuit is probably overloaded and steps should be taken to reduce the load on the circuits, or the wire size should be increased in size to accommodate the load.

Loose connections can also cause low voltage. The entire circuit should be de-energized, and each terminal of panelboard circuits, heater connections, and so on, should be checked for loose connections. A charred or blackened terminal screw is one sign that indicates this problem.

BASIC ELECTRICITY

Anyone anticipating troubleshooting electrical heating systems or the electrical/electronic controls in any type of heating system should have a good basic knowledge of electricity. The following is a brief review of the principles of electricity as applied to heating applications.

Flip a switch—a light comes on. Push a lever—bread is toasted. A live football game, being played hundreds of miles away, comes into focus at the touch of another switch. Put in the plug, pull the trigger switch, and a whole assortment of electric power tools performs immediately. Electricity is handy, convenient, taken for granted, and often not fully understood. It is well that you understand the fundamentals of electricity if any type of electric servicing will be performed while working on residential heating systems.

Understanding electric energy.   Electric energy is easier to describe by what it does rather than by what it is. Electricity is the moving of electrons from one atom to another (Fig. 7-5). The number of electrons in motion determines the amount of electric energy produced.

Electricity in its usable form is described under the following headings:

- Types of electric circuits
- Types of electric current

Types of Electric Circuits.   When a wire is moved, it cuts the magnetic lines of force and electrical potential (voltage) is generated (Fig. 7-6). An *electric circuit* is a completed path for the exchange of electrons. The circuit causes current to flow from the source of power to its use and return to the source (Fig. 7-7). Circuits are usually made of wires called *conductors* (Fig. 7-8). They are protected by *insulation* (*nonconductors*) (Fig. 7-9).

Electric circuits are identified as follows:

- Series circuit (Fig. 7-10)
- Parallel circuit (Fig. 7-11)
- Open circuit (Fig. 7-12)
- Short circuit (Fig. 7-13)

Types of Electric Current.   There are two types of electric current:

- Direct current
- Alternating current

Direct Current. Current flowing in only one direction in a circuit is called direct current (dc) (Fig. 7-14).

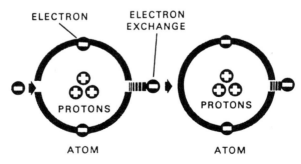

Figure 7-5 Electricity is the moving of electrons from one atom to another. (Courtesy of American Association for Vocational Instructional Materials)

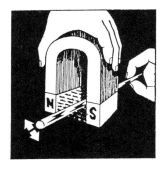

Figure 7-6 Moving a wire through magnetic lines of force generates an electric potential in the wire. (Courtesy of American Association for Vocational Instructional Materials)

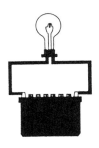

Figure 7-7 Current flows in a completed electric circuit. (Courtesy of American Association for Vocational Instructional Materials)

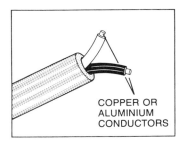

Figure 7-8 A conductor is a material that allows electron exchange. (Courtesy of American Association for Vocational Instructional Materials)

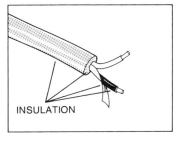

Figure 7-9 Insulation used with electric conductors is made of a material in which electrons are not exchanged. (Courtesy of American Association for Vocational Instructional Materials)

Figure 7-10 A series circuit is one in which all of the current flows throughout the entire circuit. (Courtesy of American Association for Vocational Instructional Materials

Figure 7-11 A parallel circuit provides for dividing the current flow. (Courtesy of American Association for Vocational Instructional Materials)

 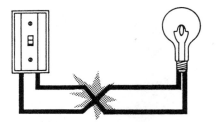

Figure 7-12   An open circuit is one that is broken and prevents current flow. (Courtesy of American Association for Vocational Instructional Materials)

Figure 7-13   A short circuit is one that allows current to return to the source without traveling throughout the entire circuit. (Courtesy of American Association for Vocational Instructional Materials)

Alternating Current. Electrons flowing first in one direction and then in another are alternating current (ac) (Fig. 7-15). Alternating current is the kind of electric energy generally made available to you by electric power suppliers.

Two special characteristics of alternating current are as follows:

1. Cycles per second (hertz)
2. Phases

1. Cycles per Second (Hertz): A cycle is the flowing of alternating current in one direction, reversing, flowing in the other direction, reversing, and starting all over again.

The number of cycles per second is the frequency of the current. The unit for frequency is hertz (Hz). The frequency generated and distributed in most countries is 60 Hz (cycles per second). However, some countries use 50-Hz current.

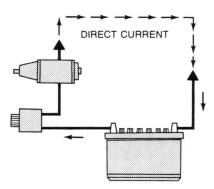 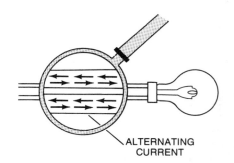

Figure 7-14   Direct current flows in one direction only. (Courtesy of American Association for Vocational Instructional Materials)

Figure 7-15   Alternating current flows in one direction and then in the other. (Courtesy of American Association for Vocational Instructional Materials)

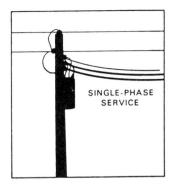

Figure 7-16   Single-phase service usually consists of three conductors between the power pole and the meter. (Courtesy of American Association for Vocational Instructional Materials)

Figure 7-17   Three-phase service generally has four wires from the power pole to the meter consisting of three "hot" wires and a neutral wire. (Courtesy of American Association for Vocational Instructional Materials)

2. Phases: Electric energy is produced in phases: single-phase, two-phase, and three-phase. Single-phase current is the flowing of alternating current (Fig. 7-16). Two-phase current is sometimes produced, but has no advantages and is not generally used. Power plant generators are designed to produce three single-phase currents, each starting and reversing one-third of a cycle apart. They are combined to produce three-phase current (Fig. 7-17). Better conductor efficiency is obtained through three-phase current than through single-phase current. Electric motors operating on three-phase current are easier to start than those operating on single-phase current. Also, they are less expensive to purchase and maintain.

How electric energy is measured.   Terms have been accepted by which electric energy can be measured. The following are some common terms:

- Ampere (A)
- Volt (V)
- Ohm (Ω)
- Watt (W)
- Kilowatt (kW)
- Megawatt (MW)
- Kilowatt-hour (kWh)

An *ampere* (A) is a unit of electric current. For example, a 100-W lamp bulb requires about 1 A of current on a 120-V system. Heat caused by friction of the electrons flowing through the lamp filament causes the lamp to glow. The instrument for measuring ampere (*amperage*) is called an ammeter (Fig. 7-18).

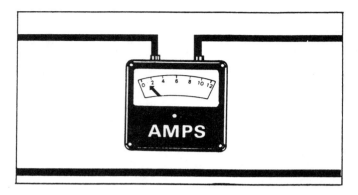

Figure 7-18 Electric current is measured in amperes with an ammeter. (Courtesy of American Association for Vocational Instructional Materials)

A unit of electric "pressure" that pushes the electrons along is a *volt;* the amount of pressure (generally referred to as *voltage*) required to push 1 ampere through 1 ohm of resistance is a volt. It is measured with a voltmeter (Fig. 7-19). The *ohm* (Ω) is a unit of resistance to current flow. Electrons do not flow freely through any conductor. There is a certain amount of resistance overcome by 1 V to cause 1 A to flow. It is measured with an ohmmeter (Fig. 7-20). Factors determining the amount of resistance in a conductor are material, size, and length (Fig. 7-21); temperature is another factor. A change in the temperature of a material changes the ease with which a conductor releases its outer electrons. For most materials the resistance increases as the temperature increases.

A *watt* (*wattage*) is a unit of electric power. It is measured with a wattmeter (Fig. 7-22). The combination of volts (pressure) and amperes (current flow) makes watts (power). Therefore,

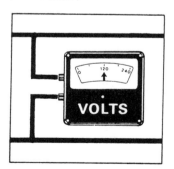

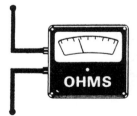

Figure 7-19 Electric voltage is measured with a voltmeter. (Courtesy of American Association for Vocational Instructional Materials)

Figure 7-20 Resistance is measured in ohms with an ohmmeter. (Courtesy of American Association for Vocational Instructional Materials)

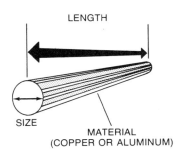

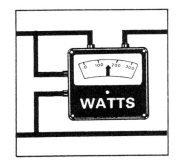

Figure 7-21 The amount of resistance in a conductor is determined by the type of material, size, and length. (Courtesy of American Association for Vocational Instructional Materials)

Figure 7-22 Electric power is measured in watts with a wattmeter. (Courtesy of American Association for Vocational Instructional Materials)

$$\text{Volts} \times \text{amperes} = \text{watts}$$

Example

120 volts $\times$ 10 amperes $-$ 1200 watts. A *kilowatt* is 1000 watts. A *megawatt* is 1,000,000 watts. A *kilowatt-hour* is the unit of measure by which electric power is marketed. Therefore,

$$\text{Kilowatts} \times \text{hours} = \text{kilowatt-hours}$$

If you operate a 1-horsepower motor (approximately 1 kW) for 2 hours, you will use about 2 kWh of electric energy.

Example

$$\text{1 Kilowatt} \times \text{2 hours} = \text{2 kilowatt-hours}$$

The meter on your electric power entrance is a kilowatt-hour meter (Fig. 7-23).

UNDERSTANDING HOW ELECTRIC ENERGY IS GENERATED

Electric current is the flowing of electrons in a circuit. Electric power is generated by causing electrons to flow. Electric energy is not created; it is converted (generated) from other forms of energy. How electric energy is generated is described next.

How electric energy is generated from chemical energy. *Batteries* are chemical generators. They have two electrodes submerged in a chemical solution (electrolyte). Electrodes are made of various types of metal or other materials. The

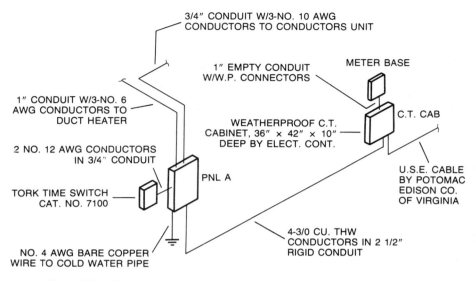

Figure 7-23 Electric energy used is measured with a kilowatt-hour meter. (Courtesy of American Association for Vocational Instructional Materials)

chemical is either acid or alkaline. Sometimes batteries are referred to as *electrochemical cells*.

The circuit is completed by connecting the two electrodes, at which time current flows within the circuit (Fig. 7-24). This flow is due to a chemical reaction of the electrolyte on the electrodes.

Batteries are made of one or more cells. The types of cells are as follows:

- Primary cells (Fig. 7-25)
- Storage cells (Fig. 7-26)
- Solar cells
- Fuel cells

How electric energy is generated from mechanical energy.   Most electric energy is generated by mechanically driven generators. They are discussed under the following headings:

- How mechanical generators work
- How mechanical generators are driven

How Mechanical Generators Work.   Passing coils of wire through a magnetic field generates electric energy mechanically. Both direct and alternating current may be generated by mechanical generators. How this is done is discussed as follows:

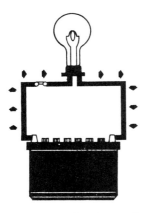

Figure 7-24 Current flows in a battery when the circuit is completed. (Courtesy of American Association for Vocational Instructional Materials)

Figure 7-25 Primary dry cell battery. (Courtesy of American Association for Vocational Instructional Materials)

- How direct-current generators work
- How alternating-current generators work

How Direct-current Generators Work. The principles of the dc mechanically driven generator are illustrated in Fig. 7-27. As magnetic lines of force travel from one pole to another, a simple horseshoe magnet forms a magnetic field. A loop of wire supported on a shaft is rotated within this magnetic field. An electric current is generated in this loop, as it turns, and the current flows to terminals (segments) on the commutator. Two stationary contacts, or brushes, touch these commutator segments as the loop of wire rotates. These brushes carry current generated in the loop to an external circuit, where it is used as electric energy.

Figure 7-26 Automotive-type battery consisting of storage cells. (Courtesy of American Association for Vocational Instructional Materials)

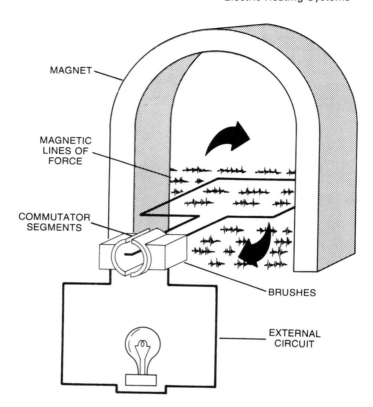

Figure 7-27 Principle of a simple direct-current generator. (Courtesy of American Association for Vocational Instructional Materials)

Note that the commutator is in two halves. The loop of wire rotates one-half turn as each brush makes contact with the other half of the commutator. This is necessary to keep the current flowing in the same direction in the circuit; thus direct current is generated.

Direct current is used principally in mobile equipment and special industrial applications (Fig. 7-28). A serious disadvantage of dc current is that it is difficult to deliver over long distances.

How Alternating-current Generators Work. An ac generator, frequently called an *alternator,* operates on much the same principle as the dc generator (Fig. 7-29). A wire loop also rotates within a magnetic field; this rotation of the loop through magnetic lines of force generates current in the loop.

Instead of being connected to segments on a commutator, the loop ends are each connected to an individual ring called a slip ring. The slip rings are fastened to the shaft and rotate with it. Stationary brushes are in contact with the slip rings. Electric energy is conducted to its point of use by the current carried through the brushes to an external circuit.

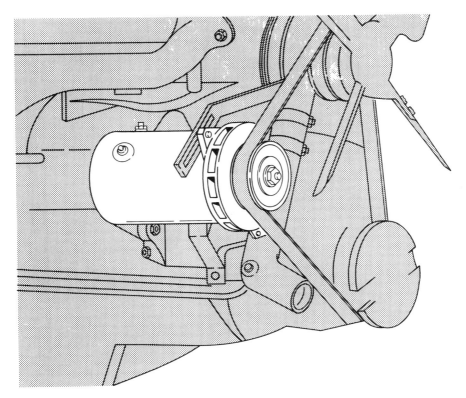

Figure 7-28 Automotive-type, direct-current generator. (Courtesy of American Association for Vocational Instructional Materials)

During one revolution of the loop, each side passes through the magnetic lines of force, first in one direction and then in the other, thus producing alternating current.

How Mechanical Generators Are Driven. Mechanical generators are driven by water power and by internal combustion engines. These methods are explained as follows:

- Water power
- Steam power
- Internal combustion engines

Water Power. Hydroelectric generation is water flowing from a higher to a lower level and being used to turn a generator. This type of electric energy generation developed very rapidly after 1910. By now, the best hydroelectric generation sites

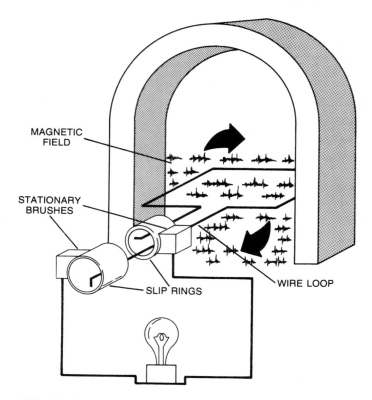

MAGNETIC
FIELD

STATIONARY
BRUSHES

SLIP RINGS

WIRE LOOP

Figure 7-29 Principle of a simple alternating-current generator. (Courtesy of American Association for Vocational Instructional Materials)

in North America have been developed. However, there are still many good sites remaining in the rest of the world.

Reservoirs are created by damming large streams, thereby providing a controlled flow of water. There may be more than one dam on the same stream. Water power uses the principle of the waterwheel to turn a generator. This "waterwheel" is made of metal and is called a *turbine wheel*. The generator is attached to the turbine shaft. Water directed against the turbine blades causes both the turbine and the generator to turn (Fig. 7-30).

Steam Power. Steam-powered generators produce about 85% of all electricity. Sometimes they are referred to as thermal-powered generators. The water is heated in a boiler until it becomes steam. At high temperatures and pressures the steam is directed against the blades or fins of the turbine, causing it to turn. The generator, being connected to the turbine, also turns (Fig. 7-31).

Heat for producing steam is supplied from the following sources of energy:

1. Fossil fuel
2. Nuclear power

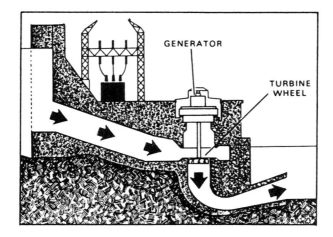

Figure 7-30   Principle of a water-powered generator. (Courtesy of American Association for Vocational Instructional Materials)

3. Geothermal energy
4. Solid wastes

The three kinds of fossil fuels are used in producing steam:

• Coal
• Oil
• Natural gas

Coal is the fuel most commonly used to make steam for generating electric energy. It can be obtained at relatively low cost and is in abundant supply. It is found in many regions of the world. When available, a 90-day supply is usually maintained at most power plants. Conveyor belts carry coal from a coal pile into the plant. Massive pulverizers literally reduce the coal to dust. Coal dust is then

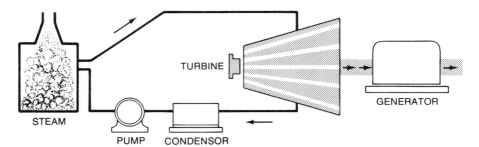

Figure 7-31   Principle of a steam-powered generator. (Courtesy of American Association for Vocational Instructional Materials)

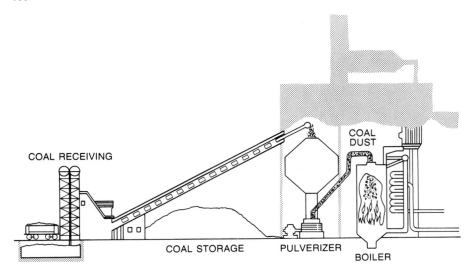

Figure 7-32 How steam is produced in a coal-burning generating plant. (Courtesy of American Association for Vocational Instructional Materials)

blown into the firebox of the boiler under high pressure. It is burned almost instantly, creating heat that produces steam (Fig. 7-32).

Oil is also used for fuel in steam-generating plants (Fig. 7-33). Heavy residual oil is used most commonly. Oil, being easier to handle and cleaner burning, was preferred over coal for many years. For that reason many plants were converted

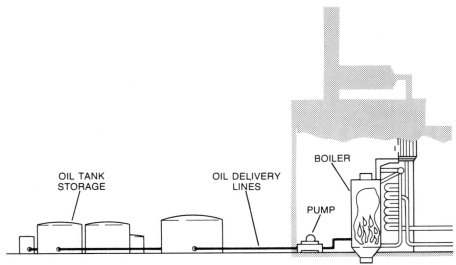

Figure 7-33 How steam is produced in an oil-burning generating plant. (Courtesy of American Association for Vocational Instructional Materials)

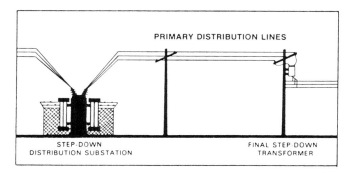

Figure 7-34   Primary distribution lines are lines carrying electric energy from a step-down transformer. (Courtesy of American Association for Vocational Instructional Materials)

from coal to oil. However, some of these plants are being converted back to coal because of the increased cost of oil and the uncertainty of an adequate supply.

Natural gas is used in some steam-generating plants. Generally, it is supplied on what is called an *interruptible* basis, whereby natural gas suppliers can limit or stop delivery during such times as the winter season when additional gas is needed for heating. At that time electric power suppliers must switch to another fuel, usually oil.

Internal Combustion Engines. A limited number of electric generators are powered by internal combustion engines. These engines may be of the following types:

1. *Internal combustion turbine.* Internal combustion turbines (heavy-duty jet engines) are used by power suppliers only when a high electrical demand is placed on the system. This limited use is because of the high cost of fuel and

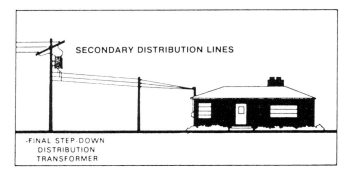

Figure 7-35   Secondary distribution lines are lines carrying electric energy from the final step-down transformer to the user. (Courtesy of American Association for Vocational Instructional Materials)

low operating efficiency for the unit. Power generated by this method may cost more than the amount charged by the power company.

2. *Diesel engines.* Standby generators operated by diesel engines are used by such facilities as hospitals and manufacturing plants in case of power failure.

3. *Gasoline engines.* Portable generators or alternators are powered by both gasoline and diesel engines. They can be mounted on trucks, tractors, trailers, skids, or carrying frames for convenience.

USE OF DISTRIBUTION LINES

Lines that fan out over the countryside distribute electric energy from stepdown distribution substations; thus power is delivered to the user. Generally, there are two types of distribution lines:

- Primary lines with voltages ranging from 2300 to 34,500 V. Typical primary line voltages are 2300, 4000, 8000, 12,000, 13,800, 20,000, 25,000, and 34,500 V (Fig. 7-34).
- Secondary lines with voltages usually of 120, 208, 240, 277, and 480 V (Fig. 7-35).

8

AIR DUCTS

Ductwork is constructed mainly from sheet metal, fiber glass, and other types of fiber. Sheet-metal ductwork is available in standard sizes already fabricated, especially in the round sizes. However, when rectangular ducts, offsets, and the like are needed, they must be made either in a sheet-metal shop or on the job—almost always requiring special equipment and tools.

Where fiber-glass ductwork is allowed, and where only a small amount of this type of work is involved, like one or two installations, the fiber-glass ductwork system is the type recommended. It can even by installed by homeowners themselves, without the need for a professional.

In dealing with ductwork systems, the following brief explanations describe some of the components of a duct system and their application. Although not complete, they should give the reader a good knowledge of the terms required to deal with such a system.

SUPPLY-AIR OUTLETS

Supply-air outlets are a major part of any air-distribution system because they provide a means of distributing properly controlled air to a room or area. To accomplish this goal, the supply-air outlets must deflect or diffuse the air, be adjustable for changing the airflow rate, be void of air noise, and be able to throw the conditioned air no less than three-fourths of the distance from the outlet to the opposite wall.

Many types of supply-air outlets are available, a sampling of which follows:

Supply-air outlet.   A supply-air outlet can be a floor, ceiling, or wall opening through which conditioned air is delivered to a room or area.

Ceiling diffuser.   The ceiling diffuser is a square, oval, circular, or semicircular facing device that covers the supply-air opening of a room or area. Most diffusers are adjustable for airflow direction and rate.

Grille.   The grille is a covering for any opening through which air passes.

Register.   The register is a covering for any opening through which air passes with a built-in damper for controlling the air passing through it.

1. A fixed-louver register is a nonadjustable register in which the air pattern is factory set.
2. An adjustable-louver register is a register with adjustable bars for directing the air in several different patterns.

Figure 8-1 shows several types of supply-air outlets and how they would appear on a working drawing.

LOCATION OF SUPPLY-AIR OUTLETS

Supply-air outlets in the area to be conditioned must be located so that sufficient air is supplied to establish and maintain comfort conditions within the area, that is, a uniform air pattern that is free of hot or cold drafts.

The location of supply-air outlets is determined after taking the following into consideration:

1. Size and shape of the room or area to be conditioned.
2. Decor of the area to be conditioned.
3. Furniture placement within the area to be conditioned.
4. Ceiling, wall, and floor finish of the area to be conditioned.
5. Budget.
6. Whether the system is designed for heating, cooling, or both (if both, the one that is used the most during the year should be given the greatest consideration).
7. Total air quantity required for the area under consideration.
8. Total load and draft conditions of the area.
9. Diffusion of spread pattern required within the space to be conditioned.
10. Level of noise allowed in the space to be conditioned.

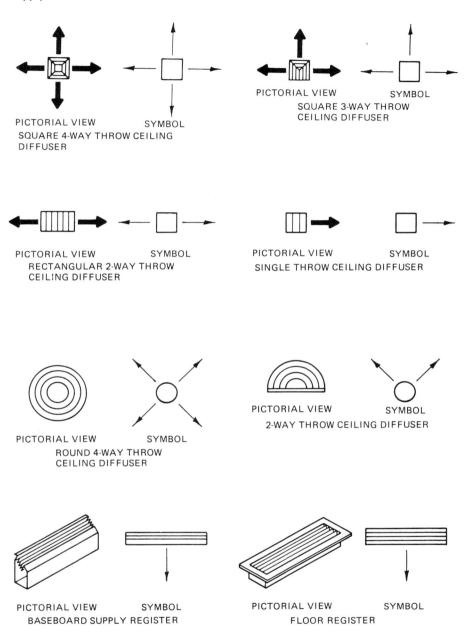

Figure 8-1 Several types of supply-air outlets and how they appear on working drawings. (Courtesy of the author)

Therefore, supply-air outlets are located according to the shape, size, use, and load concentration of the area, and according to whether the system is used in a cooling or a heating application or both.

In all cases. drawings of the areas should be made. These drawings should be studied to determine the size, shape, and use of each room or area. If architectural drawings of the home are readily available, these are excellent. However, if none are available, scale drawings must be made by measuring the various areas and then transferring these measurements to paper.

RETURN-AIR OUTLETS

The location of return-air outlets is not as critical as the location of supply-air outlets, but, as a rule of thumb, the return-air outlets should be in the opposite location from the supply-air outlets. That is, if the supply-air outlets are located in the ceiling or high on a sidewall, the return-air outlets should be located in the floor or low on a sidewall. If the supply outlets are located on the outside wall of the room, the return-air outlets should be located on an inside wall of the room, preferably on the opposite wall. If, for example, the supply outlets were located in the ceiling and the return outlets were also located in the ceiling, there is danger of short-circuiting the air from the supply outlets directly to the return outlets, as shown in Fig. 8-2.

If all supply-air outlets are located around the perimeter of a building and the air within the building is not "sealed" in each space, one centrally located return

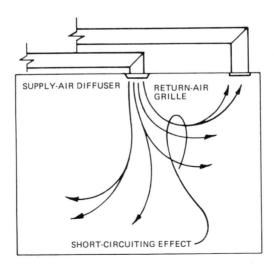

Figure 8-2 Example of short-circuited air caused by placing the supply and return outlets too close together. (Courtesy of the author)

outlet is usually satisfactory. Transfer grilles, undercut doors, or a ceiling plenum can be used to ensure that all supply air returns to the one return outlet.

The return-air system for many multistory residences is located in the stairway due to the fact that the cooler air flowing down the stairs will flow into the return outlet in the stairway; this minimizes cold-floor drafts.

When conditioned space must be sealed off, preventing one central-return outlet, the return-air outlets must be located in several areas and then transferred by duct to the air-handling apparatus.

AIR-HANDLING UNITS

Fans are used in air-handling units for the circulation of air in a heating system. They are manufactured in the four general types illustrated in Fig. 8-3. Each type of fan shown can have either a belt drive or a direct connection.

Centrifugal.   The widely used centrifugal fan, in which the air flows radially through the impeller, can efficiently move large or small quantities of air over an extended range of pressure; for this reason, it is the most versatile type in use today.

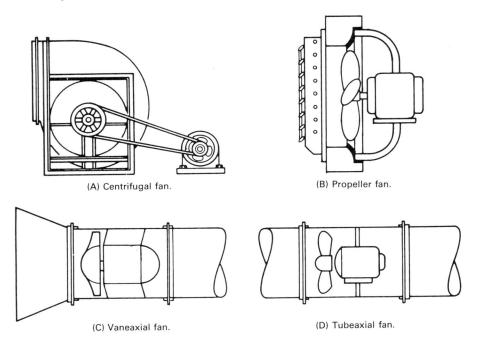

(A) Centrifugal fan.   (B) Propeller fan.

(C) Vaneaxial fan.   (D) Tubeaxial fan.

Figure 8-3 Four general types of fans used in a residential heating system. (Courtesy of the author)

Propeller.   The propeller fan can move large quantities are air, but its use is limited to areas where there is no duct system and where the resistance to airflow is low.

Vane axial.   The vane-axial fan produces an axial flow of air through the wheel and blades. It is capable of moving large or small quantities of air over a wide range of pressures. This type of fan is always used in a duct system since the wheel and its blading are located in a cylindrical housing. Air-guide vanes are used either before or after the wheel.

Tube axial.   The tube-axial fan is similar to the vane-axial fan in that the air flows axially through the impeller. It, too, is capable of moving small or large quantities of air over a wide range of pressures. However, most axial fans produce more noise than centrifugal fans and are therefore limited to use in areas where noise levels are of secondary concern.

FAN-COIL UNITS

Air-handling or blower units are used in conjunction with a heating source to move the air from the heat source to the rooms or areas to be heated. For example, in an oil-fired furnace, a blower unit moves the heated air through the ductwork.

Figure 8-4 shows an up-flow furnace with the cooling coils on the return-air

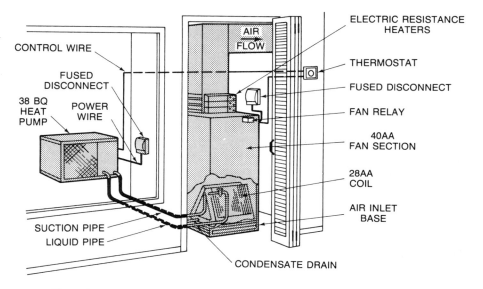

Figure 8-4   Plenum and ductwork arrangement for an up-flow residential heating/cooling system. (Courtesy of the author)

side of the furnace, which is used in conjunction with the heater to offer cool air in hot months and hot air in cold months.

PROGRAMS FOR DUCT SIZING

Most engineers and designers use a duct-sizing slide rule to obtain the proper-sized duct for a given volume of air at the correct velocity. Such calculations, however, are readily adaptable to the microcomputer. There are several approaches, two of which follow.

The BASIC program in Fig. 8-5 is designed to exactly calculate the circular equivalent of a rectangular duct for equal friction and air volume. To cover the

```
10 REM **DUCT SIZING**
20 PRINT "THIS PROGRAM IS DESIGNED TO CALCULATE THE CIRCULAR EQUIVALENTS"
30 PRINT "OF RECTANGULAR DUCTS FOR EQUAL FRICTION (INCHES & CM).
40 PRINT
50 INPUT "ENTER SHORTEST SIDE OF RECTANGULAR DUCT IN INCHES";S
60 PRINT
70 INPUT "NOW ENTER THE LONGEST SIDE OF RECTANGULAR DUCT IN INCHES";L
80 IF S<4.1 THEN 200
90 IF S<5.1 THEN 300
100 IF S<6.1 THEN 400
110 IF S<7.1 THEN 500
111 IF S<8.100001 THEN 600
112 IF S<9.100001 THEN 700
113 IF S<10.1 THEN 800
114 IF S<11.1 THEN 900
115 IF S< 12.1 THEN 1000
116 IF S<13.1 THEN 1100
117 IF S<14.1 THEN 1200
118 IF S<15.1 THEN 1300
119 IF S<16.1 THEN 1400
120 IF S<17.1 THEN 1500
121 IF S<18.1 THEN 1600
122 IF S<19.1 THEN 1700
123 IF S< 20.1 THEN 1800
124 IF S<21.1 THEN 1900
125 IF S<22.1 THEN 2000
126 IF S<23.1 THEN 2100
127 IF S<24.1 THEN 2200
137 CLS
138 PRINT "THE CIRCULAR EQUIVALENT OF A RECTANGULAR DUCTS";L;"INCHES WIDE BY"
140 IF S<10.1 THEN 800
148 PRINT ;S;" INCHES DEEP IS";C;" INCHES IN DIAMETER."
158 CLS
159 PRINT "THE CIRCULAR EQUIVALENT OF A RECTANGULAR DUCTS";L;"INCHES WIDE BY"
160 PRINT ;S;" INCHES DEEP IS";C;" INCHES IN DIAMETER."
161 PRINT
162 INPUT "DO YOU WISH TO MAKE ANOTHER CALUCATION (Y OR N)";A$
163 IF A$="Y" THEN GOTO 20
164 STOP
200 IF L<8.100001 THEN C=6.1:GOTO 158221
202 IF L<10.1 THEN C=6.8:GOTO 158
203 IF L<11.1 THEN C=7.1:GOTO 158
204 IF L<12.1 THEN C=7.4:GOTO 158
205 IF L<13.1 THEN C=7.6:GOTO 158
```

Figure 8-5

```
206 IF L<14.1 THEN C=7.9:GOTO 158
207 IF L<15.1 THEN C=8.2:GOTO 158
208 IF L<16.1 THEN C=8.399999:GOT
209 IF L<17.1 THEN C=8.600001:GOTO 158
210 IF L<18.1 THEN C=8.899999:GOTO 158
211 IF L<19.1 THEN C=9.100001:GOTO 158
212 IF L<20.1 THEN C=9.3:GOTO 158
213 IF L<22.1 THEN C=9.7:GOTO 158
214 IF L<24.1 THEN C=10!: GOTO 158
215 IF L<26.1 THEN C=10.4:GOTO 158
216 IF L<28.1 THEN C=10.8:GOTO 158
217 IF L<30.1 THEN C=11!:GOTO 158
218 IF L<32.1 THEN C=11.3:GOTO 158
219 IF L<34.1 THEN C=11.6:GOTO 158
220 IF L<36.1 THEN C=11.9:GOTO 158
221 IF L<38.1 THEN C=12.2:GOTO 158
222 IF L<40.1 THEN C=12.5:GOTO 158
223 IF L<42.1 THEN C=12.7:GOTO 158
224 IF L<44.1 THEN C=13!:GOTO 158
225 IF L<46.1 THEN C=13.3:GOTO 158
226 IF L<48.1 THEN C=13.5:GOTO 158
227 IF L<50.1 THEN C=13.7:GOTO 158
228 IF L<52.1 THEN C=13.9:GOTO 158
229 IF L<54.1 THEN C=14.1:GOTO 158
230 IF L<56.1 THEN C=14.3:GOTO 158
231 IF L<58.1 THEN C=14.6:GOTO 158
232 IF L<60.1 THEN C=14.7:GOTO 158
233 IF L<62.1 THEN C=15!:GOTO 158
234 IF L<64.1 THEN C=15.1:GOTO 158
235 IF L<66.1 THEN C=15.3:GOTO 158
240 IF L<12.1 THEN C=7.4:GOTO 158
250 IF L<13.1 THEN C=7.6:GOTO 158
260 IF L<14.1 THEN C=7.9:GOTO 158
270 IF L<15.1 THEN C=8.2:GOTO 158
280 IF L<16.1 THEN C=8.399999:GOTO 158
290 IF L<17.1 THEN C=8.600001:GOTO 158
300 GOTO 158
310 PRINT ;S;" INCHES DEEP IS";C;" INCHES IN DIAMETER."
```

Figure 8-5   (continued)

entire possible range by this method, however, would take a sizable program, so only one size has been included in this program—size $4\frac{1}{2}$ in. or smaller. The enlarging of this program would be good experience for those interested in writing their own programs.

Although not as precise as the one in Fig. 8-5, the BASIC program in Fig. 8-6, for all practical purposes, will give the circular equivalents of a rectangular duct, and in this program, the calculation is done mathematically. Figures 8-7 and 8-8 show how the monitor screen will appear when the program is run.

Other programs for duct sizing are shown in other chapters in this book. Those involved with HVAC systems should by this time try one or two programs of their own. One approach is to use an existing table and write the program around this. The computer will save much time in making such calculations.

To this point, this book has covered mainly individual programs for various HVAC applications. It is conceivable, and highly recommended, that one software package be written or obtained from which the user may select the desired calculation from a "menu" that appears on the computer monitor when the program is run.

```
10 REM **MATHEMATICAL PROGRAM FOR OBTAINING CIRCULAR EQUIVALENTS OF**
20 REM **RECTANGULAR DUCT FOR EQUAL FRICTION (INCHES AND CM)**
30 INPUT "ENTER WIDTH OF RECTANGULAR DUCT IN INCHES";W
40 PRINT
50 INPUT "ENTER DEPTH OF RECTANGULAR DUCT IN INCHES";D
60 A=W*D
70 PRINT
80 PRINT "AREA OF RECTANGULAR DUCT IS";A;"SQ. INCHES."
90 R=SQR(A/3.14)
100 C=2*R
110 PRINT "THE EQUIVALENT ROUND DUCT IS";C;"INCHES."
120 STOP
```

Figure 8-6

```
Ok
RUN
ENTER WIDTH OF RECTANGULAR DUCT IN INCHES? 4

ENTER DEPTH OF RECTANGULAR DUCT IN INCHES? 12

AREA OF RECTANGULAR DUCT IS 48 SQ. INCHES.
THE EQUIVALENT ROUND DUCT IS 7.819623 INCHES.
Break in 120
Ok
RUN "PRNSCRN
```

Figure 8-7

```
Ok
RUN
ENTER WIDTH OF RECTANGULAR DUCT IN INCHES? 24

ENTER DEPTH OF RECTANGULAR DUCT IN INCHES? 4

AREA OF RECTANGULAR DUCT IS 96 SQ. INCHES.
THE EQUIVALENT ROUND DUCT IS 11.05862 INCHES.
Break in 120
Ok
RUN "PRNSCRN
```

Figure 8-8

```
20 PRINT "THIS PROGRAM ENABLES THE USER TO DETERMINE THE FOLLOWING COSTS:"
30 PRINT "              (1) PERIOD OWNING COST"
40 PRINT "              (2) ACTUAL PERIOD OPERATING COSTS OF ELEC. SRV."
50 PRINT "              (3) COST OF WATER SERVICE"
51 PRINT "PRESS ZERO KEY WHEN NONE OF THE ABOVE ARE DESIRED"
60 PRINT
70 INPUT "WHICH OF THE ABOVE COSTS WOULD YOU LIKE TO FIND (1,2,OR 3)";A
80 IF A=1 THEN 450
90 IF A=2 THEN 250
91 CLS
92 PRINT
93 PRINT
```

Figure 8-9

```
100 PRINT "YOU HAVE CHOSEN TO DETERMINE THE COST OF WATER SERVICE, PLEASE"
110 PRINT "SUPPLY THE FOLLOWING INFORMATION."
111 PRINT
112 PRINT
120 INPUT "WATER CONSUMPTION IN GALLONS PER MINUTE";Q
130 INPUT "TOTAL OPERATING TIME, IN HOURS, DURING PERIOD";H
140 INPUT "WATER RATE OR COST IN $/1000 CU FT.";R
150 C=(Q*H*R/125)
160 PRINT
170 PRINT
180 PRINT "THE COST OF WATER FOR A TOTAL OPERATING TIME OF";H;"HOURS IS"
190 PRINT ;C;"DOLLARS."
191 PRINT
192 INPUT "DO YOU WISH TO MAKE ANOTHER CALCULATION (Y OR N)";D$
200 IF D$="Y" THEN   220
210 IF D$="N" THEN 1000
220 CLS
230 GOTO 20
240 PRINT
250 CLS
251 PRINT "YOU HAVE CHOSEN TO DETERMINE THE ACTUAL PERIOD OPERATING COST"
260 PRINT "OF ELECTRICAL SERVICE.  PLEASE SUPPLY THE FOLLOWING DATA."
270 INPUT "TOTAL BRAKE HORSEPOWER OF ELECTRIC MOTORS";B
280 INPUT "TOTAL OPERATING TIME DURING PERIOD IN HOURS";H
290 INPUT "ELECTRICAL RATE OR POWER COST, ENERGY AND DEMAND";R
300 C=(.746*B*H*R/.85)
310 PRINT
320 PRINT
330 PRINT "THE COST OF ELECTRICAL ENERGY FOR A TOTAL OPERATING TIME OF";H;
340 PRINT "HOURS IS";C;"DOLLARS."
350 PRINT
360 INPUT "DO YOU WISH TO MAKE ANOTHER CALCULATION (Y OR NO)";D$
370 IF D$="Y" THEN 220
380 IF D$="N" THEN 1000
450 CLS
460 PRINT "YOU HAVE CHOSEN TO DETERMINE THE PERIOD OWNING COST OF A HVAC"
470 PRINT "SYSTEM.  PLEASE SUPPLY THE FOLLOWING INFORMATION."
480 PRINT
490 PRINT
500 INPUT "PAYMENT ON PRINCIPAL, AS COMPUTED";P
510 INPUT "INTEREST AS COMPUTED";I
520 INPUT "TAXES AS COMPUTED";T
530 INPUT "INSURANCE AS COMPUTED";S
540 INPUT "DEPRECIATION AS COMPUTED";D
550 C=(P+I+T+S+D)
560 CLS
570 PRINT "THE TOTAL PERIOD OWNING COSTS OF THE SYSTEM IS";C;"DOLLARS"
580 PRINT
590 PRINT
600 INPUT "DO YOU WISH TO MAKE ANOTHER CALCULATION (Y OR N)";D$
610 IF D$="Y" THEN 220
620 IF D$="N" THEN 1000
1000 STOP


Ok
RUN
THIS PROGRAM ENABLES THE USER TO DETERMINE THE FOLLOWING COSTS:
          (1) PERIOD OWNING COST
          (2) ACTUAL PERIOD OPERATING COSTS OF ELEC. SRV.
          (3) COST OF WATER SERVICE
PRESS ZERO KEY WHEN NONE OF THE ABOVE ARE DESIRED

WHICH OF THE ABOVE COSTS WOULD YOU LIKE TO FIND (1,2,OR 3)?
```

Figure 8-9 (*continued*)

(1)

YOU HAVE CHOSEN TO DETERMINE THE PERIOD OWNING COST OF A HVAC
SYSTEM.   PLEASE SUPPLY THE FOLLOWING INFORMATION.

PAYMENT ON PRINCIPAL, AS COMPUTED? 5467
INTEREST AS COMPUTED? 1346
TAXES AS COMPUTED? 125
INSURANCE AS COMPUTED? 200
DEPRECIATION AS COMPUTED? 500
THE TOTAL PERIOD OWNING COSTS OF THE SYSTEM IS 7638 DOLLARS

DO YOU WISH TO MAKE ANOTHER CALCULATION (Y OR N)?

                                     (2)

YOU HAVE CHOSEN TO DETERMINE THE ACTUAL PERIOD OPERATING COST
OF ELECTRICAL SERVICE.   PLEASE SUPPLY THE FOLLOWING DATA.
TOTAL BRAKE HORSEPOWER OF ELECTRIC MOTORS? 125
TOTAL OPERATING TIME DURING PERIOD IN HOURS? 240
ELECTRICAL RATE OR POWER COST, ENERGY AND DEMAND? .0346

THE COST OF ELECTRICAL ENERGY FOR A TOTAL OPERATING TIME OF 240 HOURS IS
   910.9976 DOLLARS.

DO YOU WISH TO MAKE ANOTHER CALCULATION (Y OR NO)?

                                     (3)

YOU HAVE CHOSEN TO DETERMINE THE COST OF WATER SERVICE, PLEASE
SUPPLY THE FOLLOWING INFORMATION.

WATER CONSUMPTION IN GALLONS PER MINUTE? 12
TOTAL OPERATING TIME, IN HOURS, DURING PERIOD? 240
WATER RATE OR COST IN $/1000 CU FT.? .16

THE COST OF WATER FOR A TOTAL OPERATING TIME OF 240 HOURS IS
   3.6864 DOLLARS.

DO YOU WISH TO MAKE ANOTHER CALCULATION (Y OR N)?

Figure 8-10

Then if, say, a program on duct sizing is wanted, the operator may select this item
from the menu, or the operator may perhaps select HVAC cost programs like the
ones shown in Figs. 8-9 and 8-10.

The main reason for incorporating all programs into one package is to save
time in recalling the various programs. If each program is written individually, and
contained in various locations on the diskette, the user will first have to recall the
name of the program by first looking at the "index" of the diskette and then load
the required program. With a custom-made software package, the menu will immediately inform the user of the selections available.

9

SIZING PIPES FOR
HOT-WATER SYSTEMS

A forced hot-water heating system employs an electric pump to provide circulation so that the entire system is almost instantly supplied with hot water whenever it is needed. Also, a constant temperature can be maintained in the system to compensate for outdoor weather conditions.

Nearly all calculations dealing with pipe sizing are dependent on the following:

Pressure drop.   Pressure drop is the term that expresses the fact that power is consumed when liquids are moved through pipes, heating units, fittings, and so forth. Pressure drop is caused by friction created between the inner walls of the conveyor (pipe for example) and the moving liquid.

Head pressure.   As used in designing the capacity of a circulating pump, head pressure is the maximum pressure drop against which the pump can induce a flow of liquid. If a certain size of booster pump is connected to a tank of water as illustrated in Fig. 9-1, it will pump water to a height of 7 ft. This height, therefore, is the maximum head against which the pump can cause a flow of water.

One- and two-pipe forced hot-water systems.   Forced hot-water systems are classified as one- and two-pipe designs. Two-pipe systems are further divided into direct return and reverse return.

In a one-pipe system, as illustrated in Fig. 9-2, a single main in one or more circuits is used to circulate water. Branch pipes or risers from this main are equipped with special fittings at their connections to the main. These fittings introduce the correct amount of resistance needed to assure a proper diversion of hot water into the radiator or convector.

In the reverse-return system of a two-pipe system, as illustrated in Fig. 9-3, the first radiator of the main line is the last to return, and all radiator circuits are of equal length. Therefore, the problem of proper radiation balance is greatly simplified in this type of a system.

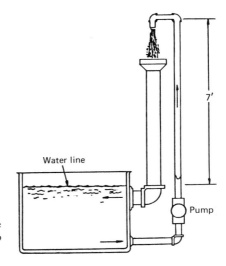

Water line

7'

Pump

Figure 9-1   Maximum pressure head is the height to which a pump can cause water to flow.

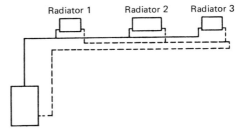

Radiator 1   Radiator 2   Radiator 3

Figure 9-2   A one-pipe forced hot-water system.

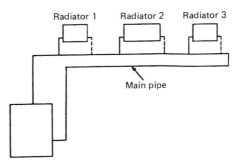

Radiator 1   Radiator 2   Radiator 3

Main pipe

Figure 9-3   A reverse-return two-pipe forced hot-water system.

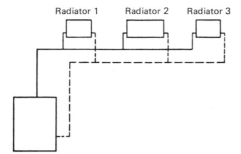

Figure 9-4   A direct-return two-pipe forced hot-water system.

In a direct-return system, as illustrated in Fig. 9-4, the first radiator taken off the main line is the first radiator to return its load. The last radiator on the line is the last to return. Consequently, the water circuits to the radiators are of unequal length and maintaining a proper balance of heat distribution can cause serious difficulties at times.

PIPING FOR REFRIGERATION SYSTEMS

Water may also be cooled by a packaged unit known as a chiller; the water is then used to cool buildings and other objects. The following are some typical applications of chilled water.

Valance cooling.   A valance cooler is a convection-operated cooling device mounted at the intersection of any wall and the ceiling. Chilled water from a chiller passes through finned heat-transfer tubing within the valance, thereby creating a convection flow of cooled air for cooling and dehumidifying a required space. The valance cooler is applicable to all air-conditioning installation, particularly where silent, draftless cooling is desired.

Fan-coil units.   A water chiller can be used to supply chilled water directly to any type of commercial air-conditioning fan and fan-coil unit.

Fresh-air units.   A water chiller, in conjunction with a hot-water boiler, can be used to furnish water to a blending tank. In turn, the blending tank supplies carefully controlled tempered water to fan-coil and filter units. This type of unit is used to provide fresh, preconditioned ventilation air for motels, schools, offices, hospitals, and other public rooms. The air is provided at preselected temperatures that are usually between 55° and 75°F.

PIPE SIZING

All the systems described require that their supply and return lines be properly sized to carry the required load and flow of liquid. A BASIC computer program can be devised to help with these calculations. However, due to the length of such a BASIC program, it might be best to consider one of the prepackaged programs for this and similar applications.

For example, the TK!Solver program, available from Software Arts, Inc., is a professional computing tool that is both useful and simple to use. These programs are available for most personal computers, such as the Wang and IBM PCs.

The TK!Solver program makes it easy to solve mathematical problems. You simply enter one or more equations and then tell the program to solve them. All the tools needed for problem solving are built into the program, including mathematical functions, facilities for converting units of measurement, and the ability to produce graphs and tables.

The TK!Solver program can solve a broad range of problems using models, consisting of sets of equations with variables of known and unknown values. Given a model and the values of the variables, the TK!Solver program solves for as many unknown values as is possible. The program's problem-solving ability is powerful and versatile enough to apply to many fields, from financial planning to architectural design to chemical analysis.

Many features of the TK!Solver program are named with familiar words. For example, in the TK!Solver program you enter information on a variety of forms displayed on the screen, just as you would write down information on sheets of paper. These forms are called sheets. The different TK!Solver sheets contain all the equations, variables, values, comments, and other information pertinent to your model.

The TK!Solver program can display either one or two sheets at a time. The sections of the screen showing the sheets are called windows because you look through them to see the sheets. The screen may show two sheets in two windows, the variable sheet in the top window and the rule sheet in the bottom window.

To demonstrate the use of the TK! package, let's take the fluid flow in pipes. The following TK! model can be used to evaluate laminar and turbulent incompressible fluid flow in pipes. Figure 9-5 shows pipe dimensions as used in the model.

ESSENTIAL INFORMATION

The model of Fig. 9-5 involves the basic fluid mechanics of incompressible, viscous, irrotational flow in pipes and tubes. Among the factors that can be analyzed with the model are pressure drops associated with incompressible flow, couplings and

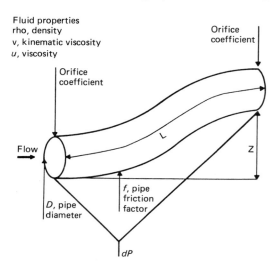

Figure 9-5   Example of pipe offset.

valves, pipe diameter and length, and pipe roughness. Two effects that can be studied with the model are (1) variations in the height of pipe ends leading to gravitationally induced pressure differences and (2) orifice effects in fittings associated with dynamic loss coefficients.

There are several considerations to keep in mind when solving the model.

1. If fluid density is entered as weight density w, the user must also enter a value of 32.1740 (in units of feet per square second) for g, the acceleration of gravity. It is possible to avoid entering this value by adding the rule $g = 32.1740$ to the rule sheet or storing this value for g in the model on the diskette.

2. If no value is given for pipe roughness, the model sets roughness to zero and calculates for smooth pipe.

3. The model calculates turbulent flow in cases where the Reynolds number is greater than 2300 and laminar flow otherwise. The type of flow is indicated by the variable flow. Where the Reynolds number is between 2000 and 4000, the flow is neither laminar nor turbulent and may exhibit transitory behavior, so the model is likely to be inaccurate. The model is also inaccurate when the Reynolds number exceeds 10^8. The variable *valid* indicates when the model is inaccurate. To see the full contents of these messages, the user must position the cursor over the output field for flow or valid.

4. The model uses Blasius's equation for smooth pipe friction factors in cases where it is accurate and the Colebrook equation otherwise. In the latter case, iterative solution is required.

5. This is a steady-state fluid model. The inertial effects of rapidly accelerating or decelerating flows and loads are not included.

6. The pump power computed in the model is the delivered fluid power. Pump inefficiencies are not included. The actual power consumed by the pump will be greater than the computed power.

7. Many solutions of this model require iteration. In particular, this is necessary whenever the Reynolds number exceeds 10^5, when nonsmooth pipes are used, or when the model is being solved for pipe diameter.

8. Several factors can cause deviations from the idealized model results, including the fluid properties fluctuating with large temperature changes and nonlinearity in viscous flows with high shear rates. Flows in the neighborhood of Reynolds number 2300 may cause the iterative solver not to converge to a solution.

SAMPLE SOLUTIONS

The following examples illustrate two typical applications of the model. Example 1 finds the maximum range of a spray pump. Example 2 determines the pressure drop and required power for a water-delivery system.

Example 1   Maximum Range

A pump for spraying paint has a nozzle with an orifice coefficient of 2.0 attached to a 600-ft smooth hose with an inside diameter of 1 in. The pump can generate a maximum of 0.2 horsepower of fluid output. The fluid has a density of 2.8 slugs/ft³ and a viscosity of 5×10^{-5} slug/ft-s. If the pump must deliver 1 gal of liquid per minute, how high from the pump can the liquid be pumped?

To solve this problem, enter the following input values for the variables indicated:

Variable Name	Input Value
L	600
D	1
Q	1
rho	2.8
u	5E-5
C	2
power	0.2
g	32.1740

Type ! to solve the model. The solution is shown in Fig. 9-6. Notice that the flow in this example is laminar.

St Input	Name	Output	Unit	Comment
				** FLUID FLOW IN PIPES **
	valid	'accurate		model validity
	flow	'laminar_		flow type
600	L		ft	length of pipe
1	D		in	pipe inside diameter
1	Q		gal/min	volume flow rate of fluid
	V	.40849771	ft/s	linear speed of fluid in pipe
	f	.03357249		friction factor of pipe
	Re	1906.3227		Reynolds number of pipe flow
2.8	rho		slug/ft©3	fluid mass density
	w	90.0872	lb/ft©3	fluid weight density
.00005	u		slug/(ft*	fluid viscosity
	v	1.7857E-5	ft©2/s	kinematic viscosity
	dP	342.85712	lb/in©2	pressure drop across pipe of length L
2	C			sum of orifice coefficients for pipe
	z	547.40838	ft	vertical height of end #2 above end #1
.2	power		hp	pump output power
	epsilon	0	ft	pipe roughness
	hf	.63203164	ft	head loss
	Area	.00545415	ft©2	cross-sectional area of pipe
32.174	g		ft/s©2	acceleration of gravity

Figure 9-6

The Reynolds number in this example is close to 2000, the accuracy limit of the model. If we decrease the pipe diameter to 0.75 in., will the model remain accurate?

To solve this problem, change the following input value for the variable indicated:

Variable Name	Input Value
D	0.75

St Input	Name	Output	Unit	Comment
				** FLUID FLOW IN PIPES **
	valid	'invalid_		model validity
	flow	'turbulen		flow type
600	L		ft	length of pipe
.75	D		in	pipe inside diameter
1	Q		gal/min	volume flow rate of fluid
	V	.72621815	ft/s	linear speed of fluid in pipe
	f	.04450444		friction factor of pipe
	Re	2541.7635		Reynolds number of pipe flow
2.8	rho		slug/ft©3	fluid mass density
	w	90.0872	lb/ft©3	fluid weight density
.00005	u		slug/(ft*	fluid viscosity
	v	1.7857E-5	ft©2/s	kinematic viscosity
	dP	342.85712	lb/in©2	pressure drop across pipe of length L
2	C			sum of orifice coefficients for pipe
	z	544.52236	ft	vertical height of end #2 above end #1
.2	power		hp	pump output power
	epsilon	0	ft	pipe roughness
	hf	3.5180495	ft	head loss
	Area	.00306796	ft©2	cross-sectional area of pipe
32.174	g		ft/s©2	acceleration of gravity

Figure 9-7

Type ! to solve the model. The solution is shown in Fig. 9-7.

By changing the pipe diameter, we have moved the Reynolds number of the flow into the critical zone, and the model cannot make an accurate prediction, as indicated by the variable valid.

Example 2   Pressure Drop and Required Power

For an irrigation system, a pump must deliver 140 gal/min of water (with a fluid weight density of 62.4 lb/ft³ and a fluid viscosity of 2.0545×10^{-5} slug/ft-s) through 300 ft of 2.5-in.-diameter pipe to a point 5 ft below the level of the pump. The sum of the orifice coefficients is 2 and the pipe has a roughness of 8.5×10 ft. Determine the pressure drop and required power.

Because rough pipes require iterative solution, it is necessary to guess at f. To solve this problem, enter the following input values and guesses for the variables indicated:

Status	Variable Name	Input Value
	L	300
	D	2.5
	Q	140
G	f	0.01
	w	62.4
	u	2.0545E-5
	C	2
	Z	-5
	epsilon	8.5E-4
	g	32.1740

St	Input	Name	Output	Unit	Comment
					** FLUID FLOW IN PIPES **
		valid	'accurate		model validity
		flow	'turbulen		flow type
	300	L		ft	length of pipe
	2.5	D		in	pipe inside diameter
	140	Q		gal/min	volume flow rate of fluid
		V	9.1503487	ft/s	linear speed of fluid in pipe
		f	.02919012		friction factor of pipe
		Re	179957.44		Reynolds number of pipe flow
		rho	1.9394542	slug/ft©3	fluid mass density
	62.4	w		lb/ft©3	fluid weight density
	2.0545E-5	u		slug/(ft*	fluid viscosity
		v	1.0593E-5	ft©2/s	kinematic viscosity
		dP	22.661705	lb/in©2	pressure drop across pipe of length L
	2	C			sum of orifice coefficients for pipe
	-5	Z		ft	vertical height of end #2 above end #1
		power	1.8507060	hp	pump output power
	.00085	epsilon		ft	pipe roughness
		hf	57.296243	ft	head loss
		Area	.03408846	ft©2	cross-sectional area of pipe
	32.174	g		ft/s©2	acceleration of gravity

Figure 9-8

Type ! to solve the model. The solution is shown in Fig. 9-8. Note that the negative value entered for Z indicates the output of the pipe is below the inflow.

CONTENTS OF THE SHEETS

Variables

Variable	Definition	Display Units (and calculation) units, if different)
valid	Model validity (message)	
flow	Flow type (message)	
L	Length of pipe	ft
D	Pipe inside diameter	in. (ft)
Q	Volume flow rate of fluid	gal/min (ft³/s)
V	Linear speed of fluid in pipe	ft/s
f	Friction factor of pipe	(dimensionless)
Re	Reynolds number of pipe flow	(dimensionless)
rho	Fluid mass density	slug/ft²
w	Fluid weight density	lb/ft³
u	Fluid viscosity	slug/ft-s
v	kinematic viscosity	ft²/s
dP	Pressure drop across pipe of length L	lb/in.² (lb/ft²)
C	Sum of orifice coefficients for pipe	(dimensionless)
Z	Vertical height of end 2 (outflow) above end 1 (inflow)	ft
power	Pump output power	hp (ft-lb/s)
epsilon	Pipe roughness	ft
hf	Head loss	ft
area	Cross-sectional area of pipe	ft²
g	Acceleration of gravity (value should be 32.1740)	ft/s²

Rules

1. Pipe cross-section area

$$\text{Area} = \frac{piD^2}{4}$$

2. Volume flow rate

$$Q = V(\text{Area})$$

3. Kinematic viscosity

$$v = \frac{u}{\text{rho}}$$

4. Reynolds number

$$Re = \frac{V(D)}{v}$$

5. Weight or mass density

$$w = (rho)g$$

6. Determines if $c = 0$ (laminar flow) or $c = 1$ (turbulent flow)

$$c = \text{step (Re, 2300)}$$

7. Bernoulli principle

$$dP = \frac{[L(f)/D + C]V^2 \, (rho)}{2 + (rho)\,(g)z}$$

8. Pump output power

$$\text{power} = Q(dP)$$

9. Head loss

$$hf = \frac{eP}{w - Z}$$

10. Sets pipe roughness to zero if not given

$$(epsilon)[given('epsilon, 0, 1)] = 0$$

11. Determines when Colebrook equation is to be used

$$M = \min[1, \text{step}(Re, 100{,}000) + |\text{sgn epsilon}|]$$

12. Friction factor or smooth pipe (Reynolds number below 10^5)

$f = \dfrac{64}{Re}$ if laminar flow, smooth pipe

$f = 0.316Re^{-0.25}$,   if turbulent flow, smooth pipe (Blasius's equation)

This appears on screen in the form:

$$(1 - M)* \ f = ((1 - c)*64/Re$$
$$+ \ c*.316*Re' - .25) *(1 - M)$$

13. Friction factor (cases not covered above): Colebrook equation

$$\frac{1}{\sqrt{f}} = 2 \log \left(\frac{epsilon}{3.7D} + \frac{2.51}{Re\sqrt{f}} \right)$$

14. Flow type

$$\text{flow} = \text{flow\_type}(c)$$

15. Model validity message

$$valid = accurate (Re)$$

Functions

1. Determines flow type

Name	flow__type
Type	Table
Usual domain	laminar/turbulent indicator
Usual range	flow type
Possible outputs	'laminar_flow,
	'turbulent_flow

2. Determines model validity

Name	accurate
Type	Step
Usual domain	Reynolds number
Usual range	validity message
Possible outputs	'accurate,
	'invalid_transitional,
	'invalid_out_of_range_
	of_Colebrook

10

MISCELLANEOUS HVAC
APPLICATIONS

This chapter covers some secondary HVAC systems that are often overlooked by many publications. Although much of the data may not be needed often, the examples further illustrate just how helpful the microcomputer can be.

The four BASIC programs at the end of this chapter are self-explanatory in that the REmark statements give the figure number and program title. Then the PRINT statement tells how to use the program. All that is necessary is for the computer to be placed in the BASIC PROGRAM mode, the data entered via the keyboard into the computer memory, and then the RUN or EXECUTE key pressed to use the programs. All the programs have been tested on both a Wang and IBM computer. All were found to operate perfectly. However, if you run into problems, which is not unusual, chances are a typo or two are present. Recheck each line of the program to find these.

REFRIGERANT PIPING

It is impractical to give rules to cover every phase of refrigeration piping and the problems that develop during the design and installation of HVAC systems. However, several basic rules should always be followed in laying out piping to provide a neat, serviceable installation. These rules include:

1. Design refrigerant lines to be as short and direct as possible.
2. Locate refrigeration piping so that access to system components is not hindered and so that refrigerant flow sight glasses can be easily observed.

3. Avoid locations where copper tube will be exposed to possible injury. If this is not feasible, enclose the tube in a protective conduit. Some codes require this.

4. Use as few joints and fittings as possible. Fittings should be of the wrought-copper, long-radius type. When possible, use wye fittings in preference to 90° connections.

5. Use a continuous length of soft copper tube bent around obstructions in inaccessible locations where it would be difficult to install tube with fittings or where obstructions would require an unusually large number of fittings. Soft tube so used must be properly supported and should never be bent more than $22\frac{1}{2}$ degrees without the use of bending tools.

6. Pitch all horizontal lines a minimum of 1/4 in. and preferably 1/2 in. in 10 ft in the direction of refrigerant flow and avoid unnecessary traps.

7. Do not expose piping to external sources of heat if it can be avoided.

8. If space does not allow a single large line, use two or more smaller lines in parallel.

SAMPLE PROBLEM

Let's assume an R-22 evaporator operates at 40°F evaporating temperature and that liquid reaches the expansion valve at 100°F. The design capacity is 75 tons, but the evaporator must operate at as low as 25-ton capacity.

The suction line is about 90 ft long. The equivalent length of its fittings is estimated to be 60 ft long, giving a total of 150 ft.

Pressure loss is not to exceed 3 psi, so the suction line size will be selected for not over (3)(100)/150 = 2 psi per 100 ft. The suction line contains a 10-ft vertical rise.

Refer to Table 10-1. For the conditions in this problem, the flow rate is 2.94 lb/min/ton. Thus the total flow at design conditions is (2.94)(75) = 200 lb/min.

From Table 10-2, the pressure drop in 3 1/8-in. copper tubing is 2 psi/100 ft when flow is about 230 lb/min; thus 3 1/8-in. tubing is satisfactory for the full capacity.

Next the suction line must be checked as to its oil return function at 25 tons. Reference to Table 10-3 shows that, at 40°F evaporating, a 3 1/8-in. line is satisfactory at as little as 20 tons.

Another consideration is if the evaporator should operate at as low as 15 tons. From Table 10-3, a 3 1/8-in. line is suitable down to 12 tons. The 10-ft vertical riser section and its two elbows would then have to be reduced to 2 5/8 in. diameter. The equivalent length of this portion of the suction line would then be nearly 25 ft.

From Table 10-2, the pressure drop in 2 5/8-in. tubing with 220 lb/min flow is about 4.3 psi/100 ft. Therefore, the loss in the 25-ft section is now about 1.1

TABLE 10-1   Flow Rate per Ton of Refrigeration for R-22

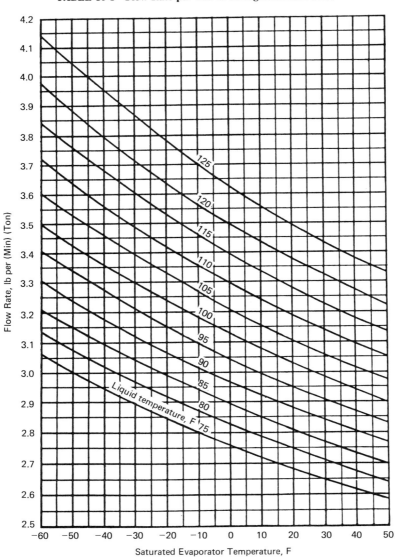

Reprinted from "Refrigerant Piping Data" published by Air-Conditioning and Refrigeration Institute.

TABLE 10-2 Pressure Drop in Copper Tubing for R-22 Vapor

Pressure drop, PSI per 100 ft

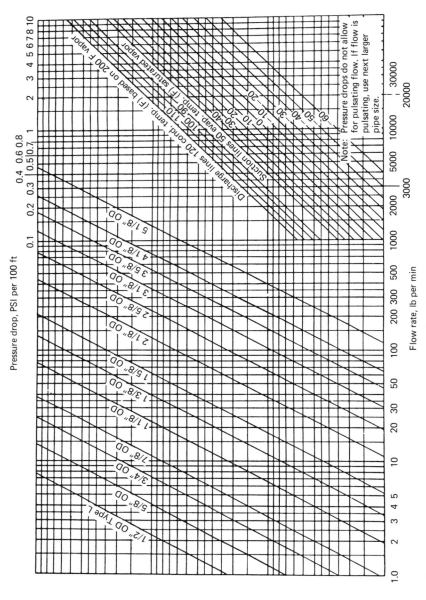

Flow rate, lb per min

TABLE 10-3 Minimum Recommended Load in Vertically Upward Refrigerant-22 Lines

Gas Condition[1]	1/2	5/8	3/4	7/8	1 1/8	1 3/8	1 5/8	2 1/8	2 5/8	3 1/8	3 5/8	4 1/8	5 1/8	6 1/8
				Copper Tube Outside Diameter, Inches										
200F and	Minimum Recommended Load for Satisfactory Oil Lift, Tons[2]													
213 psia	0.22	0.40	0.70	1.2	2.2	4.0	6.0	13.0	17.0	27.0	41	56	103	166
50F sat.	0.17	0.30	0.55	0.85	1.7	3.0	4.8	10.0	13.0	21.0	31	44	80	123
40F sat.	0.16	0.29	0.53	0.80	1.6	2.9	4.5	9.3	12.0	20.0	29	42	75	118
30F sat.	0.15	0.27	0.50	0.75	1.5	2.7	4.2	8.7	12.0	18.0	27	40	70	107
OF sat.	0.12	0.22	0.40	0.62	1.2	2.2	3.3	7.3	9.0	15.0	22	32	55	90
−50F sat.	0.08	0.14	0.26	0.40	0.8	1.4	2.2	4.7	5.7	9.3	14	20	37	57

[1] Tables, as noted are based on saturated condition for temperatures that are normal for suction, and superheated at pressure corresponding to 100F for a typical discharge condition. An increase in superheat (other conditions equal) increases tendency of gas to carry oil with it.

[2] Tons are based on: Refrigerant 22 — Three lb per min per ton. For other conditions, divide by actual lb per min per ton and multiply by 3.

psi, instead of the 0.5 psi when it was assumed to be 3 1/8-in. diameter, which is 0.6 psi more than desired.

Three alternative solutions to this problem present themselves:

1. Accept the 0.6-psi additional loss.
2. Use larger-sized tubing for the horizontal(125-ft equivalent length) portion of the suction line so that, instead of a net drop of $3.0 - 0.5 = 2.5$ psi in this portion of the line, the pressure drop will be $3.0 - 1.1 = 1.9$ psi, or $(1.9)(100)/125 = 1.5$ psi/100 ft. (See Figs. 10-1 through 10-4.) Referring to Table 10-2, a 3 5/8-in. line carries 290 lb/min/ton at this pressure loss.
3. A double suction riser may be used. This is shown in Fig. 10-5. When flow rate drops to the point that oil no longer returns up both risers, oil begins to accumulate in the trap, cutting off flow in the trapped riser. This leaves the adequate flow for oil return in the untrapped riser at the lowest capacity of operation. At higher capacity, flow takes place in both risers at an acceptable pressure loss.

In this example, a 2 5/8-in. line was found to be satisfactory for oil return at a 15-ton minimum capacity, so if a double suction riser were used, the untrapped riser would be sized at 2 5/8-in. diameter.

From Table 10-2, the flow rate through a 2 5/8-in. line at 2 psi/100 ft loss is about 145 lb/minute. If the loss at 220 lb/min is to be limited to 2 psi/100 ft, the trapped line must have that pressure loss with a flow rate of $200 - 145 = 75$ lb/min. Table 10-2 shows that a 2 1/8-in. line satisfies this condition.

DISCHARGE LINES

The function of the discharge line is to convey gas from compressor to condenser with the lowest economical pressure loss and to carry along any oil that is mixed with the gas.

```
10 REM **FIGURE 10-1**
20 REM **PRESSURE DROP PROGRAM FOR WATER**
30 PRINT "THIS PROGRAM CALCULATES THE PRESSURE DROP IN POUNDS PER"
40 PRINT "SQUARE INCH AT VARIOUS DELIVERIES PER 100 EQUIVALENT FEET"
50 PRINT "OF PIPE RUN"
60 PRINT
70 INPUT "ENTER SIZE OF PIPE (.75-IN TO 3-IN)";S
80 PRINT
90 INPUT "ENTER DELIVERY IN GALLONS PER MINUTE";G
100 IF S<1 THEN 500
110 IF S<1.25 THEN 600
120 IF S<1.5 THEN 700
130 IF S<2 THEN 800
140 IF S<2.5 THEN 900
150 IF S<3 THEN 1000
160 IF S=3 THEN 1100
170 PRINT "THE PRESSURE DROP IN A";S;"-IN PIPE WITH A DELIVERY OF";
180 PRINT G;"GALLONS PER MINUTE IS";D;"POUNDS PER SQ. IN."
190 STOP
500 IF G<1.1 THEN D=.02: GOTO 170
510 IF G<2.2 THEN D=.06:GOTO 170
520 IF G<3.1 THEN D=1:GOTO 170
530 IF G<4.1 THEN D=2:GOTO 170
540 IF G<11 THEN D=12:GOTO 170
600 IF G<1.1 THEN D=.05:GOTO 170
610 IF G<2.2 THEN D=.2:GOTO 170
620 IF G<3.1 THEN D=.42:GOTO 170
630 IF G<4.1 THEN D=.73:GOTO 170
640 IF G<11 THEN D=4!:GOTO 170
650 IF G<20 THEN D=14.5:GOTO 170
700 IF G<2.1 THEN D=.05:GOTO 170
710 IF G<3.1 THEN D=.11:GOTO 170
720 IF G<4.1 THEN D=.19:GOTO 170
730 IF G<5.1 THEN D=.28:GOTO 170
740 IF G<11 THEN D=11:GOTO 170
750 IF G<21 THEN D=3.7:GOTO 170
760 IF G<31 THEN D=7.9:GOTO 170
800 IF G<3.1 THEN D=.05:GOTO 170
810 IF G<4.1 THEN D=9.000001E-02:GOTO 170
820 IF G<5.1 THEN D=.13:GOTO 170
830 IF G<11 THEN D=.47:GOTO 170
840 IF G<21 THEN D=1.7:GOTO 170
850 IF G<31 THEN D=3.6:GOTO 170
```

```
860  IF G<41  THEN D=6.2:GOTO 170
870  IF G<51  THEN D=9.399999:GOTO 170
900  IF G<5.1 THEN D=.03:GOTO 170
910  IF G<11  THEN D=.13:GOTO 170
920  IF G<21  THEN D=.48:GOTO 170
930  IF G<31  THEN D=1:GOTO 170
940  IF G<41  THEN D=1.8:GOTO 170
950  IF G<51  THEN D=2.7:GOTO 170
960  IF G<76  THEN D=5.9:GOTO 170
970  IF G<101 THEN D=9.7:GOTO 170
1000 IF G<11  THEN D=.05:GOTO 170
1010 IF G<21  THEN D=.2:GOTO 170
1020 IF G<31  THEN D=.43:GOTO 170
1030 IF G<41  THEN D=.73:GOTO 170
1040 IF G<51  THEN D=1.1:GOTO 170
1050 IF G<76  THEN D=2.4:GOTO 170
1060 IF G<101 THEN D=4:GOTO 170
1100 IF G<21  THEN D=.07:GOTO 170
1110 IF G<31  THEN D=.14:GOTO 170
1120 IF G<41  THEN D=.24:GOTO 170
1130 IF G<51  THEN D=.37:GOTO 170
1140 IF G<76  THEN D=.83:GOTO 170
1150 IF G<101 THEN D=1.3:GOTO 170
1160 IF G<126 THEN D=21:GOTO 170
1170 IF G<151 THEN D=2.9:GOTO 170
```

```
xx??"x?????x??????°xxx??x??????????"x??x??????°???????x?x????x?????"x?°x??????
??°xxx??°?°?x????x?°????x??°????x?"????x?°????xx??x???????°x??xxx?°?
??x?x?°?°?xOk
RUN
THIS PROGRAM CALCULATES THE PRESSURE DROP IN POUNDS PER
SQUARE INCH AT VARIOUS DELIVERIES PER 100 EQUIVALENT FEET
OF PIPE RUN

ENTER SIZE OF PIPE (.75-IN TO 3-IN)? 1.5

ENTER DELIVERY IN GALLONS PER MINUTE? 10
THE PRESSURE DROP IN A 1.5 -IN PIPE WITH A DELIVERY OF 10 GALLONS PER MINUTE IS
.47 POUNDS PER SQ. IN.
Break in 190
Ok
RUN "PRNSCRN
```

Figure 10-1

```
Ok
RUN
THIS PROGRAM CALCULATES THE PRESSURE DROP IN POUNDS PER
SQUARE INCH AT VARIOUS DELIVERIES PER 100 EQUIVALENT FEET
OF PIPE RUN

ENTER SIZE OF PIPE (.75-IN TO 3-IN)? 1.25

ENTER DELIVERY IN GALLONS PER MINUTE? 3
THE PRESSURE DROP IN A 1.25 -IN PIPE WITH A DELIVERY OF 3 GALLONS PER MINUTE IS
 .11 POUNDS PER SQ. IN.
Break in 190
Ok
RUN "PRNSCRN


Ok
RUN
THIS PROGRAM CALCULATES THE PRESSURE DROP IN POUNDS PER
SQUARE INCH AT VARIOUS DELIVERIES PER 100 EQUIVALENT FEET
OF PIPE RUN

ENTER SIZE OF PIPE (.75-IN TO 3-IN)? 3

ENTER DELIVERY IN GALLONS PER MINUTE? 30
THE PRESSURE DROP IN A 3 -IN PIPE WITH A DELIVERY OF 30 GALLONS PER MINUTE IS
 .14 POUNDS PER SQ. IN.
Break in 190
Ok
RUN "PRNSCRN


Ok
RUN
THIS PROGRAM CALCULATES THE PRESSURE DROP IN POUNDS PER
SQUARE INCH AT VARIOUS DELIVERIES PER 100 EQUIVALENT FEET
OF PIPE RUN

ENTER SIZE OF PIPE (.75-IN TO 3-IN)? 2.5

ENTER DELIVERY IN GALLONS PER MINUTE? 75
THE PRESSURE DROP IN A 2.5 -IN PIPE WITH A DELIVERY OF 75 GALLONS PER MINUTE IS
 2.4 POUNDS PER SQ. IN.
Break in 190
Ok
RUN "PRNSCRN
```

Figure 10-1 (*continued*)

```
10 REM**FIGURE 10-2**
20 REM **PRESSURE DROP TABLE FOR STEAM**
30 PRINT "THIS PROGRAM CALCULATES THE MBH AT VARIOUS PRESSURE DROPS"
40 PRINT "PER 100 EQUIVALENT FEET OF PIPE RUN"
50 PRINT
60 INPUT "ENTER SIZE OF PIPE IN INCHES";S
70 PRINT
80 INPUT "ENTER PRESSURE DROP IN OUNCES (EITHER 1, 2, 4, OR 8 OUNCES)";P
90 PRINT
91 IF P=1 THEN 500
92 IF P=2 THEN 600
93 IF P=4 THEN 700
94 IF P=8 THEN 800
100 PRINT "FOR A PIPE SIZE OF";S;"INCHES, AND A PRESSURE DROP OF";P;"OUNCES"
110 PRINT "THE TOTAL MBH IS";M
111 PRINT:GOTO 30
120 IF P=1 THEN 500
130 IF P=2 THEN 600
140 IF P=4 THEN 700
150 IF P=8 THEN 800
500 IF S=1 THEN M=13.5:GOTO 100
510 IF S=1.25 THEN M=29.3:GOTO 100
520 IF S=1.5 THEN M=45.5:GOTO 100
530 IF S=2 THEN M=92.5:GOTO 100
540 IF S=2.5 THEN M=152.5:GOTO 100
550 IF S=3 THEN M=279:GOTO 100
560 IF S=4 THEN M=587:GOTO 100
570 IF S=5 THEN M=1190:GOTO 100
580 IF S=6 THEN M=1790:GOTO 100
600 IF S=1 THEN M=19
610 IF S=1.25 THEN M=41.5
620 IF S=1.5 THEN M=64.5
630 IF S=2 THEN M=131
640 IF S=2.5 THEN M=216
650 IF S=3 THEN M=395
660 IF S=4 THEN M=834
670 IF S=5 THEN M=1541
680 IF S=6 THEN M=2431
690 GOTO 100
700 IF S=1 THEN M=26.6
710 IF S=1.25 THEN M=58.8
720 IF S=1.5 THEN M=91
730 IF S=2 THEN M=185
740 IF S=2.5 THEN M=305
750 IF S=3 THEN M=560
760 IF S=4 THEN M=1180
770 IF S=5 THEN M=2180
780 IF S=6 THEN M=3699
790 GOTO 100
800 IF S=1 THEN M=37.7
810 IF S=1.25 THEN M=83
820 IF S=1.5 THEN M=129
830 IF S=2 THEN M=262
840 IF S=2.5 THEN M=430
850 IF S=3 THEN M=790
860 IF S=4 THEN M=1670
870 IF S=5 THEN M=3080
880 IF S=6 THEN M=5060
890 GOTO 100

Ok
RUN
THIS PROGRAM CALCULATES THE MBH AT VARIOUS PRESSURE DROPS
PER 100 EQUIVALENT FEET OF PIPE RUN

ENTER SIZE OF PIPE IN INCHES? 2
```

Figure 10-2

```
ENTER PRESSURE DROP IN OUNCES (EITHER 1, 2, 4, OR 8 OUNCES)? 4

FOR A PIPE SIZE OF 2 INCHES, AND A PRESSURE DROP OF 4 OUNCES
THE TOTAL MBH IS 185

THIS PROGRAM CALCULATES THE MBH AT VARIOUS PRESSURE DROPS
PER 100 EQUIVALENT FEET OF PIPE RUN

ENTER SIZE OF PIPE IN INCHES?
©C
Break in 60
Ok
RUN "PRNSCRN



Ok
RUN
THIS PROGRAM CALCULATES THE MBH AT VARIOUS PRESSURE DROPS
PER 100 EQUIVALENT FEET OF PIPE RUN

ENTER SIZE OF PIPE IN INCHES? 1.5

ENTER PRESSURE DROP IN OUNCES (EITHER 1, 2, 4, OR 8 OUNCES)? 2

FOR A PIPE SIZE OF 1.5 INCHES, AND A PRESSURE DROP OF 2 OUNCES
THE TOTAL MBH IS 64.5

THIS PROGRAM CALCULATES THE MBH AT VARIOUS PRESSURE DROPS
PER 100 EQUIVALENT FEET OF PIPE RUN

ENTER SIZE OF PIPE IN INCHES?
©C
Break in 60
Ok
RUN"PRNSCRN
```

Figure 10-2   (*continued*)


```
10 REM **FIGURE 10-3**
20 REM **WATER CAPACITY PER FOOT OF PIPE**
30 PRINT "THIS PROGRAM IS DESIGNED TO GIVE THE AMOUNT OF WATER CAPACITY"
40 PRINT "AVAILABLE IN VARIOUS SIZES OF PIPE.  TO USE, ENTER THE SIZE PIPE"
50 PRINT "WHEN PROMPTED ON THE SCREEN.  THE WATER CAPACITY PER FOOT WILL"
60 PRINT "INSTANTLY BE GIVEN."
70 PRINT
80 PRINT
90 INPUT "ENTER PIPE SIZE IN INCHES";P
100 IF P=.5 THEN G=.016
110 IF P=.75 THEN G=.023
120 IF P=1 THEN G=.04
130 IF P=1.25 THEN G=.063
140 IF P=1.5 THEN G=.102
150 IF P=2 THEN G= .17
160 IF P=2.5 THEN G=.275
170 IF P=3 THEN G=.39
180 IF P=4 THEN G=.69
190 IF P=5 THEN G=1.1
200 IF P=6 THEN G=1.5
```

Figure 10-3

```
300 PRINT
310 PRINT
320 PRINT "THE WATER CAPACITY OF A";P;"-INCH PIPE IS";G;"GALLONS PER FOOT"
330 STOP
```

Ok
RUN
THIS PROGRAM IS DESIGNED TO GIVE THE AMOUNT OF WATER CAPACITY
AVAILABLE IN VARIOUS SIZES OF PIPE. TO USE, ENTER THE SIZE PIPE
WHEN PROMPTED ON THE SCREEN. THE WATER CAPACITY PER FOOT WILL
INSTANTLY BE GIVEN.

ENTER PIPE SIZE IN INCHES? 2.5

THE WATER CAPACITY OF A 2.5 -INCH PIPE IS .275 GALLONS PER FOOT
Break in 330
Ok
RUN "PRNSCRN

Ok
RUN
THIS PROGRAM GIVES THE HEAT LOSS IN BTUH UNDER VARYING
                        CONDITIONS
SIZE OF PIPE? 1.5

AVERAGE TEMPERATURE OF WATER (IN DEGREES F.) IN PIPE? 180

THE HEAT LOSS IN A 1.5 -INCH PIPE WITH AN AVERAGE WATER
TEMPERATURE OF 180 DEGREES F. IS 126   BTUH.

THIS PROGRAM GIVES THE HEAT LOSS IN BTUH UNDER VARYING
                        CONDITIONS
SIZE OF PIPE?
©C
Break in 60
Ok
RUN "PRNSCRN
Ok
RUN

Ok
RUN
THIS PROGRAM GIVES THE HEAT LOSS IN BTUH UNDER VARYING
                        CONDITIONS
SIZE OF PIPE? 2

AVERAGE TEMPERATURE OF WATER (IN DEGREES F.) IN PIPE? 145

THE HEAT LOSS IN A 2 -INCH PIPE WITH AN AVERAGE WATER
TEMPERATURE OF 145 DEGREES F. IS 103   BTUH.

THIS PROGRAM GIVES THE HEAT LOSS IN BTUH UNDER VARYING
                        CONDITIONS
SIZE OF PIPE?
©C
Break in 60
Ok
RUN "PRNSCRN

Figure 10-3 (*continued*)

```
10 REM **FIGURE 10-4**
20 REM **HEAT EMISSION OF PIPE COILS INSTALLED HORIZONTALLY**
30 REM **                    ON SAME PLANE                    **
40 PRINT "THIS PROGRAM GIVES THE HEAT LOSS IN BTUH UNDER VARYING"
50 PRINT "                    CONDITIONS                    "
60 INPUT "SIZE OF PIPE";P
70 PRINT
80 INPUT "AVERAGE TEMPERATURE OF WATER (IN DEGREES F.) IN PIPE";T
90 IF P=.5 THEN 200
100 IF P=.75 THEN 300
110 IF P=1 THEN 400
120 IF P=1.25 THEN 500
130 IF P=1.5 THEN 600
140 IF P=2 THEN 700
150 PRINT
160 PRINT "THE HEAT LOSS IN A";P;"-INCH PIPE WITH AN AVERAGE WATER"
170 PRINT "TEMPERATURE OF";T;"DEGREES F. IS";L;" BTUH.
180 PRINT
190 PRINT
191 GOTO 30
200 IF T<121 THEN L=22.8:GOTO 150
210 IF T<151 THEN L=39.6:GOTO 150
220 IF T<181 THEN L=60:GOTO 150
230 IF T<201 THEN L=74:GOTO 150
240 IF T<211 THEN L=82:GOTO 150
250 IF T<228 THEN L=97:GOTO 150
260 GOTO 150
300 IF T<121 THEN L=27.8:GOTO 150
310 IF T<151 THEN L=48.5:GOTO 150
320 IF T<181 THEN L=73:GOTO 150
330 IF T<201 THEN L=90:GOTO 150
340 IF T<211 THEN L=100:GOTO 150
350 IF T<228 THEN L=117:GOTO 150
400 IF T<121 THEN L=34.2:GOTO 150
410 IF T<151 THEN L=59.4:GOTO 150
420 IF T<181 THEN L=90:GOTO 150
430 IF T<201 THEN L=111:GOTO 150
440 IF T<211 THEN L=123:GOTO 150
450 IF T<228 THEN L=144:GOTO 150
500 IF T<121 THEN L=42.4:GOTO 150
510 IF T<151 THEN L=73:GOTO 150
520 IF T<181 THEN L=111:GOTO 150
530 IF T<201 THEN L=138:GOTO 150
540 IF T<211 THEN L=152:GOTO 150
550 IF T<228 THEN L=178:GOTO 150
600 IF T<121 THEN L=47.8:GOTO 150
610 IF T<151 THEN L=83:GOTO 150
620 IF T<181 THEN L=126:GOTO 150
630 IF T<201 THEN L=155:GOTO 150
640 IF T<211 THEN L=172:GOTO 150
650 IF T<228 THEN L=202:GOTO 150
700 IF T<121 THEN L=59:GOTO 150
710 IF T<151 THEN L=103:GOTO 150
720 IF T<181 THEN L=155:GOTO 150
730 IF T<201 THEN L=192:GOTO 150
740 IF T<211 THEN L=212:GOTO 150
750 IF T<228 THEN L=248:GOTO 150
```

```
Ok
RUN
THIS PROGRAM GIVES THE HEAT LOSS IN BTUH UNDER VARYING
                    CONDITIONS
SIZE OF PIPE? 1.5

AVERAGE TEMPERATURE OF WATER (IN DEGREES F.) IN PIPE? 180
```

Figure 10-4

```
THE HEAT LOSS IN A 1.5 -INCH PIPE WITH AN AVERAGE WATER
TEMPERATURE OF 180 DEGREES F. IS 126  BTUH.

THIS PROGRAM GIVES THE HEAT LOSS IN BTUH UNDER VARYING
                        CONDITIONS
SIZE OF PIPE?
©C
Break in 60
Ok
RUN "PRNSCRN
```

Figure 10-4 (*continued*)

Pressure loss in the discharge line adds an equal amount to the compressor discharge pressure, increasing compressor power requirements. The decision on pipe size is based on economics. A pressure loss corresponding to about a 2°F temperature difference is reasonable. At 100°F, this represents about 6 psi for R-22.

The charts cited previously in the discussion of suction lines also include data for discharge lines.

Any upflow discharge lines carrying oil with the gas must also be sized so that, at the lowest flow rate, the oil will be carried by the gas. In those few cases where flow rate at full capacity results in excessive pressure loss through a vertical line sized for oil lift at minimum capacity, double discharge risers may be used.

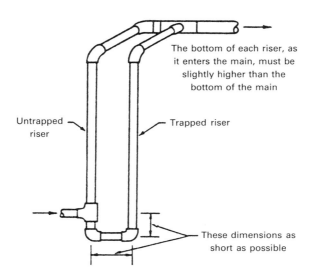

Figure 10-5 Double suction riser.

LIQUID LINES

Within reasonable limits, pressure loss in liquid lines has no effect on system capacity or power requirements. Pressure loss in liquid lines may be the result of a column of liquid when flow is upward. (When flow is downward, the liquid column is, of course, a pressure gain.)

The factors to be considered are as follows:

1. Pressure loss must not result in liquid pressure dropping below that corresponding to saturation at its existing temperature at any point before the expansion valve. If the pressure is lower, evaporation or "flashing" will occur at that point, causing higher flow resistance, and liquid may not be able to get to the evaporator at the desired rate.
2. If quick-closing solenoid valves are used, the velocity in the liquid lines should not exceed about 5 ft/s.
3. If the line passes through places where the temperature is higher than that of the liquid, insulation may be desirable; sometimes it is necessary.
4. The pressure and temperature of the liquid at the entrance to the expansion valve must be such as to result in the desired rate of flow through the existing expansion valve at the desired evaporator pressure.

Table 10-4 gives pressure loss and velocity for R-22 in copper tubing.

HVAC FAN SPEED AND HORSEPOWER SELECTION

Once the model, size, and all components of a fan-forced HVAC system are known, the correct speed and horsepower for the standard fan can be determined. First, add together the unit air resistance and the external resistances due to ductwork, grilles, and so on. When the total static pressure has been obtained by this addition, enter the fan rating table (Table 10-5) for the unit size selected, at the desired air flow, and read the fan speed and the BHP.

For convenience, Table 10-5 lists all component resistances on the basis of the velocity determined by dividing the cubic feet per minute by the unit size number. It will be recognized, since the size number in some brands of equipment is the same as the square foot face area of the cooling coil, that this is also the cooling coil face velocity. Thus one calculation only is required, and this establishes a single value of velocity in feet per minute that is used throughout the table for every item listed, and is applicable even if a cooling coil is not included.

Single zone units.   The unit air resistance is the sum of the individual resistances of each component.

Table 10-4 Velocity and Pressure Drop in Copper Tubing for R-22 Liquid

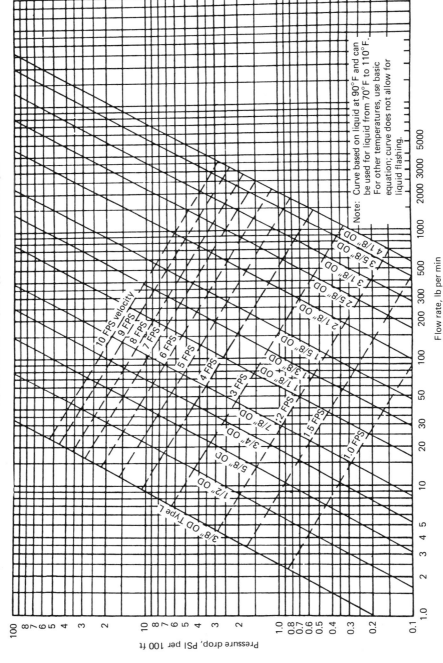

Pressure drop, PSI per 100 ft

Flow rate, lb per min

Note: Curve based on liquid at 90°F and can be used for liquid from 70°F to 110°F. For other temperatures, use basic equation; curve does not allow for liquid flashing.

TABLE 10-5   Component Resistances

Component			Face Velocity (fpm) (cfm divided by unit size no.)				
			400	450	500	550	600
Cooling coils	Wet coil resistances	4 row	0.24	0.30	0.36	0.44	0.52
		5 row	0.29	0.36	0.43	0.51	0.60
		6 row	0.32	0.40	0.47	0.57	0.67
		7 row	0.37	0.44	0.52	0.63	0.74
		8 row	0.40	0.49	0.58	0.69	0.81
Heating coils	CV, CVN, CH, CHN	1 row	0.04	0.05	0.06	0.07	0.09
		2 row	0.09	0.12	0.14	0.16	0.19
	CM	1 row	0.13	0.16	0.20	0.24	0.27
		2 row	0.28	0.37	0.41	0.49	0.57
Filters (2 in. thick)	Flat box	Throwaway	0.15	0.19	0.22		
		Cleanable	0.07	0.09	0.12	0.14	0.18
	Oversize flat box	Throwaway	0.08	0.10	0.13	0.15	0.18
		Cleanable	0.04	0.05	0.06	0.07	0.09
	Angle box	Throwaway	0.04	0.06	0.07	0.09	0.10
		Cleanable	0.03	0.03	0.04	0.04	0.05
Cabinet	CV, CVN: 1.66 to 9.06		0.05	0.06	0.08	0.09	0.11
	CV, CVN: 10.16 to 32 with 2 to 8 rows total		0.04	0.05	0.06	0.07	0.09
	with 9 to 10 rows total		0.07	0.09	0.11	0.14	0.17
	with 11 to 12 rows total		0.11	0.14	0.17	0.20	0.25
	CH, CHN: all sizes		0.00	0.00	0.00	0.00	0.00
	CM: all sizes		0.13	0.16	0.20	0.24	0.30

Multi zone or blow-through double deck units.   The unit air resistance is the sum of the individual resistances of each component, except that only one coil resistance is counted, this being either the cooling or heating coil, whichever is greater.

Consistent with other data, the fan ratings are listed according to face velocity, with the cubic feet per minute and outlet velocity shown in direct relation (if outlet velocity from the CM unit is desired, this may be calcuted based on zone damper opening sizes). Ratings cover the standard low-pressure forward-curved-blade fans. Ratings for the optional medium-pressure fans are available on request from the factory and cover a range up to approximately 5 in. total static pressure.

ABSORPTION CHILLER

An absorption chiller is shown diagrammatically in Fig. 10-6. This machine consists of two vessels stacked vertically. The upper vessel contains the absorber and evaporator. The lower, smaller vessel contains the condenser, generator, and heat exchanger. The refrigeration effect or chilling takes place in the evaporator. Refrigerant (water) supplied to the evaporator section is sprayed by the refrigerant pump over a tube bundle through which passes the water to be chilled. The refrigerant evaporates on the tube surface. The heat required to evaporate the refrigerant is taken from the water in the tubes, thereby chilling the water. The evaporator is maintained at 0.25 in. of mercury, a pressure low enough that the boiling temperature of the refrigerant is sufficiently low to produce the desired temperature of chilled water.

The pressure of the evaporator is maintained at this desired level by drawing off the refrigerant vapor as it is produced. This vapor is accomplished by locating an absorbent adjacent to the evaporator in the absorber section. The absorbent, called solution, has a great affinity for water vapor and will take this vapor into solution as it is produced. The solution used is lithium bromide brine at about 62% concentration. Lithium bromide is sprayed by the absorber pump into the absorber to provide as large a liquid surface as possible, since the absorption process is one of contact with the water vapor. As the solution falls from the sprays, it contacts and passes through a tube bundle. This bundle cools the solution and removes the heat liberated to the solution when the refrigerant vapor is absorbed and returns to its liquid state. It is through this heat exchange that the heat removed from the chilled water is rejected from the machine and passed to a cooling tower or other heat sink.

As the absorption process continues, the solution in the absorber becomes more dilute, and its tendency is to lose its ability to absorb at the same rate as vapor is produced. Therefore, the absorber solution is replenished with strong solution to maintain the required concentration. An equivalent amount of weak solution from the absorber pan drops down pipe 1 in Fig. 10-6. by gravity and flows through one side of the heat exchanger into the generator, where heat is applied inside a tube bundle from low-pressure steam or hot water. The heat applied raises the weak solution to its boiling point and drives off the water vapor. The solution becomes strong again and flows out of the generator through the other side of the heat exchanger and is drawn into a flow-mixer. It mixes with intermediate-strength solution in the flow-mixer and is pumped back to the absorber to do more work.

The refrigerant vapor driven off in the generator flows into the condenser,

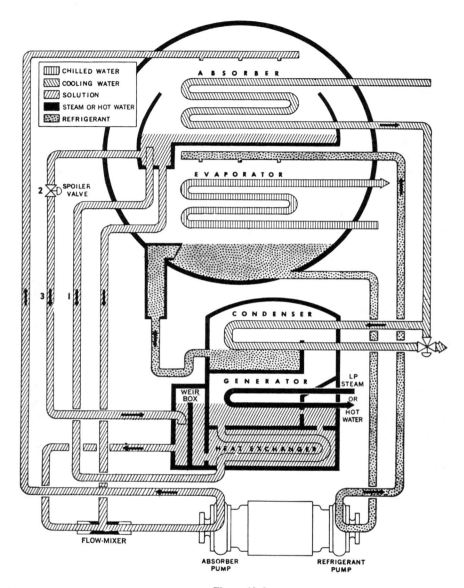

Figure 10-6

where it is condensed. The condensing medium is the same water that was used to cool the solution in the absorber.

The condensed refrigerant accumulates in the condenser pan and is forced by pressure difference back to the evaporator.

The heat exchanger removes heat from the hot strong solution, which must be cooled to work in the absorber, and transfers it to the weak solution, which must be heated before it can be concentrated.

The cycle is now complete, and the process will continue as long as heat is available and flows are maintained.

SIMPLIFIED CONTROL SYSTEM

Spoiler-valve capacity control. The machine is controlled by matching the absorber capacity to the chiller load. Absorber capacity is varied by modulating its mean solution concentration. This concentration is controlled by varying the amount of strong solution that may be withdrawn from the generator. The flow-mixer is a constant flow device and takes whatever solution is available from the weir box. When less than full capacity is required, weak solution from the absorber is bled into the weir box. This weak solution displaces the strong solution, preventing the strong solution from flowing into the flow-mixer. The end result is a weakening of the absorber-solution strength. This "spoilage" is accomplished by modulating a valve (2) in the bleed line (3) in accordance with leaving chilled water temperature.

Head-pressure regulation. The chiller does not require constant cooling water inlet temperature and can easily tolerate the temperature fluctuations normally encountered with cooling-tower operation. Instead, control is from the temperature of the water leaving the condenser so as to maintain a reasonably constant condensing pressure. To accomplish this, cooling water is automatically bypassed around the condenser.

Inherent generator regulation. The generator output is inherently limited by the rate of withdrawal of strong solution. As the rate of withdrawal is reduced, as occurs at part-load conditions, the strong solution in the generator increases in concentration. This reduces the available temperature difference between the boiling strong solution and the condensing steam and so reduces the heat being put into the system. At the same time, the cooling water regulation described previously tends to maintain constant condensing pressure. This, in turn, limits the extent to which the solution increases in concentration. Crystallization is not required to take place in the generator in order to permit operation at part load, even though no throttle is applied to the inlet stream.

The condensate leaving the generator is subcooled in the generator. The discharge is automatically controlled by a temperature-regulating valve so that condensate finally leaves subcooled to a temperature of 200° to 210°F. Heat produced by this subcooling is put to beneficial use in the generator, rather than being wasted in an external flash cooler or other device.

11

HVAC GRAPHIC SYMBOLS

The purpose of an HVAC drawing is to show the location of air-handling and other HVAC equipment; the sizes and routes of the various ductwork (both supply and return air); the air outlets, including the volume and velocity of air from each; and other necessary information required in a duct system. Furthermore, water circulating lines or controls and other pertinent information may be found. In the preparation of such drawings, symbols are used to simply the draftman's work and to save time. Figures 11-1 and 11-2 illustrate this.

Figures 11-3 through 11-54 show HVAC symbols along with a practical application.

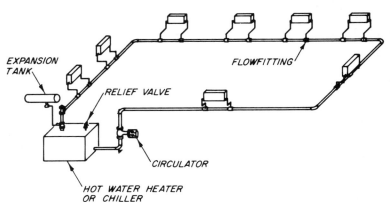

EXPANSION TANK

FLOWFITTING

RELIEF VALVE

CIRCULATOR

HOT WATER HEATER OR CHILLER

Figure 11-1 Pictorial drawing of a heating system.

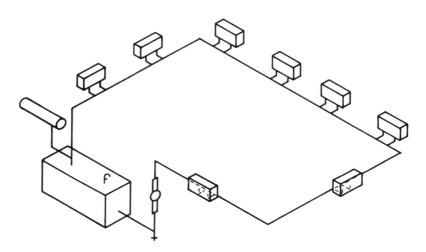

Figure 11-2   Pictorial drawing of a heating system using symbols and simplified lines.

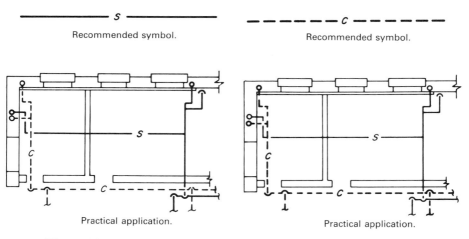

Figure 11-3   Steam pipes.   **Figure 11-4**   Condensate return pipe.

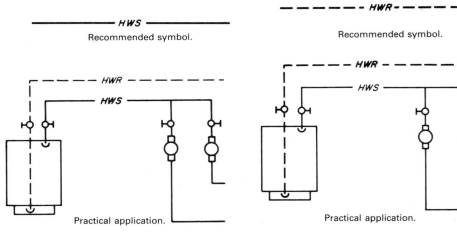

Figure 11-5   Hot-water supply pipe.

Figure 11-6   Hot-water return pipe.

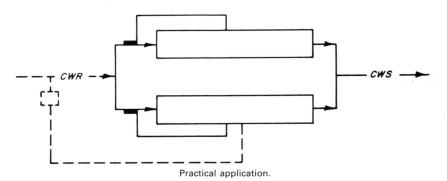

Figure 11-7   Chilled-water supply pipe.

— — — — — · *CWR* · — — — — —

Recommended symbol.

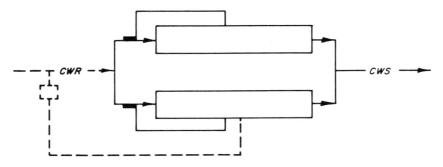

Practical application.

Figure 11-8   Chilled-water return pipe.

———————— *HCS* ————————

Recommended symbol.

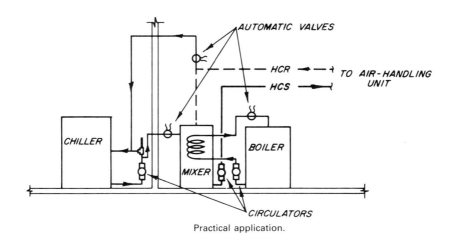

Practical application.

Figure 11-9   Combination hot- and chilled-water supply pipe.

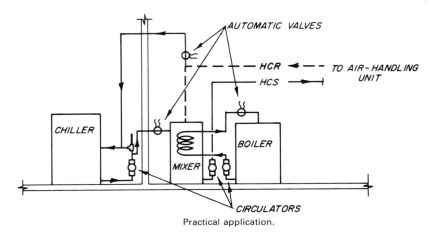

Figure 11-10   Combination hot- and chilled-water return pipe.

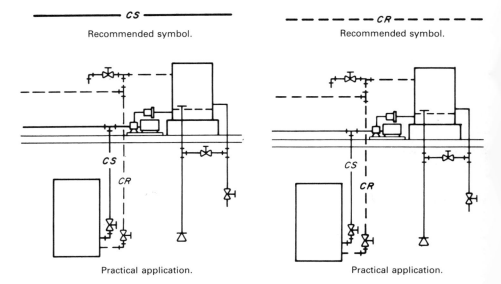

Figure 11-11   Condenser water supply pipe.   **Figure 11-12**   Condenser water return pipe.

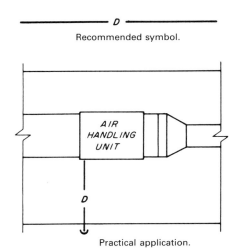

Recommended symbol.

Practical application.

Figure 11-13   Drain pipe from cooling coil.

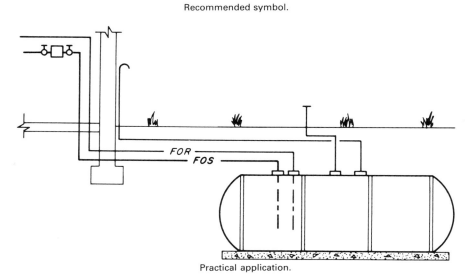

Recommended symbol.

Practical application.

Figure 11-14   Fuel oil supply pipe.

FOR

Recommended symbol.

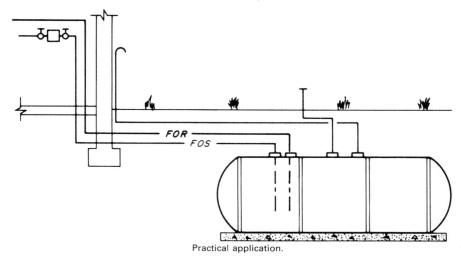

Practical application.

Figure 11-15   Fuel oil return pipe.

R

Recommended symbol.

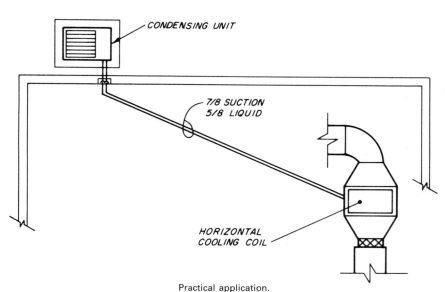

Practical application.

Figure 11-16   Refrigerant pipe.

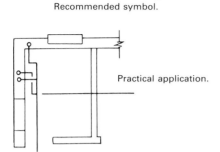

Figure 11-17 Pipe rising.

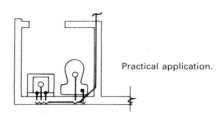

Figure 11-18 Pipe turning down.

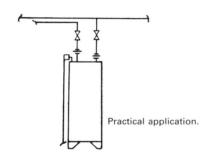

Figure 11-19 Union.

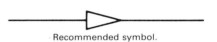

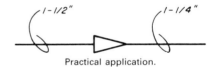

Figure 11-20 Reducer-concentric.

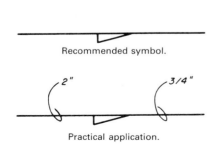

Figure 11-21 Reducer-eccentric.

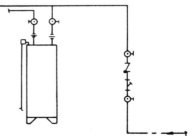

Figure 11-22 Strainer.

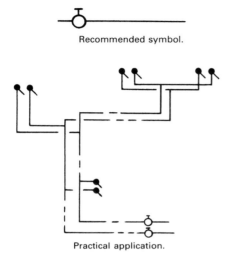

Figure 11-23   Gate valve.

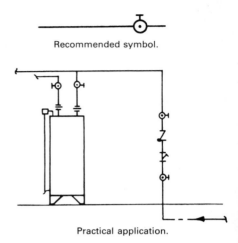

Figure 11-24   Globe valve.

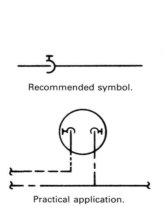

Figure 11-25   Valve in riser.

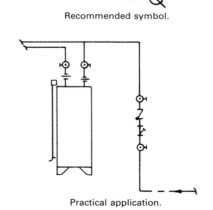

Figure 11-26   Check valve.

Recommended symbol.

Recommended symbol.

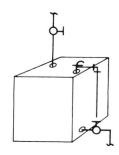

Practical application.

Figure 11-27   Pressure-reducing valve.

Practical application.

Figure 11-28   Pressure-relief valve.

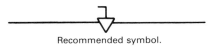

Recommended symbol.

Recommended symbol.

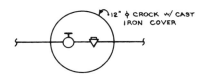

Practical application.

Figure 11-29   Square head cock.

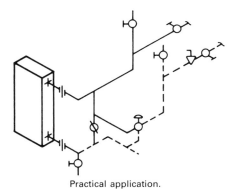

Practical application.

Figure 11-30   Balancing valve.

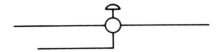

Recommended symbol.

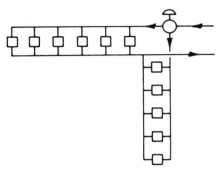

Practical application.

Figure 11-31 Three-way control valve.

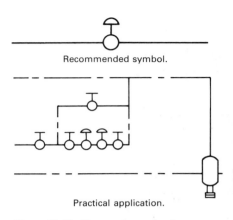

Recommended symbol.

Practical application.

Figure 11-32 Two-way control valve.

Recommended symbol.

Practical application.

Figure 11-33 Pipe pitched minimum 1″/40′.

Recommended symbol.

Figure 11-34 Anchor location.

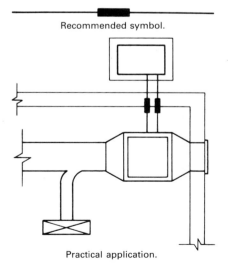

Recommended symbol.

Practical application.

Figure 11-35 Flexible pipe connection.

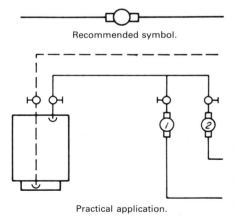

Recommended symbol.

Practical application.

Figure 11-36 In-line pump.

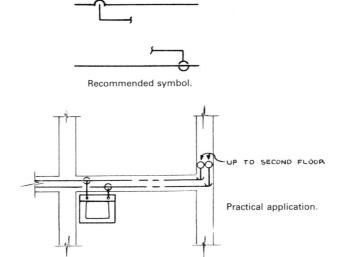

Recommended symbol.

Practical application.

Figure 11-37   Top and bottom takeoff.

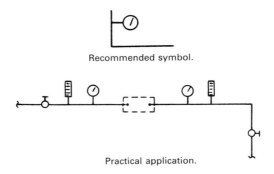

Recommended symbol.

Practical application.

Figure 11-38   Pressure gauge.

Recommended symbol.

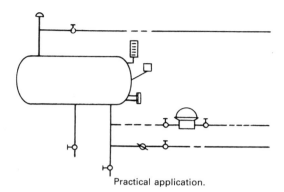

Practical application.

Figure 11-39   Thermometer.

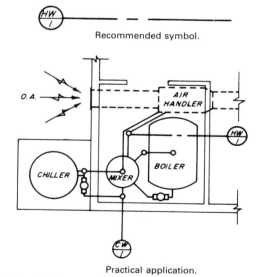

Practical application.

Figure 11-40   Hot-water riser.

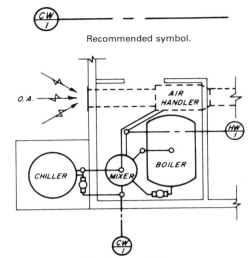

Recommended symbol.

Practical application.

Figure 11-41 Chilled-water riser.

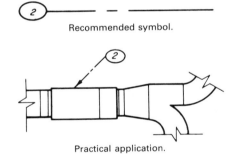

Recommended symbol.

Practical application.

Figure 11-42 Fan-coil unit.

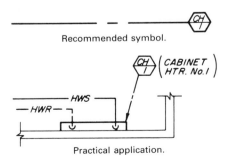

Recommended symbol.

Practical application.

Figure 11-43 Equipment as indicated.

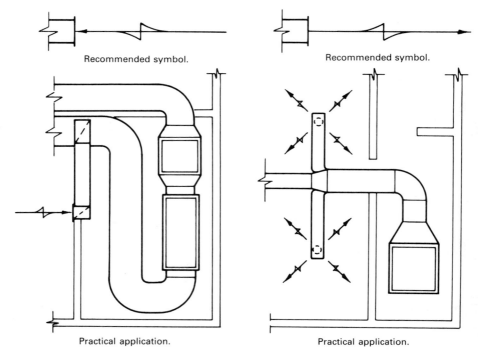

Recommended symbol.

Practical application.

Figure 11-44 Air into register.

Recommended symbol.

Practical application.

Figure 11-45 Air out of register.

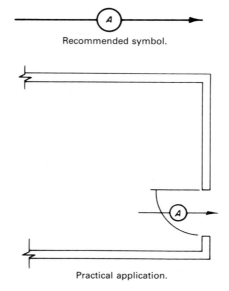

Recommended symbol.

Practical application.

Figure 11-46 Airflow through undercut or louvered door.

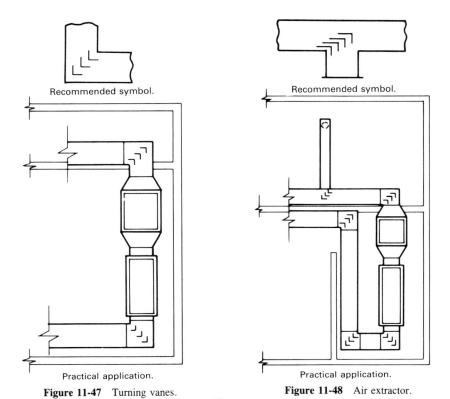

Recommended symbol.

Practical application.

Figure 11-47 Turning vanes.

Recommended symbol.

Practical application.

Figure 11-48 Air extractor.

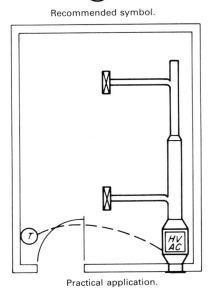

Recommended symbol.

Practical application.

Figure 11-49 Various kinds of thermostats.

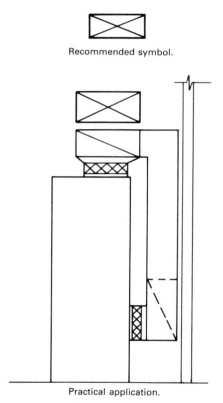

Recommended symbol.

Practical application.

Figure 11-50 Supply-air duct system.

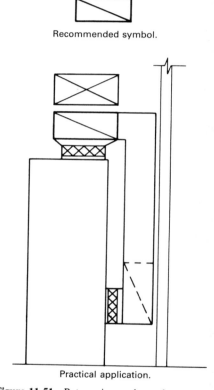

Recommended symbol.

Practical application.

Figure 11-51 Return-air or exhaust duct system.

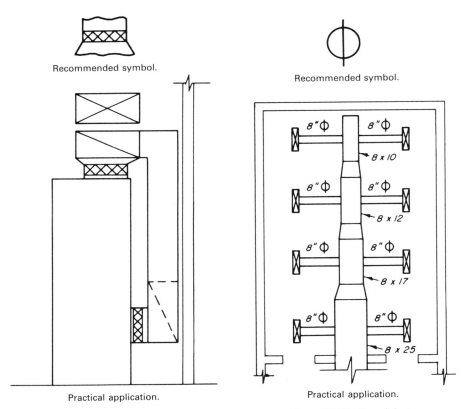

Recommended symbol.

Practical application.

Figure 11-52 Flexible duct connection.

Recommended symbol.

Practical application.

Figure 11-53 Round duct.

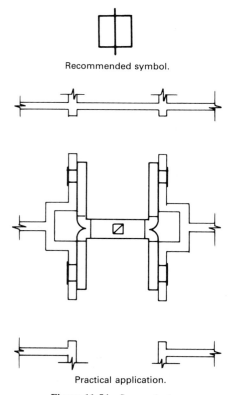

Recommended symbol.

Practical application.

Figure 11-54 Square duct.

12

ELECTRICITY BASICS

Many different electrical power supplies are encountered while working with motor controls. The type supplied is dependent on either the power company's distribution network and transformer hook-up or else the manufacturing plant's generation system.

Electric power is normally distributed at high voltages for economical reasons; that is, the higher the voltage, the smaller wire size required to carry the same amount of power. The power company uses transformers at the generators to step up the voltage for cross-country distribution, and then transformers are again used at substations or at the point of utilization to step the voltage down to the amount required. Most of the power is generated as three phase, with one of the phases used to obtain single phase.

From a practical standpoint, those involved with motor controls need only be concerned with the power supply on the secondary (usage) side of the transformer, as this determines the characteristic of the power supply for use in the building or on the premises.

Two general arrangements of transformers and secondaries are in common use. The first arrangement is the sectional form, in which a unit of load, such as one city street or city block, is served by a fixed length of secondary, with the transformer located in the middle. The second arrangement is the continuous form in which the secondary is installed in one long continuous run, with transformers spaced along it at the most suitable points. As the load grows or shifts, the transformers spaced along it can be moved or rearranged, if desired. In sectional arrangement, such a load can be cared for only by changing to a larger size of transformer or installing an additional unit in the same section.

One of the greatest advantages of the secondary bank is that the starting currents of motors are divided among transformers, reducing voltage drop and also diminishing the resulting lamp flicker at the various outlets.

Power companies all over the United States and Canada are now trying to incorporate networks into their secondary power systems, especially in areas where a high degree of service reliability is necessary. Around cities and industrial applications, most secondary circuits are three phase, either 120/208 V or 480/208 V and wye-connected. Usually, two to four primary feeders are run into the area, and transformers are connected alternately to them. The feeders are interconnected in a grid, or network, so that if any feeder goes out of service the load is still carried by the remaining feeders.

The primary feeders supplying networks are run from substations at the usual primary voltage for the system, such as 4160, 4800, 6900, or 13,200 V. Higher voltages are practicable if the loads are large enough to warrant them.

COMMON POWER SUPPLIES

The most common power supply used for residential and small commercial applications is the 120/240 V, single-phase service; it is used primarily for light and power, including single-phase motors up to about $7\frac{1}{2}$ hp. A diagram of this service is shown in Fig. 12-1.

Four-wire delta-connected secondaries (Fig. 12-2) and four-wire, wye-connected secondaries (Fig. 12-3) are common around industrial and large commercial applications.

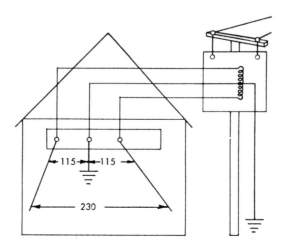

Figure 12-1   Single-phase three-wire, 120/240V service. (Courtesy Borg-Warner Air Conditioning)

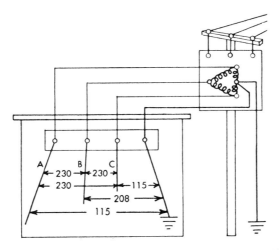

Figure 12-2 Four-wire delta-connected secondary. (Courtesy Borg-Warner Air Conditioning)

TRANSFORMERS

The main purpose of a power transformer is to obtain a voltage supply that is different from the main voltage available. A transformer's capacity is rated in kilovolt-amperes (kVA). A transformer must be designed for the frequency (hertz, Hz) of the system involved.

To obtain a certain voltage when the available supply is other than the voltage required, either a step-up or step-down transformer may be used, depending on the

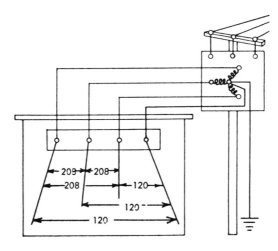

Figure 12-3 Four-wire, Wye-connected secondary. (Courtesy Borg-Warner Air Conditioning)

circumstance. Each type is interchangeable; that is, primary and secondary windings may be reversed.

When selecting transformers, determine the supply line voltage, load voltage requirement, and the load amperage requirement. Then consult manufacturers' catalogs and/or manufacturers' representatives for a specific selection.

At times it may be necessary to obtain a relatively small voltage correction when dealing with motors and motor controls. For example, a motor rated for 240 V may be connected to a 208-V power supply. To obtain this additional voltage, a buck and boost transformer may be used. In our examples, it is used to boost the voltage. If the reverse were true (a 208-V motor used on a 240-V supply), the transformer would be used to buck the voltage (lower it).

In general, a buck and boost transformer is a four-winding isolated transformer designed so that the independent windings may be interconnected to function as an autotransformer. Connected in this manner, all power for the load must pass through the transformer windings as shown in Fig. 12-4. Then, by proper interconnection of the windings, the output voltage may be increased or decreased from the input voltage depending on the ratio between the primary and secondary windings.

Connected as an autotransformer, the largest part of the power goes directly to the load, with only that part bucking or boosting being involved in transformation. See Fig. 12-5. If, say, only 10% of the voltage must undergo transformation, the autotransformer rating is increased approximately 10 times the normal rating of the corresponding isolated transformer.

An approximate transformer size can be determined by multiplying the volts (buck or boost) times the load amperes. This can only be an approximation due to the wide requirement for voltage change and the amperage used. It is possible for this method to exceed the transformer rating.

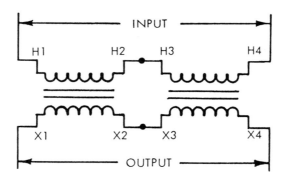

Figure 12-4   Buck and boost transformer. (Courtesy Borg-Warner Air Conditioning)

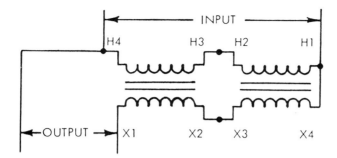

Figure 12-5 Autotransformer. (Courtesy Borg-Warner Air Conditioning)

CONTROL CIRCUIT TRANSFORMERS

Low-voltage control circuit transformers (class 2) are used extensively in control circuits to obtain a lower voltage than is available from the power supply. For example, many control circuits operate at 24 V, and normally 120 V is the lowest voltage used in any electrical system for building construction. Therefore, a transformer is used to reduce the 120-V circuit to the required 24 V. In selecting such a transformer, class 2 low-voltage control systems are limited to transformers with a maximum output capacity of 75 VA (watts). If a control transformer is overloaded for any great length of time, the transformer will fail. Therefore, systems that require the addition of controls should be checked to assure that the rating of the transformer is not exceeded. A typical control circuit is shown in Fig. 12-6, showing the load of the holding coils, which totals 22 VA. Since a 45-VA transformer is used, 23 VA (45 minus 22) is available for additional field-installed controls.

MOTOR STARTERS

A motor starter provides a means to make and break all power supply lines running to a motor and also provides motor overload protection. A typical motor starter is shown in Fig. 12-7.

The main purpose of the overload protection is to protect the motor and its controls from overheating due to motor overloads. Such protection should be selected to trip at not more than 125% full-load motor current for hermetic compressor motors and also motors with a temperature rise of not over 40°C. When the value specified for motor overcurrent protection does not correspond to a standard-sized protector, the next higher rating may be used, but not greater than 140% of full-load current rating.

For all other motors, the trip should be selected at not more than 115% full-load motor current, except where the value specified does not correspond to a

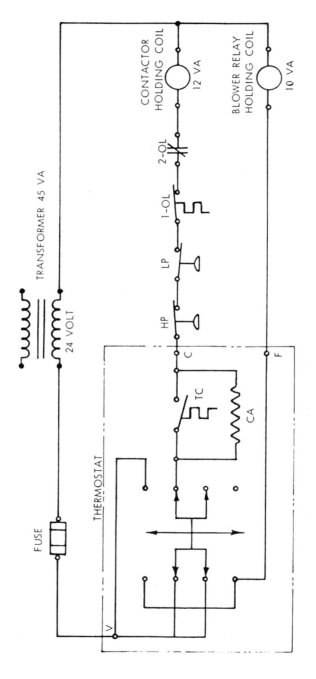

Figure 12-6 Typical control circuit. (Courtesy Borg-Warner Air Conditioning)

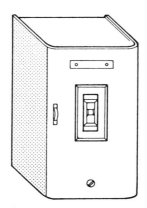

Figure 12-7 Typical motor starter. (Courtesy Borg-Warner Air Conditioning)

standard-sized protector. Then the next higher rating may be used, but not greater than 130% of full-load current rating.

The motor starter is also rated in amperes or horsepower and must be selected with a capacity rating greater than the load in which it serves. If a motor load is only slightly less than the rated capacity of the starter, a longer contact life can be obtained by selecting the next size larger starter.

Motor starters are normally available with two-, three-, or 4-pole contacts. The holding coil may be for use with line voltage or 24-V controls circuits. The schematic drawing in Fig. 12-8 demonstrates the operation of a motor starter. Starting at the top of the drawing, note that the power circuit is protected with a fused disconnect switch and that three-phase is used to power the motor. This power supply runs through the motor starter prior to connecting to the motor itself. Note that this particular starter has four poles, but only three are being used.

The drawing in Fig. 12-8 represents a control circuit for an air-conditioning system. The holding coil, which controls making and breaking the contacts, is connected in series with the thermostat and safety controls. When the thermostat closes and all safety control contacts are closed, the holding coil is energized, closing the starter contacts and supplying power to the compressor motor. When the thermostat is satisfied, its contact opens to de-energize the holding coil and interrupt the power supply to the compressor. If any one of the power legs should exceed the current rating of the overload element, the corresponding overload contact opens to de-energize the holding coil. The extra starter contact in this control could be used for control of a remote motor such as a cooling tower pump or the like.

The VA requirement of the holding coil varies depending on the type, size, and manufacturer of the starter. Typical holding coil ratings are as follows:

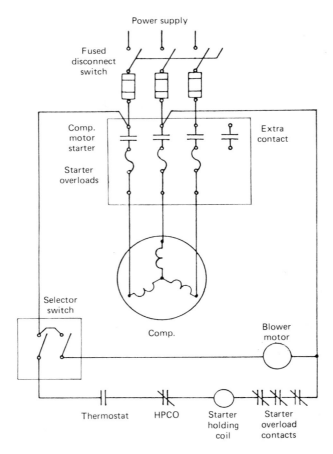

Figure 12-8 Schematic showing the operation of a motor starter. (Courtesy Borg-Warner Air Conditioning)

30 amperes: 9 to 11 VA

60 amperes: 17 to 20 VA

To select a motor starter, in general, first obtain the motor characteristics from manufacturer's data or from the nameplate on the motor. For example, assume a 5-hp motor with a full-load ampere rating of 17.4 at 240 V. Checking in a typical motor control catalog, a NEMA size 1 starter (for 5-hp motor) would be chosen. Overload elements are then selected to trip at 21.8 A (1.25 × 17.4). The holding coil could be rated at full line voltage or 240 V. If the motor is designed for three-phase operation, at least a three-pole starter should be utilized; a two-pole starter would suffice for a single-phase motor.

CONTACTORS

The purpose of contactors is to provide a means to make and break all power supply lines running to a load. In the case of electric motors, the load is inductive. Contactors must be selected with a capacity rating greater than the load that they serve. If a load is only slightly less than the rated capacity of the contactor, a longer contact life can be obtained by selecting the next size larger contactor, and this is recommended when specifying definite-purpose devices.

The contactor holding coil may be for either line voltage or low-voltage control circuits, depending on the application. Starters are available with two, three, or four contacts for various applications. For example, refer to Fig. 12-9, where a four-pole contactor is utilized. Note that the contacts are connected in series with the power supply to the load. The holding coil, which controls the making and

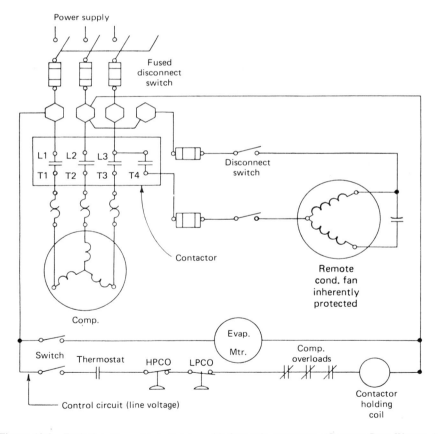

Figure 12-9 Typical system wiring diagram with four-pole contractor. (Courtesy Borg-Warner Air Conditioning)

breaking of the contacts, is connected in series in the control circuit with the thermostat and safety controls. When the thermostat closes and all safety control contacts are closed, the holding coil is energized, closing the contacts of the contactor to supply power to the load. Once the thermostat is satisfied, its contact opens to de-energize the holding coil, which interrupts the power supply to the load. The extra fourth contact is used to control the power supply to a small remote motor operating a condenser fan.

The VA requirement of the holding coil varies depending on the type, size, and manufacturer of the contactor. Typical ratings are in the range from 9 to 20 VA.

PROTECTOR RELAY (LOCKOUT) CONTROL CIRCUIT

The purpose of the lockout relay in a control circuit is to prevent a certain motor from operating out of sequence due to the opening and closing of the control circuit by any of the automatic reset safety controls. If the lockout relay has been activated, the system may be reset for normal operation only by interrupting the power supply to the control circuit either by the thermostat (in the case of a HVAC system) or by the main power switch.

In the circuit in Fig. 12-10, the coil, due to its high resistance, is not energized during normal operation. However, when any one of the safety controls opens the circuit to the compressor contactor coil, current flows through the lockout relay coil, causing it to become energized and to open its contact. This contact then remains open, keeping the compressor contactor circuit open until the power is interrupted either by the thermostat or the main power switch after the safety control has reset. Performance depends on the resistance of the lockout relay coil being much greater than the resistance of the compressor contactor coil. If the lockout relay becomes defective, it should be replaced with an exact duplicate to maintain the proper resistance balance.

It is permissible to add a control relay coil in parallel with the contactor coil when a system demands another control. The resistance of the contactor coil and the relay coil in parallel decreases the total resistance and does not affect the operation of the lockout relay. However, never put additional lockout relays, lights, or other load devices in parallel with the lockout relay coil.

TIME-DELAY RELAY

The purpose of the time-delay relay is to delay, for a predetermined length of time after the control system has been energized, the normal operation of a control or group of controls. The length of delay depends on the time built into the relay coil and may vary from a fraction of a second to several minutes.

Electrical systems utilizing several motors may use such a delay device to

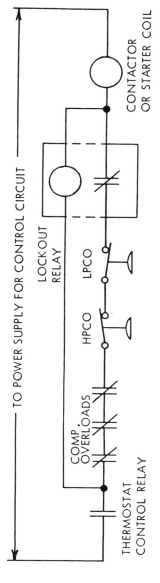

Figure 12-10 Control circuit with lockout relay. (Courtesy Borg-Warner Air Conditioning)

179

start the motors one at a time to limit inrush current. For example, the schematic drawing in Fig. 12-11 shows four compressor control circuits with time-delay relays for sequencing the starting of each. In this design, if all three stages of the thermostat are closed and electrical power is supplied to the units, compressor contactor coil 1 and the time-delay coil 1 become energized to start the compressor 1. After the specified time delay, the contacts of time delay relay 1 close to energize compressor contactor coil 2 and time delay coil 2, which starts compressor 2, and so on, until all four compressors are in operation.

Another application of time-delay relays is on HVAC systems with air-cooled condensers operating with zero-degree low-ambient accessories. A time-delay relay may be used, for example, to bypass the automatic low-pressure cutout for a sufficient length of time to permit the suction pressure to build up and close the contacts of the cutout.

DISCONNECT SWITCH

Every motor circuit must have a disconnect switch to disconnect the power supply from the motor for complete shutdown or servicing of the unit. The disconnect also provides a means of overcurrent protection for the electrical conductors and controls in the circuit.

Each motor must have a disconnect switch and this switch must be readily accessible to the load that it serves. Disconnect switches are rated in amperes and horsepower, and each should be selected with a capacity rating greater than that of the load it serves The recommended switch rating is 125% of the full-load motor current. Therefore, if a motor has a full-load ampere rating of, say, 20.5 A, the switch should be rated at $20.5 \times 1.25 = 25.62$ A. The smallest disconnect switch now made is rated for 30 A, so this would suffice for this load in question.

When circuit protection is not required at the motor location, nonfusible disconnects are available at a lower price than the fusible types. Two-pole disconnects are used on single-phase circuits, and three-pole disconnects are used for three-phase circuits.

When circuit protection is desired, fuses are utilized to protect the electrical circuit from damage due to high or dangerous temperatures resulting from excessive current. Two types are common: the plug fuse and the cartridge fuse.

The plug fuse is rated only to 30 A and to 125 V and may be used only on very small motors. It screws into a conventional Edison base bulb holder.

Several types of cartridge fuses are currently in use. The two major physical characteristics are the contact fuse with end caps and the type with blades. The type with end caps is rated from 0 to 60 A and from 0 to 600 V. The blade types are rated from around 70 to 600 A and from 0 to 600 V.

Besides the outside physical characteristics of cartridge fuses, they also differ internally. The one-time cartridge fuse has a permanently connected fuse link, and

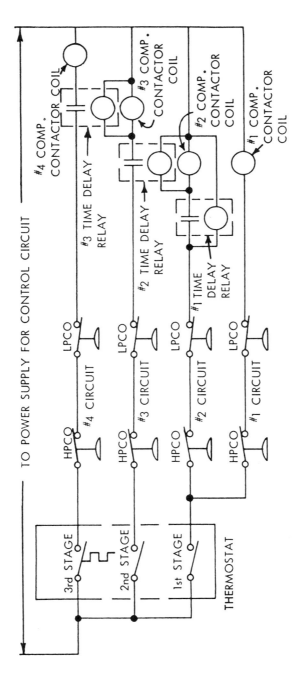

Figure 12-11 Schematic showing four compressor control circuits with time-delay relays. (Courtesy Borg-Warner Air Conditioning)

when this link opens, it must be discarded. Renewable-link fuses are similar, but they have replaceable fuse links. Therefore, when the link opens, it may be replaced with a new one.

For motor applications, the dual-element fuse (either plug or cartridge type) is the recommended type in most cases. This type of fuse has a fusible link and also a thermal cutout connected in series. The fusibile link protects against short circuits, while the thermal cutout protects against overloads. When a motor is started, higher amperage occurs in the circuit than during normal running operation. Therefore, a long time lag built into the fuse prevents opening the circuit on a normal motor start-up.

Fuse ratings are based on the current that trips the thermal cutout. Their use permits selecting a smaller fuse size to afford close overload protection, yet provides trip-free motor starting current. The *National Electric Code®* and manufacturers' catalogs provide the recommended maximum fuse sizes for each application.

SOLENOID VALVE

A solenoid valve is used in liquid lines and is electrically opened or closed to control the flow of the fluid. It is commonly used in manufacturing processes, in the liquid line to an evaporator to control the flow of refrigerant in an HVAC system, and in other uses.

In most cases, the solenoid coil opens the valve when energized and allows the valve to close when de-energized. It almost always operates at line voltage since the VA rating is normally too large for a 24-V control system.

When the control circuit is energized, the relay contacts close to supply power to the solenoid coil, which causes the valve to open. When the control circuit is de-energized, the relay contacts open to interrupt the power supplying the coil, causing the valve to close.

In selecting solenoid valves, the following must be determined:

1. Fluid to be controlled
2. Quantity of fluid valve must allow to flow
3. Allowable pressure drop
4. Maximum operating pressure differential
5. Maximum working pressure
6. Electrical characteristics for coil operation

A typical schematic wiring diagram for a solenoid valve is shown in Fig. 12-12.

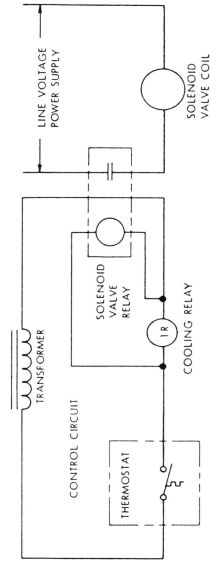

Figure 12-12 Typical schematic wiring diagram for a solenoid valve. (Courtesy Borg-Warner Air Conditioning)

ELECTRICAL LINE CURRENT CAPACITY

Electrical conductors must be sized according to the *National Electric Code®* and good wiring practices. Besides the information given in tables as to the amperes allowed to flow through any given wire size, the wire should also be sized to limit the voltage drop to a maximum of 2% in any electrical circuit. This ensures efficient operation of both controls and equipment.

Even when sizing wire for low-voltage (24-V) systems, the voltage drop should be limited to 3% because excessive voltage drop causes:

1. Failure to control coil to activate
2. Control contact chatter
3. Erratic operation of controls
4. Control coil burnout
5. Contact burnout

A table that may be used to size low-voltage wire is shown in Fig. 12-13. To use, assume a load of 35 VA with a 50-ft run for a 24-V control circuit. Referring to the table, scan the 50-ft column. Note that No. 18 AWG wire will carry 29 VA and No. 16 wire will carry 43 VA while still maintaining a maximum of 3% voltage drop. In this case, No. 16 wire would be the size to use.

When the length of wire is other than listed in the table, the capacity may be determined by the following equation:

$$\text{VA capacity} = \frac{\text{length of circuit (from table)}}{\text{length of circuit (actual)}} \times \text{VA (from table)}$$

The 3% voltage drop limitation is imposed to assure proper operation when the power supply is below the rated voltage. For example, if the rated 240-V supply is 10% low (216 V), the transformer does not produce 24 V but rather 21.6 V. When normal voltage drop is taken from this 21.6 V, it approaches the lower operating limit of most controls. If it is assured that the primary voltage to the

AWG Wire Size	Length of Circuit, One Way (ft)											
	25	50	75	100	125	150	175	200	225	250	275	300
20	29	14	10	7.2	5.8	4.8	4.1	3.6	3.2	2.9	2.6	2.4
18	58	29	19	14	11	9.6	8.2	7.2	6.4	5.8	5.2	4.8
16	86	43	29	22	17	14	12	11	9.6	8.7	7.8	7.2
14	133	67	44	33	27	22	19	17	15	13	12	11

Figure 12-13 Table that may be used to size low-voltage wire. (Courtesy Borg-Warner Air Conditioning)

transformer will always be at rated value or above, the control circuit will operate satisfactorily with more than a 3% voltage drop.

In most installations, several lines connect the transformer to the control circuit. One line usually carries the full load of the control circuit from the hot side of the transformer to one control with the return, perhaps through several lines of the various other controls. Therefore, the line from the hot side of the transformer is the most critical regarding voltage drop and VA capacity and must be properly sized.

When low-voltage lines are installed, it is suggested that one extra line be run for emergency purposes. This can be substituted for any one of the existing lines that may become defective. Also it is possible to parallel this extra line with the existing line carrying the full load of the control circuit if the length of run affects control operation caused by voltage drop. In many cases this will reduce the voltage drop and permit satisfactory operation.

CONTROL RELAY

In general, the purpose of a control relay is to energize or de-energize an electrical circuit to obtain a specific operation of a component. It may be used to control a motor, heater, solenoid valve, or another relay.

In selecting a control relay, determine the voltage to be applied to the coil. Then determine the voltage and current characteristics of the load to be controlled by the contacts and whether the load is resistive or inductive. Determine the coil VA rating (this is especially important on low-voltage systems) and then consult a manufacturer's catalog to select a relay to meet the requirements.

TEMPERATURE CONTROLS

Low-voltage thermostats are available to provide many different combinations of control.

1. One- or two-stage cooling
2. One- or two-stage heating
3. Manual or automatic changeover between cooling and heating
4. Constant or automatic fan operation

Any combination of these operations may be incorporated into a single thermostat.

Figure 12-14 shows a two-stage cool, two-stage heat thermostat circuit with automatic changeover. During installation, conductors are to be connected to the terminals as shown in this diagram. While studying this drawing, note that a jumper is connected between terminals V and M to use a single low-voltage power supply for both cooling and heating. If two low-voltage power supplies were used instead of one, this jumper may be removed. The cooling power supply may then be

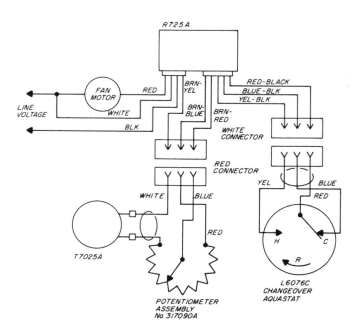

Figure 12-14 Wiring diagram of an HVAC control system containing a changeover aquastat.

connected to terminal V and the heating power supply to terminal M.

A cold anticipator, consisting of a small resistance heater located on the thermostat, introduces artificial heat to the sensing element when the cooling contact is open and not calling for cooling. In use, the thermostat reacts to the space temperature and artificial heat to return the cooling unit to the ON cycle sooner than normal. The cold anticipator causes the thermostat to cycle more often and thereby maintain a more even space temperature. The size of the heater is determined by the resistance of the other controls that are in series with it.

For longer OFF periods, an anticipator may be used with a higher amperage range, and for shorter periods in the OFF mode, an anticipator with a lower amperage range may be used.

A heat anticipator is a small resistance heater located in the thermostat that introduces artificial heat to the sensing element when the heating contact is closed (calling for heat). In use, the thermostat reacts to the space temperature and the artificial heat to turn off the heating supply sooner than normal to minimize over-heating and thereby maintain a more even space temperature.

The heater size (amperage range) is determined by the resistance of the other controls that are in series with it. In most cases, the amperage rating of the heater should match the amperage rating of the primary control. For longer ON periods, an anticipator should be used with a higher amperage range. For shorter ON periods, an anticipator with a lower amperage range should be used.

Appendix A

GLOSSARY

A

Accessible: Capable of being removed or exposed without damaging the building structure or finish, or not permanently closed in by the structure or finish of the building.
Air cleaner: Device used for removal of airborne impurities.
Air diffuser: Air-distribution outlet designed to direct airflow into desired patterns.
Ambient temperature: Temperature of fluid (usually air) that surrounds an object on all sides.
Antisiphon trap: Trap in a drainage system designed to preserve a water seal by defeating siphonage.
Automatic: Self-acting, operating by its own mechanism when actuated by some impersonal influence, such as a change in current strength, pressure, temperature, or mechanical configuration.

B

Back pressure: Pressure in the low side of a refrigerating system; also called suction pressure or low-side pressure.
Barometer: Instrument for measuring atmospheric pressure.
Beam: Horizontal member of wood, reinforced concrete, steel, or other material used to span the space between posts, columns, girders, or over an opening in a wall.

Boiler: Closed container in which a liquid may be heated and vaporized.

Boiling point: Temperature at which a liquid boils or generates bubbles of vapor when heated.

British thermal unit (Btu):   Quantity of heat required to raise the temperature of 1 point of water 1 degree fahrenheit.

Burner: Device in which combustion of fuel takes place.

Butane: Liquid hydrocarbon commonly used as fuel for heating purposes.

Bypass: Passage at one side of or around a regular passage.

C

Calorie: Heat required to raise temperature of 1 gram of water 1 degree Celsius.

Carbon dioxide: Compound of carbon and oxygen that is sometimes used as a refrigerant.

Carbon filter: Air filter using activated carbon as air-cleansing agent.

Celsius: The metric system's temperature scale (replaces centigrade scale). Freezing point of water is 0 degrees; boiling point is 100 degrees.

Centigrade scale: Obsolete temperature scale.

Chase: Recess in inner face of masonry wall providing space for pipes and/or ducts.

Check valve: Device that permits fluid flow only in one direction.

Chimney effect: Tendency of air or gas to rise when heated.

Code installation: Installation that conforms to local and/or national codes for safe and efficient installation.

Comfort zone: Area on psychrometric chart that shows conditions of temperature, humidity, and sometimes air movement in which most people are comfortable.

Compressor: The pump of a refrigerating mechanism that draws a vacuum or low pressure on the cooling side of a refrigerant cycle and squeezes or compresses the gas into the high pressure or condensing side of the cycle.

Control, temperature: Thermostatic device that automatically stops and starts a motor, the operation of which is based on temperature changes.

Cooling tower: Device that cools water by evaporation in air. Water is cooled to the wet bulb temperature of air.

Crawl space: Shallow space between the first tier of beams and the ground (no basement).

Critical temperature: Temperature at which vapor and liquid have the same properties.

Cycle: Interval of time during which a sequence or a recurring succession of events is completed.

D

Damper: Valve for controlling airflow.

Density: Closeness of texture or consistency.

Draft gauge: Instrument used to measure air movement.

Draft indicator: Instrument used to indicate or measure chimney draft or combustion gas movement.

Duct: Tube or channel through which air is conveyed or moved.

Duct, continuous: Service requirement that demands operation at a substantially constant load for an indefinitely long time.

Duty, intermittent: Service requirement that demands operation for alternate intervals of load and no load; load and rest; or load, no load, and rest.

E

Effective temperature: Overall effect on a person of air temperature, humidity, and air movement.

Electric heating: House heating system in which heat from electrical resistance units is used to heat rooms.

Electric water valve: Solenoid type (electrically operated) valve used to turn water flow on and off.

Elevation: Drawing showing the projection of a building on a vertical plane.

Enclosed: Surrounded by a case that will prevent anyone from accidentally touching live parts.

Equipment: General term including material, fittings, devices, appliances, fixtures, apparatus, and the like used as part of, or in connection with, an electrical installation.

Evaporation: Changing of a liquid to a gas. Heat is absorbed in this process.

Evaporator: Part of a refrigerating mechanism in which the refrigerant vaporizes and absorbs heat.

Expansion valve: Device in a refrigerating system that maintains a pressure difference between the high side and low side and is operated by pressure.

F

Fan: Radial or axial flow device used for moving or producing artificial currents of air.

Filter: Porous article through which a gas or liquid is passed to separate out matter in suspension; a circuit or devices that pass one frequency or frequency band while blocking others, or vice versa.

Firebrick: Brick made to withstand high temperatures that is used for lining chimneys, incinerators, and similar structures.

Fireproof wood: Chemically treated wood; fire-resistive; used where incombustible materials are required.

Flapper valve: Type of valve used in refrigeration compressors that allows gaseous refrigerants to flow in only one direction.

Flash point: Lowest temperature at which vapors above a volatile combustible substance ignite in air when exposed to flame.

Flooding: Act of filling a space with a liquid.

Flow Meter: Instrument used to measure velocity or volume of fluid movement.

Forced convection: Movement of fluid by mechanical force such as fans or pumps.

G

Gas: Vapor phase or state of substance.

H

Head pressure: Pressure that exists in the condensing side of a refrigerating system.

Heat: Added energy that causes substances to rise in temperature; energy associated with random motion of molecules.

Heat exchanger: Device used to transfer heat from a warm or hot surface to a cold or cooler surface. Evaporators and condensers are heat exchangers.

Heating value: Amount of heat that may be obtained by burning a fuel; usually expressed in Btu per pound or gallon.

Heat load: Amount of heat, measured in Btu, that is removed during a period of 24 hours.

Heat of compression: Mechanical energy of pressure transformed into heat energy.

Heat pressure control: Pressure-operated control that opens an electrical circuit if high-side pressure becomes excessive.

Heat pump: Compression cycle system used to supply heat to a temperature-controlled space, which can also remove heat from the same space.

Heat transfer: Movement of heat from one body or substance to another. Heat may be transferred by radiation, conduction, convection, or a combination of these.

Hermetic motor: Compressor drive motor sealed within the same casing that contains the compressor.

Hermetic system: Refrigeration system that has a compressor driven by a motor contained in a compressor dome or housing.

High side: Parts of a refrigerating system that are under condensing or high-side pressure.

Hot gas bypass: Piping system in a refrigerating unit that moves hot refrigerant gas from a condenser into the low-pressure side.

Humidity: Moisture, dampness. Relative humidity is the ratio of the quantity of vapor present in the air to the greatest amount possible at a given temperature.

Hydrometer: Floating instrument used to measure specific gravity of a liquid. Specific gravity is the ratio of the density of a material to the density of a substance accepted as a standard.

Hydronic: Type of heating system that circulates a heated fluid, usually water, through baseboard coils. The circulating pump is usually controlled by a thermostat.

Hygrometer: Instrument used to measure the degree of moisture in the atmosphere.

L

Latent heat: Heat given off or absorbed in a process (as vaporization or fusion) other than a change in temperature.

Limit control: Control used to open or close electrical circuits as temperature or pressure limits are reached.

N

Natural convection: Movement of a fluid or air caused by temperature differences.

Normal charge: Thermal element charge that is part liquid and part gas under all operating conditions.

O

Orifice: Accurately sized opening for controlling fluid flow.

P

Pressure: Energy impact on a unit area; force or thrust exerted on a surface.

Primary control: Device that directly controls the operation of a heating system.

Pump down: Act of using a compressor or pump to reduce the pressure in a container or system.

Pyrometer: Instrument for measuring high temperatures.

Q

Qualified person: One familiar with the construction and operation of the apparatus and the hazards involved.

R

Radiant heating: Heating system in which warm or hot surfaces are used to radiate heat into the space to be conditioned.

Radiation: The process of emitting radiant energy in the form of waves or particles.

Refrigerant: Substance used in refrigerating mechanism to absorb heat in an evaporator coil and to release heat in a condenser as the substance goes from a gaseous state back to a liquid state.

Register: Combination grille and damper assembly covering on an air opening or end of an air duct.

Relative humidity: Ratio of amount of water vapor present in air to greatest amount possible at same temperature.

Relay: An electromechanical switching device that can be used as a remote control.

Relief valve: Safety device to permit the escape of steam or hot water subjected to excessive pressures or temperatures.

Riser valve: Device used to manually control flow of refrigerant in vertical piping.

S

Saddle valve: Valve body shaped so it may be silver brazed to a refrigerant tubing surface.

Safety control: Device that stops the refrigerating unit if unsafe pressures and/or temperatures are reached.

Safety plug: Device that releases the contents of a container above normal pressure conditions and before rupture pressures are reached.

Sensible heat: Heat that causes a change in temperature of a substance.

Sequence controls: Devices that act in series or in time order.

Solar heat: Heat from visible and invisible energy waves from the sun.

Specific heat: Ratio of the quantity of heat required to raise the temperature of a body 1 degree to that required to raise the temperature of an equal mass of water 1 degree.

Steam: Water in vapor state.

Steam heating: Heating system in which steam from a boiler is conducted to radiators in a space to be heated.

T

Tachometer: An instrument for measuring revolutions per minute.

Temperature: Degree of hotness or coldness as measured by a thermometer.

Temperature humidity index: Actual temperature and humidity of a sample of air compared to air at standard conditions.

Therm: Quantity of heat equivalent to 100,000 Btu.

Thermodynamics: Science that deals with the relationships between heat and mechanical energy and their interconversion.

Thermometer: Device for measuring temperatures.

Thermostat: Device responsive to ambient temperature conditions.

Thermostatic expansion valve: A control valve operated by temperature and pressure within an evaporator coil, which controls the flow of refrigerant.

Thermostatic valve: Valve controlled by thermostatic elements.

Thermostatic water valve: Valve used to control flow of water through a system, actuated by temperature difference; used in units such as a water-cooled compressor or condenser.

Timer-thermostat: Thermostat control that includes a clock mechanism. Unit automatically controls room temperature and changes it according to the time of day.

V

Valve: Device used for controlling fluid flow.

Valve, expansion: Type of refrigerant control that maintains a pressure difference between high-side and low-side pressure in a refrigerating mechanism. The valve operates by pressure in the low or suction side.

Valve, solenoid: Valve actuated by magnetic action by means of an electrically energized coil.

Vapor: Word usually used to denote vaporized refrigerant rather than gas.

Vapor lock: Condition where liquid is trapped in line because of a bend or improper installation that prevents the vapor from flowing.

Vapor, saturated: A vapor condition that results in condensation into liquid droplets as vapor temperature is reduced.

Velocimeter: Instrument used to measure air velocities using a direct-reading airspeed-indicating dial.

Ventilation: Circulation of air; system or means of providing fresh air.

Viscosity: Resistance to flow of fluids.

W

Wet bulb: Device used in measurement of relative humidity.

Appendix B

HEATING AND VENTILATING SPECIFICATIONS

The specifications for a building or project are the written description of what is required by the owner, architect, or engineer. Together with the drawings, the specifications form the basis of the contract requirements for the construction. The following sample illustrates the general wording and contents of a typical heating and ventilating specification.

DIVISION 15 — MECHANICAL

HEATING AND VENTILATING

1. GENERAL:
   (A) The "Instructions to Bidders," "General Conditions" of the architectural specifications govern work under this Section.
   (B) It is understood and agreed that the Contractor has, by careful examination, satisfied himself as to the nature and location of the work under this Section and all conditions which must be met in order to carry out the work under this Section of the Specifications.
   (C) The Drawings are diagrammatic and indicate generally the locations of materials and equipment. These drawings shall be followed as closely as possible. The architectural, structural, and drawings of other trades shall be checked for dimensions and clearance before installation of any work under this Section. The heating and ventilating contractor shall cooperate with the other trades involved in carrying out the work in order to eliminate interference between the trades.
   (D) The Drawings and Specifications are complementary each to the other, and work required by either shall be included in the Contract as if called for by both.
   (E) It shall be the responsibility of the Heating and Ventilating Contractor to obtain drawings of equipment and materials which are to be furnished by the Owner under separate contract, to which this Contractor is to connect, and for which it is necessary that the Heating and Ventilating Contractor coordinate the work under this Section.
   (F) All services that are interrupted or disconnected shall be rerouted and reconnected in order to provide a complete installation.
   (G) All work shall be performed by mechanics skilled in the particular class or phase of work involved.
   (H) All equipment shall be installed in strict accordance with the respective manufacturer's instructions or recommendations.
   (I) Where appropriate, all equipment shall be UL approved.
   (J) The Heating and Ventilating Contractor shall present five (5) copies of shop drawings or brochures for all fixtures, equipment, and fabricated items to the Engineer for the Engineer's approval. The Heating and Ventilating Contractor shall not proceed with ordering, purchasing, fabricating, or installing any equipment prior to the Engineer's approval of the shop drawings and brochures. Checking is only for general conformance with the design concept of the project and for general compliance with the information given in the contract documents. Any action shown is subject to the requirements of the Plans and Specifications. The contractor is responsible for dimensions that shall be confirmed and correlated at the job site, fabrication processes and techniques of construction, coordination of his work with that of all other trades, and the satisfactory performance of his work.
   (K) All materials and equipment shall be new and undamaged and shall be fully protected throughout the construction period in order that all equipment and materials shall be in perfect condition at the time of acceptance of the building by the Owner. It shall be the responsibility of the Heating and Ventilating Contractor to replace any damaged equipment or materials he is furnishing.
   (L) The naming of a certain brand or manufacturer in the Specifications is to establish a quality standard for the article desired. This Contractor is not restricted to the use of the specific brand or manufacturer named. However, where a substitution is requested, a substitution will be permitted only with the written approval of the Engineer. The Heating and Ventilating Contractor shall assume all responsibility for additional expenses as required in any way to meet changes from the original materials or equipment specified. If notice of substitution is not furnished to the Engineer within fifteen days after the General Contract is awarded, then equipment named in the Specifications and materials named in the Specifications are to be used.
   (M) EXCAVATION AND BACKFILLING:
       (1) The Heating and Ventilating Contractor shall do necessary excavation, shoring, and backfilling to complete the work under this Section of the Specifications under the supervision of the Gen-

Courtesy John Traister Associates.

eral Contractor. No foundation or structural member shall be undermined or weakened by cutting, unless provisions are made to strengthen the member so weakened as necessary.

(2) Excavation shall be cut to provide firm support for all underground conduit, pipe, etc.

(3) Backfill shall be provided as specified under *Backfilling.*

(N) CODES AND STANDARDS: All materials and workmanship shall comply with all applicable codes, specifications, industry standards, and utility company regulations.

(1) In cases of differences between the building codes, Specifications, state laws, industry standards, and utility company regulations in the Contract Documents, the most stringent shall govern. The Contractor shall promptly notify the Architect in writing of any such existing difference.

(2) *Noncompliance:* Should the Contractor perform any work that does not comply with the requirements of the applicable building codes, state laws, industry standards, and utility company regulations, he shall bear the cost arising from the correction of the deficiency.

(3) Applicable codes and all standards shall include all state laws, utility company regulations, and applicable requirements of the following nationally accepted codes and standards:
  a. National Building Code
  b. National Electrical Code
  c. Industry codes, Standards, and Specifications:
     1. AMCA—Air Moving and Conditioning Association
     2. ASHRAE—American Society of Heating, Refrigeration, and Air Conditioning Engineers
     3. SMACNA—Sheet Metal and Air Condition Contractors' National Association

(O) This Contractor shall do all cutting and patching of work as necessary to complete the work under this Section. All finished work in conjunction with this work shall be repaired to perfectly match adjoining finished work. This work shall conform to each respective specification section for the particular phase involved. The Heating and Ventilating Contractor shall employ tradesmen skilled in the particular trade involved in carrying out this work. This work shall proceed only with the approval of the Architect. This Contractor shall perform the work under this Section of the Contract in such a way that the amount of cutting and patching of other work shall be kept to an absolute minimum.

(P) This Contractor shall obtain all permits and arrange for all inspections necessary for the installation of this work. All fees in this relation shall be paid for by the Heating and Ventilating Contractor. This Contractor shall provide the Owner with certificates of inspection from all authorities having jurisdiction. This Contractor shall be responsible for notifying the authorities having jurisdiction at each inspection stage, and no work shall progress until the inspection has been completed and the work approved.

(Q) COORDINATION:
(1) It is called to the Heating and Ventilating Contractor's attention that the ductwork and piping shown on the base bid plan have extremely close clearance.

(2) It shall be the responsibility of the Heating and Ventilating Contractor to coordinate the work under this Section with the Plumbing, and electrical Contractor and other subcontractors.

(3) This Contractor shall check approved equipment drawings of other trades so that all roughing-in work shall be of proper size and in the proper location, for all specific equipment used.

(4) The Heating and Ventilating Contractor shall furnish necessary information to the related trades and shall properly coordinate this information.

(5) The Heating and Ventilating Contractor shall cooperate with the other trades involved in order to eliminate any interference between the trades. This Contractor shall make minor field adjustments to accomplish this.

(6) This Contractor shall cooperate with the other subcontractors in order to establish the responsibilities of each so that work can be completed without delay or interference by this Contractor.

2. WORK INCLUDED:
(A) The work in this Section shall include furnishing all labor, equipment, materials, supplies, and components for complete heating and ventilating systems as indicated on the Drawings and Specifications.

3. ELECTRICAL WORK:
(A) The Heating and Ventilating Contractor is to furnish and attach all necessary components for the heating and control system. The control wiring is to be performed by a qualified electricial contractor employed by the Heating and Ventilating Contractor.

(B) The Heating and Ventilating Contractor is to furnish all motor starters and control components that are specified in the mechanical section of these specifications or shown in schedules on the drawings.

(C) The Electrical Contractor shall furnish all other starters and disconnect switches. The Heating and Ventilating Contractor shall be responsible for the electrical connections and for the electrical wiring between the elements of the pneumatic control system.

(D) The Electrical Contractor shall furnish all conduit, fittings, and materials for the electrical work to connect to the heating and ventilating equipment.

(E) The electrical work required in the Heating and Ventilating Section shall conform to all requirements of the Electrical Section of these Specifications.

(F) All equipment shall be suitable for 208-volt, three-phase, 60-hertz electrical characteristics except motors under ½ hp, which are to be 120-volt, single-phase, 60-hertz. Motors of other characteristics are to be used only where specifically indicated.

4. EQUIPMENT:
(A) VENTILATING UNITS:
(1) Ventilating units shall be the draw-through type as scheduled on the drawings.

(2) Units shall be installed in accordance with the manufacturer's recommendations and be factory assembled and tested.

(3) Casings shall be constructed of steel, reinforced and braced for maximum rigidity. Casings shall be of sectionalized construction and have removable panels for access to all internal parts.

(4) Fans shall be DIDW Class 1 centrifugal and shall be statically and dynamically balanced at the factory. Fan shafts shall run in grease-lubricated ball bearings, the grease line for internal bearings being brought out to the exterior of the casing.

(5) The interior of the unit casing shall be insulated with 1-inch blanket fiber glass insulation, coated to prevent erosion.

(6) Casings and all accessories, with the exception of the coils described in the following paragraphs, shall be galvanized steel or shall be given a protective baked-enamel finish over a suitable rust inhibitor.

(7) Coils shall have seamless copper tubes and aluminum fins. Fins shall be bonded to tubes by mechanical expansion of the tubes. No soldering or tinning shall be used in the bonding process. Coils shall have a galvanized steel casing no lighter than 16 gauge, shall be mounted so that they are accessible for service, and shall be removable without dismantling the entire unit. Steam coils shall be a nonfreeze, distributing type. Hot-water coils shall be type WS, and the steam coils shall be type NS steam distributing.

(8) Heating coils for hot-water service shall be pitched in the unit casing for proper drainage, and tested at 250 psig air pressure under water.

(9) Each unit shall be provided with an adjustable-speed V-belt drive, having a variable-pitch motor sheath to provide approximately ten-percent variation in speed above and below the factory setting. Drive shall be protected by a suitable guard with openings at fan and motor shafts for use of a tachometer.

(10) Motor shall be general-purpose, squirrel-cage type with same type bearings as air-handling unit. Nameplate rating of motor shall not be exceeded by fan BHP requirements.

(11) See details on drawings for mounting and isolation of units.

(12) Filter boxes shall be furnished with throwaway filters, as scheduled. Filter area shall be such that filter velocity is in accordance with the filter manufacturer's recommendation. Filter boxes shall have access doors on both sides. Filters shall fit snugly to prevent air bypass. Both sides of the filter box shall be flanged for fastener holes. Filter shall be not less than 2 inches thick.

(B) CONVERTOR:

(1) Convertor shall be designed for heating hot water with steam. The unit shall be constructed in accordance with ASME Code and labeled for 150-psi working pressure in shell and tubes.

(2) Materials of construction shall be as follows:
a. Water chamber—cast iron.
b. Shell—carbon steel.
c. Tube sheet—rolled steel.
d. Support and Cradles—steel or cast iron.
e. Tubes—¾ inch O.D. 18-gauge seamless drawn copper.
f. Tube Spaces—soft bronze or copper alloy.

(3) Capacity given in schedule on drawings shall be based on a fouling factor of 0.0005.

(4) A valved _____ No. 60 vacuum breaker shall be provided on shell. At each convertor in water piping, a _____ Series 240 Relief valve, ASME rated and sized for full capacity of convertor, shall be installed and set to relieve at pressure shown on Drawings. Valve shall be located so it cannot be valved off from convertor. Pipe discharge shall be full size to the floor drain.

(5) The Contractor shall provide a stand for support of convertor, constructed of welded structural steel or steel pipe.

(6) Convertor shall be as manufactured by _____ Company, Type SU1.

(C) PUMPS:

(1) Base-mounted pumps shall be _____ "Universal" of vertical split-case design, equipped with mechanical seals for 225°F operating temperature and built for not less than 125-psi working pressure. Motor shall be 1750 RPM, drip proof and specifically designed for quiet operation. The coupler between motor and pump shall be _____ flexible type. Spring-type couplers will not be acceptable. Pump and motor shall have oil-lubricated bronze sleeve bearings. Pump shall have removable bearings to permit disassembly of pump without disconnection of piping, hydraulically balanced bronze impeller, and solid cast-iron volute. Pump and motor shall be mounted on a steel base plate.

(2) Base-mounted pumps shall have pump connectors as manufactured by _____ and shall be stainless steel, Type SPCF. They shall be sized the same as the connecting pipe.

(D) CABINET UNIT HEATERS:

(1) Cabinet unit heaters shall be self-contained and factory assembled, and shall consist generally of a filter, heating coil, fan with driving motor, and casing. Heater element shall consist of nonferrous fuses and fins.

(2) Cabinet shall be of steel and be wall mounted or ceiling mounted as indicated on the Drawings.

(3) Front of cabinet shall be removable and not lighter than 16-gauge steel. The back shall be not less than 18-gauge steel. Cabinet shall be provided with steel supports for fan, heating coil, and filter, and shall be steel reinforced members as required to provide a rigid exposed casing and silent operation.

(4) Enclosures shall be complete with inlet and outlet grilles and with doors for access to valves. The element shall be easily accessible for repair after installation of unit. Enclosures shall be galvanized, bonderized, or painted with rust-inhibiting paint at factory, and finished in baked enamel in standard color selected.

(5) Fans shall be centrifugal type with one or more wheels mounted on a single shaft. Fan wheels, shaft, bearings, and fan housing shall be mounted as an integral assembly on a heavy steel mounting plate and securely fastened to enclosures. Bearings of fan and motor shall be self-aligning, permanently lubricated ball type, or sleeve type with ample provision for lubrication and oil reservoirs. Bearings shall be effectively sealed against loss of oil and entrance of dirt.

(6) Filters shall be of the permanent type, mounted in tight-fitting slide-out frames arranged to permit filter renewal or cleaning without removal of front panel.

(7) Heaters shall be tested and rated in accordance with standard test codes adopted jointly by the Unit Heater Division, Air Moving and Conditioning Association, Inc., and the American Society of Heating, Refrigerating, & Air Conditioning Engineers.

(8) Motors shall be resilient mounted on a cushion base, shall be for constant or multispeed operation, and shall have overload protection.

(9) See drawings for capacity, type, and arrangement.

(E) FIN-TUBE RADIATION: Fin-tube heating elements and enclosures, together with required mounting components and accessories, shall be furnished and installed as indicated on plans. Material shall be as manufactured by _____ Radiator Company or approved equal.

(1) *Nonferrous Heating Elements:* Nonferrous heating elements shall consist of full-hard aluminum plate fins, permanently bonded to copper seamless-drawn tube and guaranteed for working pressure at 300°F not less than 150 psi for 1-inch tube and 200 psi for 1¼-inch tube. Fins shall be embedded in copper tube at least .007 inch.

(2) *Enclosures and Accessories:* Enclosures and accessories shall be of style and dimensions indicated on plans and shall be fabricated from electrozinc-coated, rust-resistant, bonderized steel. Enclosures shall be 14 gauge. Enclosure louvers shall be "pencil-proof" type. On wall-to-wall application, enclosures shall be furnished in one piece up to a maximum of 10-feet enclosure length for rooms or spaces measuring a maximum of 10 feet 10 inches in wall length, and a 6-inch end trim shall be used at each end. Enclosures shall be furnished in two or more lengths for wall lengths exceeding 10 feet 10 inches. Corners and end enclosures shall have same method of joining.

End trims, furnished with roll-flanged edges, shall be used between ends of enclosures and walls on wall-to-wall applications. End trims shall be 6-inches maximum length and shall be attached without visible fasteners. Corners and end enclosures shall be furnished where indicated, shall be the same gauge as enclosures, and shall fit flush with enclosures.

(3) *Enclosure-Supports:* Type-A Dura-Mount Back: Enclosures shall be supported at top by means of a 20-gauge roll-formed continuous mounting channel fabricated from electrozinc-coated, rust-resistant, bonderized steel. There shall be a minimum of eight bends forming strengthening ribs running the length of the channel. The top projection of channel shall position the enclosure ⅞ inch from wall to prevent "gouging" of walls when enclosure is installed or removed. A sponge-rubber dirt sealer shall be provided to the offset section of channel permanently anchored to wall, allowing enclosure installation or removal without disturbing the sealer. Dirt sealers attached to rear flange of enclosure are not permitted.

(4) *Enclosure Brackets and Element Hangers:*

a. Enclosure brackets and element hangers shall be installed not farther than 4 feet. Brackets shall be die-formed from 3⁄16-inch-thick stock, 1½ inches wide, and shall be lanced to support and position lower flange of enclosure. Enclosures shall be firmly attached to brackets by setscrews, operated from under the enclosure. Devices that do not provide positive fastening of enclosures are not acceptable. Brackets shall be inserted in prepunched slots in mounting channel to ensure correct alignment and shall be fastened securely to wall at bottom.

b. Sliding saddles shall support heating element and provide positive positioning of element in enclosure to ensure maximum heating efficiency while preventing any possibility of fin impingement on brackets or enclosure joints during expansion or contraction. Element supports shall be double-saddle design fabricated from 16-gauge electrozinc-coated, rust-resistant, bonderized steel. Saddle shall slide freely on saddle support arm bolted to support bracket. Support arm shall allow 1½-inch height adjustment for pitch. The element support saddle shall allow 1⅝-inch lateral movement for expansion and contraction of heating element. Rod or wire hangers are not acceptable.

(5) *Access Doors:* Access doors shall be provided where noted on plans. Doors shall be at least 8 by 8 inches, shall be located in 12-inch-long access panels, and shall have the same gauge as enclosures.

(6) *Enclosure Dampers:* Enclosure dampers shall be provided where indicated. Damper blades shall be fabricated from 18-gauge electrozinc-coated, rust-resistant, bonderized steel, flanged for added rigidity, and shall be permanently attached to enclosures. Threaded damper screw and trunnion shall provide positive operation of blade in any position between open and closed. Damper shall be operated by knob.

(F) FANS: Fans shall be provided as shown and scheduled on drawings. Care shall be taken when mounting in-line fans between joists to provide access to all parts of the fan. (No fans shall be mounted on roof.)

(1) *In-Line Fans:* All these fans shall be equal to _____ "Square Line Centrifugal Fan" with backward-inclined centrifugal wheel, belt-driven Model SQ. B. See Schedule on drawings.

(2) *Fume Centrifugal Fan:* (Welding Fumes) This fan shall be equal to "ILG" Type PE-Belted with cast-iron wheel. See drawings for capacity and mounting.

(3) *Propeller Fans:* See drawings for location and capacity.

(4) Note: See drawings for mounting and isolation.

(G) UNDERGROUND PIPE CONDUIT: (See Alternate A)

(1) *Scope:* The underground conduit shall include reinforced concrete foundation slabs, unit cast-iron pipe supports, unit sleeve-alignment guides, unit pipe anchors and tile conduit envelope, and shall be insulated as specified in these Specifications.

(2) The tile shall be "Therm-O-Tile," or approved equal, and shall be vitrified and equal to or better than "extra-strength" clay pipe of the same diameter as per ASTM Specification C-278. All joints in the conduit envelope shall be sealed with _____ cement mortar mixed in the proportion of one part _____ cement to two parts clean, sharp sand, and coated after cement has set with "Therm-O-Mastic" compound. Additional weatherproofing consisting of one layer of 30-pound felt shall be applied completely over the tile and lapped over the concrete foundation slab. Laps shall be at least 3 inches and shall be sealed with "Therm-O-Mastic" or hot asphalt.

(3) *Tile Conduit Foundation:* The foundation slab shall be at least 4-inch-thick concrete as specified under Section 3, reinforced with 6 by 6 by No. 10 welded wire mesh, and shall have an emergency drain throughout its run. The foundation slab shall extend through building or manhole walls and shall rest on the masonry of these walls. The emergency drain shall be continued to building or manhole sumps, to sewers, to dry wells, or to outfalls. Where con-

duit passes under roadway, it shall be reinforced with an envelope of concrete, 4-inches thick.

(4) *Pipe Supports, Anchors, and Guides:* These accessories shall be as regularly furnished by the manufacturer of the "Therm-O-Tile" conduit and especially designed to fit within the conduit envelope. Location shall be as shown on the Plot Plan. There shall be two guides on each side of each drop.

(5) Conduit shall be sized per the manufacturer's recommendation for the pipe sizes enclosed.

(6) *Shop Drawings:* The successful contractor for the conduit work will be required to furnish, for approval, scale drawings showing cross sections through each separate conduit run and giving all required dimensions of the conduit and centers on which each pipe line will be located within it.

(7) *Wall Openings:* The space around the conduit where it enters walls shall be closed with brick and mortar and completely covered with weatherproof mastic. The space on the inside of the conduit on the inside of building or manhole wall shall be filled with brick and mortar.

(8) *Backfilling:* Backfilling shall be done carefully, and the surface restored to its original condition. Backfilling and tamping shall proceed simultaneously on both sides of the conduit (lengthwise of the trench) until the arch is covered to a depth of at least 18 inches. Rock or stone that might damage the tile shall not be used in the backfill. Backfilling shall comply with Section 2 of the Specifications.

(9) Expansion joints shall be furnished or installed where indicated on Drawings. Model and size shall be as shown on Drawings. Expansion joints shall be as manufactured by _____ Corporation.

(10) Conduit and accessories shall be installed in accordance with the manufacturer's recommendations.

(H) STEAM PRESSURE REDUCING VALVE ASSEMBLY:

(1) *SPRV:* Valve shall be as manufactured by _____ Specialty Manufacturing Corp. Valve body shall be iron and shall have flanged connections. Valve shall be single seated and shall have a stainless-steel valve and seat and deep gland packed stuffing box for minimum friction on valve stem. Valve shall have maximum working pressure of 250 psig, an initial pressure of 75 psig, and a reduced pressure of 10 psig. All parts shall be renewable and interchangeable, and valve seat and disc shall be such that they can be changed without removing valve body from the line. Valve shall be _____ No. 7000 3-inch size, capacity 8600 pounds condensate per hour.

(2) Components of pressure-reducing valves shall be installed as recommended by the manufacturer. See diagram on Drawing M-5.

(3) Safety valve on reduced-pressure side of pressure-reducing station shall be as manufactured by _____ Company, ASME tested and rated, having cast-iron body and 250-pound flanged inlet connection. Valve shall be Catalog No. 630 and shall have capacity indicated on Drawings based on a 3-percent accumulation. Pipe discharge of safety valve shall be full size to exterior of building.

(I) STEAM SPECIALTIES:

(1) *High-Pressure Steam:* Traps shall be _____ side inlet inverted bucket traps. Traps shall be built for up to 125-psig working steam pressure.

(2) *Low-Pressure Steam:* Traps shall be _____ B series, float and thermostatic type, built for up to 15-psig working steam pressure. Traps shall be sized at ¼-pound of differential.

(3) Traps shall have cast-iron or semisteel body with stainless-steel trim.

(4) Flash tank shall be as detailed on the Drawings.

(J) HEATING WATER SPECIALTIES:

(1) Hot-water expansion tank shall be _____ built for 125-pounds water working pressure, and shall be equipped with proper size "Airtrol" tank fitting and air charger fitting. Tank shall be _____, ASME of size as indicated on drawings.

(2) Air separators shall be _____ "Rolairtrol." They shall be installed as instructed by manufacturer and shall afford adequate clearance to remove built-in strainer.

(3) Water makeup pressure-reducing valves shall be _____ Type 12, with screwed ends.

(4) Air vents installed on heating coils and at high points in water piping and on all upfeed radiation units shall consist of an air chamber and manual air vent of a type suitable for the particular application where used. See detail on drawings.

(5) *Balancing Fittings:* The Heating and Ventilating Contractor shall furnish and install _____ Series 700 flow meter fittings as a permanent part of the water piping systems for use with _____ No. SD-400-4 flow meter in determining and balancing water flow in all systems. These fittings shall be at points indicated on Drawings and shall be located so as to provide 15 diameters upstream and 5 diameters downstream of uninterrupted straight pipe. The systems shall be balanced as closely as practicable by use of the aforementioned flow meter.

(6) Water relief valves shall be _____ Series 230 or 240 as indicated on Drawings. Valves shall be set to relieve at the pressures indicated on Drawings. Pipe discharge shall be full size to floor drain.

(7) *Thermometers:* Thermometers shall be _____, Type 105 straight form or Type 115-90 degree back angle form, as applicable, industrial type, with standard separable socket, 9-inch scale, 30°F to 240°F range, cast aluminum case, with red-reading mercury tube.

(8) *Pressure Gauges:* Pressure gauges for pipe lines shall be _____ drawn case gauges, No. 1000 for pressure, No. 1002 for vacuum, and No. 1004 for compound. Pressure gauges shall have brass bourdon tube soldered to socket and tip, brass movement, and white-coated metal dial 3½ inches in diameter, graduated to meet system design requirements, normal operating pressure being indicated middial. _____ No. 1106B brass pulsation dampener shall be provided on gauges near pumps and _____ No. 1092 T-handled cock in ¼-inch line to all pressure gauges. No. 1100 pigtail siphon shall be provided on all steam gauges.

(K) CONDENSATE PUMP:

(1) One duplex condensation pump shall be furnished and installed where shown on the Plans. The

pump shall be manufactured by the _____ Co. The pump shall be driven by open, drip-protected ball-bearing motors, rated for single-phase, 60-hertz, 120-volt ac operation. Each pumping unit shall have capacity at 205°F as indicated. The Heating and Ventilating Contractor shall furnish combination starters with disconnect switch and motor overload protection.

(2) The equipment is to include one cast-iron receiving tank, two pumping units, and accessories listed below:

a. The pumping units shall be bronze fitted throughout, shall be of the centrifugal type, and shall have rotating parts that have been dynamically balanced. The receiving tank, pumping units, and motors shall be assembled by the manufacturer to form an integral unit. A strainer with movable screen is to be installed in the receiving tank.

b. Automatic controls shall consist of a float switch, combination starters, and alternator. Controls shall provide automatic alternation between one pump motor and the other.

(3) If requested, the installing contractor shall secure from the pump manufacturer a factory test report which is to be submitted to the specifying engineer for approval. This report shall show the actual condensate capacity for the pumping units and the power input to the units, all as determined by tests of the actual equipment furnished. The test report is to be certified by the manufacturer as to its correctness and all particulars.

(L) DIFFUSERS, REGISTERS, AND GRILLES:

(1) *Diffusers:* Diffuser shall be _____ type SFSV with deflectrol, No. 7 finish. Dropped Collar shall be provided where called for on drawings.

(2) *Exhaust Registers:* Exhaust registers shall be _____ type GMRV or GFRV, No. 4 finish. Grille in Dark Room shall be light tight.

(3) *Supply Registers:* Supply registers shall be _____ type GMAV with No. 4 finish.

(4) *Exhaust Grilles:* Exhaust grilles shall be _____ type EMR or GFR with No. 7 finish.

(5) *Door Grilles:* Shall be provided by General Contractor. (See Drawing for location only.)

(M) MECHANICAL EXPANSION JOINTS: Mechanical expansion joints shall be provided as called for on drawings. Size, capacity, and type are given on drawings. Expansion joints and guides shall be equal to _____.

(N) FLEXIBLE CONNECTIONS: Bronze unbraided flexible metal nipples shall be provided to connect to steel heating piping below floor and shall extend from ¾-inch inlet to fin tube radiation above floor. See detail on drawings. Nipples shall be furnished in 18-inch length, ¾-inch hex male end, and suitable for temperatures up to 350°F.

(O) UNIT HEATERS: Horizontal hot-water–type heaters shall be provided by _____ or equal. See drawing for Model number, size, and capacity.

(P) FAN-COIL UNITS: Two units of the following type and capacity shall be provided: Model OH 600, 4.2 GPM, 42.2 mbh, 200°F EWT, 180°F LWT, P.D. - 12 feet, 3-speed, and a return-air plenum with permanent filter and a fan control switch. Motor shall have split capacitor, 1/20 hp, 120 volt/1 hp.

(Q) AUTOMATIC TEMPERATURE CONTROLS:

(1) *General:* The System shall be a complete system of automatic temperature regulation of the pneumatic type with electric accessories and components as indicated. Component parts of the system shall be manufactured by _____; the base bid shall be _____ and can be considered as an alternate at the option of the Contractor. The entire system shall be installed by the Control Manufacturer. All control items except room thermostats shall be properly identified with engraved plastic nameplates permanently attached. Room thermostat locations shall be coordinated to align vertically or horizontally with adjacent light switches or control instruments. Room thermostats shall be 5 feet 6 inches (nominal) above the floor. Room thermostat covers shall be open.

(2) MATERIALS: (Thermostats)

a. Firestats shall be UL approved, manual-reset type T-7602 with an adjustable temperature setting. Range hood shall be set at 250°F; all others at 125°F.

b. Freezestats shall be T-7606 with 20-foot temperature-sensitive element, located downstream from the coil. If any portion of the element senses a temperature below its setting, the contacts shall break.

c. Unit heater thermostats for space mounting shall be T-7162, line-voltage type with SP-ST switching action rated 6 amperes for full load and rated 36 amperes at 120 volts for lock rotor.

d. Surface-mounted aquastats shall be type T-7912 with adjustable set point and 10° differential. Contacts shall be rated 10 amperes at 120 volts.

e. Thermostatic sensors shall be T-5210 style "B" bulbs with 5½-inch and 4-foot capillaries or 8-foot and 17-foot averaging element. Sensors shall be designed to measure a temperature and to convert the measurement to an air-pressure signal that is transmitted to a receiver, a 3- to 15-psi signal. The sensor shall have pneumatic feedback.

f. Fluidic controlling receivers shall be T-9000. The instrument shall accept a 3- to 15-psi pneumatic signal from one or two temperature-relative humidity or pressure transmitters, and have pneumatic feedback and enclosed fluidic circuitry.

g. Receiver controller shall be T-5312 and shall accept a 3- to 15-psi signal from a remote transmitter.

h. Pneumatic thermometer shall be T-5500 to provide visual indication of the temperature. The thermometer shall accept a 3- to 15-psi signal from a remote transmitter. The T-5500 shall be for flush-mounted applications.

i. Day-night thermostats shall be T-4502 equipped with two (2) separate bimetallic elements for day and night operation. The thermostats shall be equipped with an indexing switch for changing the thermostat to day or night operation as desired, or from a control location by changing the air pressure from 15 to 20 pounds.

j. Remote capillary pneumatic thermostats shall be T-8000 for direct or reverse acting. The T-8000 shall be equipped with the proper capillary, *B* bulb for sensing outside air and water temperature and also of the averaging type for all other applications.

k. Remote capillary pneumatic thermostats for two-position applications shall be T-8000.

(3) VALVES:

a. Valves shall be sized by the control manufacturer and shall have threaded connections, except valves over 2 inches shall have flanged connections. Valve packing shall be U-cap silicone except where indicated. Maximum allowable pressure drop shall be 5-feet water column for water valves and 60-percent steam pressure.

b. Valve operators for valve ½ inch to 2 inches shall be V-3000 piston operated. The diaphragm shall be manufactured of Butyl rubber enclosed in a heavy die-cast aluminum housing.

c. Valves for steam or water service shall be V-3752 normally open type. The valve shall be equipped with a V-3000 piston operator. The V-3752 bodies shall be of high-grade cast red brass in sizes ½ inch through 2 inches and shall have a back-setting feature that permits changing the stem packing without interrupting service to the system. The modulating plug shall have a replaceable composition disc, especially compounded for steam or hot water, and shall provide an equal percentage relationship between valve lift and flow at a constant pressure drop.

d. Connector valves shall be V-3800 for steam or water with restrictor mounting space. The valve shall be equipped with a heavy-duty moulded rubber diaphragm of the oval piston type. The valve body shall be of cast red brass in sizes ½ inch through 2 and ¾ inch.

e. Valve for steam or water service shall be V-3970 normally closed type. The valve shall be equipped with a V-3000 piston operator. The V-3870 bodies shall be of high-grade cast red brass in sizes ½ inch through 2 inches and shall have a back-setting feature that permits changing the stem packing without interrupting service to the system. The modulating plug shall have a replaceable compulsion disc especially compounded for steam or hot water, and shall provide an equal percentage relationship between valve lift and flow at a constant pressure drop.

f. Three-way mixing valves shall be V-4322 and ½ inch through 2 inches in size. The body shall be three-way with screwed ends and made of high-grade cast red brass. The body shall be suitable for pressure to 150 psi.

(4) DAMPERS AND DAMPER MOTORS:

a. Automatic control dampers shall be interlocking and airtight. They shall be of opposed-blade construction for modulating service and of parallel-blade construction for two-position service. Dampers shall be of the multilouver construction with brass bearings, channel iron frame, and maximum width of 6 feet.

b. Control dampers shall be D-1200 or D-1300 and manufactured specifically to control the airflow in heating, ventilating, and air-conditioning systems.

c. Frames shall be made of No. 13 galvanized sheet steel, formed into channels and riveted. In addition to the rigid frame construction,

corner brackets shall be used to maintain perfect alignment of the damper.

d. Blades shall consist of two formed No. 22 galvanized sheets, spot-welded together for strength to withstand high velocities and static pressures. Square blade pins shall be furnished to ensure nonslip pivoting of the blades when a damper is used as a single module or when it is interconnected with others.

e. Bushings shall be made of oil-impregnated sintered bronze and shall provide constant lubrication.

f. Synthetic elastomer seals shall be provided on the blade edges and on the top, bottom, and sides of the frame, and shall be capable of withstanding air temperatures from −20 to 200°F or from −65 to 400°F, as required for the application. The material and extruded form of the blade edge seals shall create a positive seal when the blades are closed. The seals shall be replaceable if they become damaged. Leakage shall be less than 0.5 percent when closing against 4-inch w.g. static pressure, based on conventional velocity of 2000 FPM.

g. Damper motors shall be provided for all automatic dampers and shall be of sufficient capacity to operate the connected damper. Where required, damper motors shall be equipped with positive positioners.

h. Automatic control dampers are specified to be provided as an integral part of the air units.

(5) PANELS:

a. Control cabinets shall be furnished where specified. In general, it is the intention of this specification that control cabinets be furnished for each air-handling unit, major equipment components, and elsewhere as specified. Control cabinets shall be fabricated of extruded aluminum or steel. The cabinets shall have a face panel for flush-mounting gauges and a subpanel for mounting of controllers, relays, etc. Those controls which require manual positioning or visual indication shall be flush mounted and identified with engraved nameplates on the face panel. The controls that must be accessible for maintenance and calibration only are to be mounted on the subpanel inside cabinet. Each item shall be identified by engraved nameplates.

(6) CONTROL PIPING:

a. Control piping shall be hard-drawn copper tubing where exposed and may be either hard- or soft-drawn copper tubing where it is to be concealed. Either solder or compression fitting shall be used. Tubing shall be run in a neat and workmanlike manner and shall be fastened securely to the building structure. All tubing in finished rooms shall be concealed. Where exposed in unfinished rooms, tubing shall be run either parallel to or at right angles to the building structure. In lieu of copper tubing, plastic tubing may be used in end compartment of unit and in control panel.

b. *Plastic Tubing:* In lieu of copper tubing, high-density virgin polyethylene may be substituted, subject to the following requirements. The tubing shall be rated 600-psi burst pressure at 72°F and 300-psi burst pressure at 140°F. Each tube shall be individually numbered at intervals not exceeding 1 inch. All tubing except tubing in control panels and junction boxes shall be installed in EMT conduit in sizes of ½ inch through 2 inches. Standard electrical fittings shall be used. All bends for conduit 1 inch and larger shall be standard purchased bends. There shall not be more than three 90-degree bends between pull boxes. Termination shall be made in standard electric junction boxes or enclosed control panels. Where connections are made from plastic to copper, protective grommets shall be used to prevent electrolysis. The conduit installation shall conform to the same standard as set forth in the copper piping requirements.

(7) INSTALLATION:

a. EXPOSED:

    1. Single polyethylene tubing and soft copper aluminum tubing may be run exposed for a length of 18 inches or less. For lengths that exceed 18 inches, the lines shall be run within enclosed trough or conduit, and this tube carrier system shall be installed in a workmanlike manner, parallel to building lines, adequately supported, etc. All connections, except for terminal connections to valves, damper operators, etc., shall be made inside troughs, junction boxes, or control cabinets.

    2. Factory-manufactured bundles of polyethylene tubing, with protective outer sheath and hard copper or aluminum tubing, may be installed without an additional trough or conduit envelope, provided that the tube system is installed in same workmanlike manner as specified above for trough and conduit systems.

b. CONCEALED-ACCESSIBLE:

    1. Single polyethylene tubing and soft copper or aluminum tubing, either individual or bundled, shall be installed in a workmanlike manner, securely fastened to fixed members of the building structure at sufficient points to avoid excessive freedom of movement. Field-fabricated bundles shall be tied together with a sufficient number of nylon ties to present a neat, uniform appearance.

c. *Concealed-Inaccessible:* Single polyethylene tubes shall be run within enclosed trough or conduit. Factory-manufactured bundles of polyethylene tubing, with protective outer sheath and soft copper or aluminum tubing, may be installed without an additional trough or conduit envelope. Fitting connections to polyethylene tubing shall not be made within the inaccessible area.

d. *Piping Test:* The piping system shall be tested and made tight under pressure of 30 psi. Leakage will not exceed 10 psi in 12 hours.

(8) Miscellaneous relays, pressure switches, disconnect switches, PE and EP relays, time clocks and other items shall be provided as required for the sequence of control indicated. Time clock shall be seven-day type. The PE relays shall be located within 5 feet of the motor control device.

(9) *Air Compressor:* Air compressor shall be of the electric type complete with tank, gauges, combination pressure-reducing valves, low-pressure relief valve, filter assembly, and necessary accessories. The unit shall be of ample capacity to automatically maintain the desired air pressure with an idle period equal to at least twice that of the operating period. Compressor shall be single-stage, high-pressure (60- to 75-psi) type fitted with galvanized ASME reservoir. Motor shall be provided with built-in overload protection. Compressor and motor shall be sized so that their capacity is sufficient for future addition to building.

(10) WORK BY OTHERS:

a. Dampers and valves will be installed by the Mechanical Contractor.

b. Temperature-control wiring shall be the responsibility of the Temperature Control Contractor. This responsibility shall consist of wiring the following items:

    1. P.E. switches

    2. E.P. switches

    3. Firestats

    4. Freezestats

    5. Air compressor

    6. All interlocking wiring required for the system to function properly.

c. The electrical contractor shall be responsible for all power wiring to the equipment.

(11) SEQUENCE OF OPERATION:

a. *Air-Handling Unit Control:* When the unit fan is started, EP-1 is energized to position the outdoor air damper open through D-1 and through PE-1 on units 7 and 8 which energize their respective exhaust fans. When the unit fan is stopped, PE-1 is de-energized and the outdoor air damper is positioned fully closed. Firestat T-3, located in the filter discharge, stops the fan if the discharge temperature rises above 125°F. T-1, located in the discharge duct, controls V-1 modulater to bypass an increasing amount of water around the coil. T-2, with its element located on the face of the heating coil, prevents the discharge temperature from falling below 35°F by overriding T-1 and modulating V-1. Five (5) units have hot-water coils and require three-way valves; three (3) units are steam coils and require steam valves.

b. *Radiation Control:* During the day operation, T-1 controls V-1 to maintain the desired space temperature. During the night operation, T-1 controls V-1 to maintain a reduced night temperature of 60°F.

c. *Exhaust Fan Control:* T-1, located in the intake of each exhaust fan, stops the unit fan should the intake temperature rise above 125°F.

d. *Pump Bypass Control:* T-1, with its sensor located in the supply and return lines, controls V-1 to maintain the desired differential pump pressure.

e. *Convertor Control:* T-1, with its sensor TT-2 located in the convertor supply, is reset inversely with changes in the outside air temperature by TT-1, to control V-1 and maintain the desired convertor discharge temperature inversely with changes in the outside air temperature. T-2 located in the outside air, stops the pump should the outside air temperature rise above 70°F. When the pump is stopped, EP-1 is de-energized to position V-1, fully closed.

f. *Domestic Hot-Water Control:* T-1, located in the discharge of the convertor, controls V-1 to maintain the desired domestic hot-water temperature. T-2, located in the tank, starts the circulating pump if the temperature rises above a predetermined setting. Aquastat T-3 starts the recirculating pump if the temperature rises above the predetermined setting.

g. *Air Supply:* During the day, seven-day time clock C-1 is energized. It, in turn, energizes EP-1 which positions VA-1 to supply 15 pounds of air to day-night thermostats for day operation. During the night operation, C-1 is de-energized. It, in turn, de-energizes EP-1 which positions VA-1 to supply 20 pounds of air to day-night thermostats for night operation.

h. *Valve and Mechanical Rooms Exhaust-Fan Control:* T-1 cycles the fan to maintain a desired temperature of 85°F. A motorized damper, located at the outside air intake louver, interlocks with fan to open when fan is energized and to close when fan is de-energized. A low-limit thermostat, located downstream of the damper in the outside air duct, shuts off fan if temperature drops below 35°F.

i. *Fan-Coil, Unit-Heater, and Cabinet Unit-Heater Control:* T-1 cycles fans to maintain the space temperature. Aquastat T-2 stops the fans if the supply-water temperature falls below 90°F.

(12) *Service and Guarantee:* The entire control system shall be serviced and maintained in first-class condition by the control manufacturer for a period of one year after acceptance at no extra cost to the Owner. At the end of the one-year guarantee period, the Control Contractor must be capable of furnishing emergency service within a normal requested time.

5. DUCTWORK:

(A) Duct thickness, duct breaking, duct joints (both longitudinal and transverse), duct hangers, and all general ductwork shall be in accordance with the recommendations of "Duct Manual and Sheet Metal Construction for Ventilating and Air-Conditoning Systems," as prepared by the Sheet Metal and Air-Conditioning Contractors' National Association.

(B) Ductwork shall be galvanized steel, manufactured in gauges recommended in the above manual.

(C) Duct fittings shall be equivalent to Air Distribution Institute Standard fittings as a minimum requirement.

(D) Where mains split, splitter dampers must be furnished.

(E) All duct joints are to be airtight at ½-inch water pressure.

(F) *Turning Vanes:* _____ or _____ air-turns are to be used in all elbows except round pipes.

(G) EXTERNAL DUCT INSULATION:

(1) *Exposed Ductwork:* Supply ducts and outside air ducts shall be insulated on the outside with 1-inch-thick J-M No. 814, nonflexible, SPIN-GLAS fiber glass duct insulation. Insulation shall have

factory-applied facing—FSK (Foil Skrim Kraft). Insulation shall have an average thermal conductivity not to exceed .23 Btu-inch per square foot per °F per hour at a mean temperature of 75°F. All insulation shall be applied with edges tightly butted. Insulation shall be impaled on pins welded to the duct and secured with speed clips. Pins shall be clipped off close to speed clips. Spacing of pins shall be as required to hold insulation firmly against duct surface, but not less than one pin per square foot. All joints and speed clips shall be sealed with _____ 207 glass fabric set in _____ 30-35, on a 3-inch-wide strip of same facing adhered with _____ 85-20 adhesive.

(2) *Concealed Ductwork:* Supply ducts and outside air ducts shall be insulated on the outside with 1-inch-thick J-M flexible Microlite or approved equal. Insulation shall be cut slightly longer than the perimeter of the duct to ensure full thickness at corners. The insulation shall have an average thermal conductivity not to exceed 0.25 Btu-inch per square foot per °F per hour at a mean temperature of 75°F. All insulation shall be applied with edges tightly butted. Insulation shall be secured with _____ 85-20 adhesive. Adhesive shall be applied so that insulation conforms to duct surface uniformly and firmly. All joints shall be taped and sealed with 3-inch-wide strips of the facing applied with 85-20 adhesive.

(H) Where ducts change shape, enlarge, or reduce, transition is to be made with a maximum angle of 15 degrees, except where it is specifically shown otherwise.

(I) *Volume-Control Duct Dampers and Duct Damper Hardware:* Volume-control duct dampers shall be placed as indicated on drawings and constructed as shown in the SMACNA Duct Manual, Plate No. 28 and multiple-plate volume dampers SMACNA Manual, Plate No. 29. Vent-lok control hardware shall be appropriate for specific use.

(J) FIRE DAMPERS:

(1) Fire dampers shall be installed at locations indicated on the Plans, in full conformance with NFPA Bulletin No. 90-A, and in complete accordance with city, state, and local codes.

(2) All fire dampers shall bear label of UL and be listed under the continuing inspection service of UL, where applicable, and shall have been successfully tested for 1½ hours, up to 1800°F. In mounting conditions not in conformance with UL testing, units shall be built in full conformance with standards of the American Insurance Association and the NFPA Bulletin No. 90-A.

(3) Fire dampers shall be manufactured by "Fire-Seal" damper. Dampers shall be provided with interlocking blades to form a solid coating of steel when closed. When open, the blades are to be completely concealed in the head of the frame, allowing 100-percent-free undisturbed airflow with minimum turbulence. Entire assembly shall be galvanized for corrosion resistance and shall conform to ASTM Specification A-90-63-T.

(K) *Control Dampers:* Control dampers shall be furnished to the Mechanical Contractor by the Control Manufacturer and shall be installed in accordance with the Control Manufacturer's instructions in the duct system.

(L) *Canvas Connections:* Canvas connections shall be Vent-Fabric "Vent-Fab," 20-ounce waterproof and fireproof canvas approved by Underwriters' Laboratories. Each air-handling unit return and supply shall be connected with canvas connection.

(M) *Sawdust Ductwork:* Sawdust ductwork shall be round, 16 gauge with fittings as shown. Ductwork shall be equal to _____. All joints shall be welded airtight. Welding frame fume exhaust shall be of same material.

(N) Flexible metal exhaust duct shall be equal to _____ or _____.

(O) This Contractor shall provide all louvers equal to Air Balance, 4 inches deep, rain and storm check, and of all-aluminum construction. Installation in wall shall be done by the General Contractor.

(P) *Paint Spray Booth Vent:* Paint spray booth vent shall be fabricated of No. 20 gauge galvanized sheet steel equal to vent manufactured by _____. Vent shall be furnished with a roof flange and weather canopy with rain guard, as manufactured by _____. See drawings for support detail.

6. WIRING DIAGRAMS:

(A) This Contractor shall furnish to the Architect for the Architect's approval five (5) copies of wiring diagrams (i.e., all individual wires diagrammed) showing the complete control wiring system diagram for the heating and ventilating system. The Contractor shall furnish a framed, glass-protected copy of this wiring diagram for the complete system *as installed*. This Contractor shall place this wiring diagram in the Equipment Room.

7. TESTS, CLEANING, AND GUARANTEE:

(A) This Contractor shall provide all pumps, gauges, and other instruments necessary to perform tests as required.

(B) This Contractor shall hydrostatically test the piping of the steam system and heating-water system, to a pressure of 150 percent of the system working pressures. The pressure test shall be for at least 8 hours, at which time pressure shall remain constant without additional pumping. After satisfactorily completing tests and before permanently connecting equipment, this Contractor shall blow and flush piping thoroughly so that interiors of all piping shall be free of foreign matter. All traps, strainers, etc., shall be cleaned at the time of flushing.

(C) The Contractor shall adjust and regulate the completed system under actual heating and ventilating conditions to produce a satisfactory system. All automatic temperature controls shall be adjusted for satisfactory operation during the first heating and ventilating seasons. This Contractor shall make all necessary adjustments during the first heating and ventilating seasons without additional cost to the Owner. (This does not mean that the Heating and Ventilating Contractor is responsible for any negligence of operation by the Owner.)

(A) This Contractor shall furnish complete instructions covering the operation of the heating, ventilating, and control systems.

(B) A framed, glass-protected copy of operating instructions is to be placed in the Mechanical Equipment Room by this Contractor.

9. PERFORMANCE TESTS:

(A) This Contractor shall provide all necessary instruments to perform tests as required.

(B) The Heating and Ventilating Contractor shall conduct the following tests upon completion of installation of the system under the direction of the Architect.

(1) *Air Distribution System:* Performance test after proper balancing of system, showing airflow measurements through each supply and return.

(2) *Ventilation System:* Performance test after proper balancing, showing airflow measurements through each exhaust grille.

(3) *Heating System:* Operating test of the entire system during cold weather with fiinal adjustment to outdoor design conditions as necessary and to the heating system. In the event the weather prevents testing before acceptance of the building, the building will be accepted subject to successful completion of the above tests.

(4) *Air-Handling Equipment:* Airflow tabulation and listing of outlet and inlet temperatures and heating medium inlet-outlet temperatures.

(C) Performance tests shall include the complete heating and ventilating systems and all their parts, including thermostatic and electrical controls, in order to determine that the systems are in compliance with the Contract. Tests shall show that the heating and ventilating systems are acceptable before the installation is approved for acceptance by the Owner. The Contractor shall furnish the Owner with four (4) copies of the finds of the approved texts, including tabulation of all readings for the job and computations. Final payment to the Contractor, less an amount to cover the cost of certain tests, shall be made when weather conditions have caused postponement of certain tests.

(D) The heating units shall be checked for performance to determine that the Specifications are met in every respect.

(E) This Contractor shall guarantee all materials and equipment installed by him, and all workmanship for a period of one year after final acceptance of the heating work against all defects occurring during that period.

(F) The heating and ventilating system shall be tested under operating conditions for a period of five 8-hour days or as necessary to demonstrate that the requirements of the Contract are fulfilled.

(G) This Contractor shall adjust and regulate the completed system under actual heating conditions to produce a satisfactory system. All automatic temperature controls shall be adjusted for satisfactory operation in the first heating season. This Contractor shall make all necessary adjustments in the first heating season without additional cost to Owner. (This does not mean that the Heating Contractor is responsible for any negligence in operation by Owner.)

10. MARKING OF CONTROLS, VALVES, AND ELECTRIC CONTROLS:

(A) All valves, electric controls, and electric starters and switches are to be marked with permanent metal tags. The tags shall be black enamel finish with engraved, white enameled letters that are at least ¼ inch high.

(B) The location at ceiling of all damper electric controls and balancing valves and duct balancing dampers shall be marked above the ceiling with tag, as described above and screwed to the metal ceiling runners at each location.

11. TEMPORARY HEATING:

(A) The General Contractor shall be responsible for furnishing temporary heating throughout the period of construction of the building.

12. PAINTING:

(A) Factory-painted equipment and materials shall receive primer coat and two coats of enamel, factory applied.

(B) Factory-painted equipment shall be touched up as necessary and where factory-painted color does not match the Architect's color scheme in finished areas.

(C) Factory-primed equipment and materials shall be painted with two coats of enamel in accordance with the Painting Section of these Specifications. This paint shall be applied by the Painting Contractor who shall use experienced painters for this purpose in accordance with the Painting Section of these Specifications.

(D) Unpainted equipment and materials shall receive one coat of primer and two coats of enamel in accordance with the requirements of the Painting Section of these Specifications for exposed metal. This paint shall be applied by the Painting Contractor who shall use experienced painters for this purpose in accord-

ance with the Painting Section of these Specifications.

(E) The inside of all ductwork visible in finished building shall be painted dull black, the paint to be applied in accordance with Painting Section of the Specifications.

(F) All colors shall be as approved by the Architect.

13. TEMPORARY POWER:

(A) The General Contractor shall provide, as required, 208/120-volt, single-phase, 60-hertz temporary power for use of the Heating and Ventilating Contractor.

14. LUBRICATION PRIOR TO START-UP:

(A) Prior to start-up, the Heating and Ventilating Contractor shall fully lubricate all equipment under this Section in accordance with the respective manufacturers' recommendations.

Appendix C

SUPPLY AND RETURN AIR OUTLETS

Manufacturers of diffusers, registers, and grilles usually provide tables that show the proper size according to CFM requirements. Typical examples are shown herein. All Tables courtesy York Air Conditioning & Refrigeration, Division of Borg-Warner.

Table C-1. Side Wall Registers

CFM	Size	Throw-Feet
60	10 x 4	10
80	10 x 6	12
100	14 x 6	14
120	14 x 6	16
140	16 x 6	16
160	16 x 6	18
180	20 x 6	14
200	20 x 6	16
220	20 x 6	18
240	20 x 6	20
260	24 x 6	20
280	30 x 6	18
300	30 x 6	20

Table C-2. Round Ceiling Diffusers

CFM	Diameter (in)
100	6
120	8
140	8
160	8
180	8
200	10
220	10
240	10

Table C-3. Floor Outlets

CFM	Size	Spread (ft)
60	2¼ x 10	7
80	2¼ x 12	11
100	2¼ x 14	11
120	4 x 10	11
140	4 x 10	13
160	4 x 12	13

Table C-4. Return Air Grilles

CFM	Free Area Sq in	Side Wall Return Grilles	Floor Grilles
60- 140	40	10 x 6	4 x 14
140- 170	48	12 x 6	4 x 18 or 6 x 10
170- 190	55	10 x 8	4 x 18 or 6 x 12
190- 235	67	12 x 8	6 x 14
235- 260	74	18 x 6	6 x 16 or 8 x 14
260- 370	106	12 x 12	8 x 20
370- 560	162	18 x 12	8 x 30
560- 760	218	24 x 12	10 x 30 or 12 x 24
760- 870	252	18 x 18	12 x 30
870- 960	276	30 x 12	12 x 30
960-1170	340	24 x 18	
1170-1470	423	30 x 18	18 x 30 14 x 30
1470-1580	455	24 x 24	20 x 30
1580-1770	510	36 x 18	22 x 30
1770-1990	572	30 x 24	24 x 30
1990-2400	690	36 x 24	24 x 36
2400-3020	870	36 x 30	30 x 36

INDEX